MASTER YOUR ATTACHMENT STYLE

CREATE A SECURE AND LOVING RELATIONSHIP FROM ANXIOUS, AVOIDANT, AND DISORGANIZED PATTERNS

ELIZA BENNETT

CONTENTS

ANXIOUS ATTACHMENT RECOVERY

FREEDOM FROM AVOIDANT ATTACHMENT

FREEDOM FROM DISORGANIZED ATTACHMENT

ELIZA BENNETT

ANXIOUS ATTACHMENT
Recovery

Proven Steps to Conquer Relationship Anxiety,
Rebuild Trust, and Cultivate Lasting Love

INTRODUCTION

I will never forget one night I was sitting alone at home, staring at my phone, my anxiety and panic increasing with each minute that passed without a text. I had a sinking feeling in my stomach. I was convinced that my partner's silence had a secret meaning—that they were pulling away, losing interest, or worse. I knew it was not rational, but the fear gripped me, making it hard to breathe or think clearly. It was a moment of intense relationship anxiety, a feeling many of us know all too well.

Moments like these and my recovery journey led me to write this book. My name is Eliza Bennett, and I have walked the path of overcoming relationship anxiety. I have not only delved into academic research in psychology and attachment theory, but I have also grappled with personal struggles with anxious attachment. I have felt the same fears and struggled with similar insecurities that you may have. This shared experience drives me to provide you with the tools and insights you need to transform your anxious attachment style.

With this experience, I have committed to providing the tools and insights you need to transform your anxious attachment style. Over the years, I have met countless people who have worked through understanding and conquering the difficulties of anxious attachment to have more secure and fulfilling relationships.

WHO THIS BOOKS IS FOR

This book is for anyone who has ever felt anxiety in their relationships. If you often find yourself overthinking messages, worrying about your partner's feelings, or second-guessing your worth, know that you are not alone. This guide is specially crafted for those of us who experience anxious attachment, whether you are in a long-term relationship, dating, or navigating the complexities of love and connection. If you find it hard to trust others or feel insecure about your partner's commitment, this book will provide the insights and strategies you need to navigate these turbulent emotions with confidence.

It is also for those seeking to deepen their knowledge of attachment styles and how they affect their relationships. Whether you are a seasoned psychology reader or new to these concepts, I have used approachable language and well-researched content that will resonate with you. My book aims to empower those who wish to break free from the patterns of anxiety and insecurity that have held them back, offering a roadmap to healthier, more fulfilling connections.

Furthermore, this book will be valuable if you value personal growth and self-awareness. It encourages introspection and offers tools to heal emotional wounds and nurture a sense of inner security. By addressing the roots of anxious attachment, you will embark on a journey toward improving your relationship and overall well-being. Ultimately, this book is for anyone ready to embrace change and take proactive steps toward secure, loving relationships filled with trust and fulfillment.

WHAT TO EXPECT FROM THIS BOOK

In these pages, you will comprehensively understand anxious attachment, its roots, and its impact on your relationships and self-esteem. More importantly, you will discover practical steps to break free from the cycle of anxiety and insecurity. These valuable strategies are theoretical concepts and tools you can apply daily to develop healthier, more secure connections. I wrote this book to equip you with the knowledge and skills to overcome anxious attachment.

This book is structured to take you on a step-by-step journey to understanding and overcoming anxious attachment. Each chapter explores different aspects of this journey, providing actionable steps to implement the strategies daily.

I will first provide a comprehensive overview of anxious attachment, exploring its psychological and neuroscientific underpinnings. You will discover how to identify the specific signs and behaviors linked to this attachment style, both in yourself and others.

After that, I will give you practical strategies and approaches for managing overthinking, anxiety, and jealousy in relationships.

Then, we will explore connecting with and healing our inner child.

We will discuss rebuilding and strengthening our emotional security and trust in our relationships. I will also provide techniques for improving long-term emotional regulation and balance.

I will also guide you in strengthening relationships, including setting the proper boundaries essential to any secure attachment and healthy relationship. The other key topics I will cover in this book include enhancing self-awareness and fostering ongoing personal growth.

HOW TO USE THIS BOOK

To effectively use this book, start by setting aside dedicated time for reading and reflection. Create a quiet, comfortable space to fully engage with the material without distractions. As you read, note key concepts that resonate with you and reflect on your experiences and emotions related to the topics discussed. This process will help you internalize and apply the lessons to your life.

Additionally, consider approaching each chapter with an open mind and a willingness to learn. Some sections may challenge your beliefs or require you to confront difficult emotions. Allow yourself to process these feelings and recognize that discomfort is often a part of growth. After completing a chapter, take the time to journal about your thoughts and any insights you gained. This practice will deepen your understanding and reinforce the ideas presented.

Finally, do not hesitate to revisit certain book sections as needed. Healing and personal growth are non-linear journeys, and different passages resonate with you at various stages of your process. Repeatedly engaging with the material can provide new perspectives and reinforce your commitment to cultivating secure attachments and healthier relationships. Remember, this book is a tool to support you on your path, so use it in a way that feels empowering and nurturing.

EMBRACING THE JOURNEY OF RECOVERY

Anxious attachment is more than just a label—it is a deeply ingrained pattern that shapes how we connect with others, often leaving us feeling vulnerable, insecure, and longing for reassurance in our relationships. Rooted in early experiences and carried into adulthood, this attachment style can create cycles of fear, doubt, and emotional turmoil that impact our romantic partnerships and sense of self-worth. Yet, the fact that anxious attachment stems from learned behaviors means you can unlearn it. I will guide you to understanding these patterns, breaking free from them, and cultivating healthier, more secure relationships. Whether you have struggled with relationship anxiety, experienced recurring trust issues, or felt trapped in a loop of emotional uncertainty, this journey is about reclaiming your emotional balance, rebuilding trust, and creating lasting love—not just with others but also with yourself.

If you are reading this, you are probably looking for comfort, answers, and ways to break free from the cycle of anxiety that has imprisoned you. It is important to remember that you are never alone. Yes, there are many challenges on this journey of healing and personal growth, but the rewards can transform your life. I encourage you to commit to this journey with an open heart and mind. The path to recovery and secure attachment is within your reach. Embrace the process, take each step with intention, and know you can achieve secure connections and lasting love. The adventure toward a more fulfilling and secure relationship starts now.

CHAPTER 1
UNDERSTANDING ANXIOUS ATTACHMENT

ONE EVENING, AFTER A MINOR DISAGREEMENT WITH MY PARTNER, I found myself in a downward spiral of anxiety and worry. I replayed our conversation over and over again, scrutinizing every word. I tormented myself with the idea that this minor conflict signaled the end of our relationship. I could not sleep, my mind racing with thoughts of abandonment and rejection. I experienced raw anxiety, a feeling that many of us with anxious attachment know all too well.

In this chapter, we will explore what anxious attachment is and the roots of feelings like these, giving you insights into why we experience them and how they affect our relationships.

WHAT IS ANXIOUS ATTACHMENT?

Anxious attachment is a term rooted in psychology and neuroscience. It describes a pattern that includes a deep fear of abandonment, as well as an overwhelming need for closeness and reassurance. Negative experiences in childhood are what usually lead us to this attachment style, and it is shaped by our interactions with caregivers. If we have inconsistent or unpredictable bonds with our caregivers when we are children, the seeds of anxious attachment are sown. This can lead to behaviors that tend to disrupt our relationships in adulthood.

Some of the most common signs of being anxiously attached are frequent worrying about what your partner feels and does, constantly seeking validation, and feeling insecure even when there are no apparent issues in the relationship. People with anxious attachments might overthink every conversation, feel intensely jealous for no reason, and look for constant reassurance that they are loved and valued.

Research shows that those with anxious attachment are more likely to experience relationship dissatisfaction, emotional turmoil, and lower self-esteem. Further studies show that nearly 20% of adults exhibit anxious attachment behaviors. If you are among them, you will have enormous difficulty forming stable and fulfilling connections. If you have an anxious attachment style, you will have to do significant work addressing and managing your emotions and the roots of the problem if you want to build healthier, more secure relationships.

THE ROOTS OF ANXIOUS ATTACHMENT

The tendency for humans to develop anxious attachment styles is deeply rooted in our evolutionary past. In early human societies, survival depended on close-knit relationships, and caregiver availability was crucial for the survival of infants. Infants who maintained proximity to a caregiver were more likely to survive, as caregivers provided protection, nourishment, and learning opportunities. This need for closeness and security became hardwired into our brains, ensuring that infants would signal distress when separated, thereby ensuring their caregivers' return.

From an evolutionary perspective, attachment behaviors such as clinging to caregivers and showing distress during separation were advantageous. Infants who exhibited these behaviors were more likely to receive the attention and care they needed, ultimately increasing their chances of survival. Over generations, these behaviors became a fundamental part of human development, shaping how we bond and form relationships.

John Bowlby, a pioneer in attachment theory, underscored the evolutionary perspective. His research revealed that early attachment behaviors served a purpose beyond immediate survival: they helped form a secure base from which a child could explore the world and develop confidence. Bowlby's work laid the foundation for understanding how attachment styles form and persist throughout life, enlightening us about the profound impact of early experiences on our development.

Mary Ainsworth, a colleague of Bowlby, further advanced the field with her pioneering research. Her famous Strange Situation experiment identified three primary attachment styles:

- Secure
- Avoidant
- Anxious

This structured observational study subjected infants to separations and reunions with their caregivers. Securely attached infants showed distress when separated but quickly calmed upon reunion. In contrast, anxiously attached infants exhibited intense distress during separation and had difficulty calming down even when the caregiver returned. Ainsworth's work underscored the variability in attachment behaviors, providing a framework for understanding anxious attachment. We owe much to Ainsworth's pioneering research, which has advanced our understanding of attachment styles.

HOW CHILDHOOD EXPERIENCES SHAPE ATTACHMENT STYLES

While the evolutionary roots of anxious attachment provide an overarching framework, a child's individual experiences with caregivers significantly shape their attachment style. Children develop secure attachments when they experience consistent and responsive caregiving. This means that their caregivers quickly and reliably meet their needs, responding appropriately to their cries and signals. When children feel they can depend on their caregivers, they develop trust, forming the foundation of secure attachment.

However, children may develop an anxious attachment style when caregiving is inconsistent or neglectful. When a child's needs are met sporadically or unpredictably, the child becomes hyper-vigilant and constantly seeks reassurance, fearing abandonment. These behaviors are adaptive responses to the early experiences of unreliable caregiving.

For example, suppose a caregiver is affectionate and responsive at times but distant or unavailable at other times. In that case, it creates a confusing environment for the child. This inconsistency makes relationships feel unpredictable and unreliable, leading to the development of anxious attachment. Conversely, children who experience consistent emotional support from caregivers are likelier to develop secure attachment styles.

Traumatic childhood experiences, such as emotional or physical abuse, can also significantly impact attachment. When caregivers are abusive or neglectful, children learn that the people who are supposed to provide love and safety may also cause pain and fear. This duality can create a turbulent internal world where love and anxiety become intertwined. Similarly, parental separation or loss can disrupt a child's sense of stability, leading to anxious behaviors in future relationships. A trauma-informed approach to anxiety attachment recovery with a therapist or counselor can be highly beneficial if this is the case.

Another critical factor is the transmission of attachment styles across generations. As the primary caregivers and role models, parents unconsciously pass down their attachment patterns to their children. For instance, a parent with anxious attachment may exhibit overprotective or inconsistent behaviors, which the child may internalize and model. This cycle of attachment behaviors can perpetuate anxious attachment across generations.

There is hope for adults who have developed anxious attachment patterns due to their childhood experiences. Inner child healing exercises offer a practical approach. They involve reconnecting with the wounded inner child and providing the nurturing missed during childhood. We will cover this inner healing in more depth in Chapter 4.

THE NEUROSCIENCE BEHIND ATTACHMENT STYLES

Understanding the neuroscience that plays a pivotal part in attachment styles is essential. You will better understand why we act and feel the way we do in our relationships. Our brain wiring is a complex system that governs how we think, feel, and react, as well as the nature of our attachments. The amygdala is located deep within our brain. It is a small structure shaped like an almond, and it plays a fundamental role in how we process emotional responses. It becomes significantly activated when we are experiencing intense anxiety or fear, which can trigger a fight-or-flight response. When we feel an intense fear of abandonment, it is caused by our amygdala activating. Its purpose is to prepare our body to react to a perceived threat. This response has deep roots in our evolutionary past when we needed to react quickly to threats to survive.

Your prefrontal cortex is situated at the front of your brain. It carries out higher-order functions, such as emotional regulation, impulse control, and decision-making. This area also plays a part in letting us assess situations in a rational way and make logical decisions. If you are a person with anxious attachment, you have a weaker connection between the prefrontal cortex and the amygdala. This means it is harder to regulate your emotions during stressful moments. Also, you will be prone to overthinking and have trouble calming down if you feel there are threats to your relationship.

We often call oxytocin the "love hormone." It plays a significant role in bonding and attachment, and it is released during physical touch, such as hugging or holding hands. This hormone enhances feelings of trust and connection, which is crucial for establishing and maintaining strong bonds between people in relationships. If you have an anxious attachment style, the craving to have physical contact and reassurance is probably partially a result of craving oxytocin release. This biological drive helps us better understand how vital physical affection can be in forging secure attachments and reducing anxiety.

Other complex processes include the neurochemical interactions that form the basis for attachment and emotional responses. Dopamine and serotonin are neurotransmitters fundamental to mood regulation and emotional well-being. Dopamine is linked to pleasure and reward. It reinforces positive behaviors that make us feel good, such as spending time with loved ones. Serotonin is a little bit different. It focuses more on stabilizing our mood by helping us feel calm and happy. If you have an imbalance in these neurotransmitters, you will probably feel anxious and emotionally unstable. Both these emotions are significant in anxious attachment.

Additionally, stress hormones like cortisol play a role in responding to perceived threats. When cortisol levels increase, people tend to feel high levels of vigilance and anxiety. This makes it much harder for them to feel relaxed and have secure attachments.

Luckily, our brains have neuroplasticity, which allows them to reorganize and form new neural connections. This is a significant source of hope when changing our attachment patterns. We can rewire our brains by consciously adopting new thought patterns and behaviors. Our brains' adaptable nature helps us overcome anxious attachment styles and achieve security in our relationships. Treatment like cognitive behavioral therapy (CBT) can help reinforce these new neural pathways, promoting greater emotional regulation and stability.

As we have seen, neuroscience research has given us essential information on attachment styles. Brain imaging studies have demonstrated that people with different attachment styles show different brain activity patterns. As we have discussed, people with anxious attachment will often show heightened activity in the amygdala and lower connectivity with the prefrontal cortex. In longitudinal studies keeping track of people over time, it has been demonstrated how attachment-related brain changes tend to impact emotional and relational outcomes. It has also been found that specific genetic factors may make people more prone to particular attachment styles. However, environmental factors are highly significant.

I want you to understand that the neuroscience of attachment has practical implications for managing anxious attachment. If you have an anxious attachment style, one helpful strategy you can use to manage its effects is mindfulness practice. Practicing mindfulness can help calm your amygdala and strengthen the regulatory functioning of the prefrontal cortex, promoting better balance in your emotional responses. Neurofeedback is another therapeutic intervention that trains you to alter your brain activity.

It may help people with anxious attachments develop better emotional stability. Also, changing your lifestyle, such as getting enough sleep, eating healthy food, and regularly exercising, can support your brain health and may improve attachment security.

If you incorporate these strategies, you should be able to leverage your brain plasticity to develop healthier, more secure attachment patterns. Throughout this book, specifically in Chapter 3, we will explore these practical healing techniques, like CBT, mindfulness practices, and self-compassion exercises, in more depth—all effective in healing attachment wounds.

THE EMOTIONAL IMPACT OF ANXIOUS ATTACHMENT

If you have an anxious attachment style, you probably feel like you are living in a constant storm of emotions. You may be so frequently worried and fearful of abandonment that it is difficult to think or focus. You might experience intense anxiety just because there is a slight change in the tone of your partner's voice or a delay in a text message. You often feel on edge because you constantly fear being left alone. You have a constant feeling of insecurity in every part of your relationship.

There is even more emotional turmoil beyond that. For example, people with anxious attachments often experience dramatic emotional changes and mood swings. Intense emotional highs and lows leave you (and your partner) feeling drained and exhausted. Stability seems unattainable as you are in a perpetual state of emotional flux. You will find that your mental and physical well-being are negatively impacted over time.

Anxious attachment also commonly causes overthinking and obsessive thoughts about your relationship. You may replay past conversations, ruminating over every word and gesture, looking for hidden meanings. You might find it challenging to relax and sleep. Overthinking tends to cause anxiety, and you can end up in a vicious cycle that is difficult to break. I have struggled through this experience and know that your mind makes you feel like a prisoner, trapping you in an endless loop of anxiety and doubt. This makes it very challenging to enjoy the present moment or think positively about the future.

Before I took steps to address my anxious attachment, I found that it had a devastating impact on my self-esteem and sense of self-worth. One of the damaging aspects of frequently craving validation from others to have positive feelings about yourself is that your self-esteem becomes dependent on other people. This makes you too vulnerable to feelings of inadequacy and self-doubt, as you tend to believe you are inadequate when you are on your own. This might manifest in feeling inferior in social settings and underestimating your abilities. If you have this problem, you may negatively compare yourself to others and hold yourself back from trying new challenges.

Anxious attachment styles also put an enormous strain on relationships. The tendency toward jealousy and possessiveness can cause misunderstandings and conflict. A typical scenario is that you tend to be anxious about everything your partner does, seeing their interactions with other people as threats. When this kind of jealousy is present in a relationship, it can be toxic for both partners. Trust will erode, and it will likely cause an emotional distance. Many case studies have demonstrated how this kind of behavior can destroy the stability of a relationship, causing a cycle of conflict and reconciliation that will likely leave you feeling exhausted and disconnected.

You can do several different things to change these emotional responses and cultivate emotional security. You will find it easier to stay grounded and calm even during challenging moments when you use emotional regulation techniques. This involves methods such as deep breathing exercises and developing better self-compassion and self-care. Being kind to yourself and prioritizing your well-being means you can strengthen your sense of self-worth, so you are not depending on external validation. Mindfulness practices will also help you create better emotional resilience, making coping with anxiety and having more stable relationships much more manageable. We will thoroughly cover more detailed techniques and processes for long-term emotional stability throughout the rest of the book.

It takes a lot of work to achieve emotional security. It does not happen overnight. You must exert continual effort, be willing to face your fears, use the right strategies, and deeply consider how anxious attachment impacts you emotionally. In this way, you can start to transform your emotional responses. Making these changes means you can feel safe and secure in your relationships, with high trust and mutual support. You will create a feeling of peace within yourself and a sense of stability in your interpersonal interactions.

CHAPTER 2

IDENTIFYING ANXIOUS ATTACHMENT AND EMOTIONAL TRIGGERS

THERE WAS A TIME SEVERAL YEARS AGO WHEN I WAS CONSTANTLY feeling anxious and on edge. It felt like I was being tested every time I spoke to my partner. I was continually seeking reassurance that I would not lose their affection. On one occasion, there was a particularly intense argument. It plunged me into self-doubt. I could not understand why I would react so dramatically and always seemed to fear the worst. It only took a short amount of introspection to realize that I needed to understand myself for any chance of healing.

My goal in this chapter is to help you become self-aware. I will show you how to reveal the causes of your anxious attachment and suggest tools to identify and understand them so that you can manage them. As I mentioned in the previous chapter, exploring the source of anxious attachment may bring up traumatic events in your life. So, contact professional therapists or counselors if you need support.

SELF-IDENTIFYING AND UNDERSTANDING ANXIOUS ATTACHMENT

You need insight into your attachment style to achieve emotional health and personal growth, especially in relationships. I recommend using self-assessment tools to understand how you behave and respond emotionally.

You can start by doing online quizzes and assessments. If you look for these tools, stick to reputable psychology websites. When you take these quizzes, remember that they are designed to help you understand your current attachment style. They will usually ask several questions about your behaviors and emotions in relationships. For example, questionnaires may prompt you to reflect on your feelings and relationship behaviors. For instance, there might be questions such as "Do you often worry that your partner does not love you?" or "How frequently do you seek reassurance from your partner?" You may also be asked to reflect on your reactions when your partner does not respond to a message as quickly as you would like. Answering these questions honestly can provide a clearer picture of your attachment style.

The next step to take is interpreting your assessment results. Quizzes or formal inventories you take may give you a scoring method to categorize your attachment style. Make sure that you understand the score breakdowns. You might have an anxious attachment style if you get a high score on the fear of abandonment questions. It is helpful to compare your results with known attachment styles to get more insight. If you get an indication that you tend to have an anxious attachment, you then need to know about the behaviors and feelings linked to this style.

After that, you need to identify the areas where you can improve. Do you constantly feel like you need reassurance or have obstacles to trust? By focusing on these areas, you can improve your efforts to make specific changes.

Your fundamental transformation can begin by connecting your assessment results to your daily relationship patterns and behaviors. If you have an assessment that shows intense anxiety in relationships, you probably overthink everything your partner says and does, looking for constant validation. You can see illustrations of the dynamics at work by imagining specific scenarios. For example, if your partner is busy at work and does not send an immediate response to your texts, you may have an anxious attachment style if you feel worried that they do not care or are losing interest. You will see patterns you must address more efficiently by understanding how your assessment results link to your behavior.

There are also more reflective self-questionnaires you can do. One benefit is how they require reflection on emotions and behavior, thus assisting you in understanding your potential patterns and triggers. Some questions you might need to answer include, "What are your emotions when your partner is not around?" and "What are the biggest fears you tend to have in relationships?" When you answer these questions, you will achieve much better clarity in understanding your attachment style. A more in-depth option is an attachment-style inventory. If you go to a therapist, you will likely be asked to answer the questions for one of these. They are used to assess your attachment style. They ask about your childhood experiences and relationship history.

You could also consult a checklist of common anxious attachment behaviors as a quick reference. Some behaviors include the tendency to overthink and ruminate about your relationships. These checklists will help you recognize typical signs and symptoms of anxious attachment. As alluded to above, you probably show an excessive need for reassurance if you have this attachment style. For example, you might constantly look for validation from your partner, asking questions like, "Do you still love me?" or "Are you mad at me?" The root of this constant need for affirmation tends to be caused by a deep-seated fear of abandonment. There are various ways that this fear may manifest, such as imagining that neutral behavior means rejection or anxious feelings when a partner is not immediately available. You may replay conversations in your mind often, dissecting every word and action, looking for hidden meanings. You probably worry about potential problems in the relationship's future, even if there are no apparent issues.

Reflective journaling is another helpful practice for identifying anxious attachment, which prompts you to examine and deeply understand your experiences and emotions. For example, you could write using prompts such as "What tends to cause anxiety for you in relationships?" and "How do you react when you feel fearful of being abandoned?" Using these reflective questions will help increase your self-awareness. They can help you better understand your attachment style and uncover patterns by tracking your emotions and thoughts.

You can also do mirror exercises to reflect on your feelings and inner world. To do this, look at yourself in the mirror and have an honest conversation with yourself about your fears and insecurities. Doing this exercise is helpful with confronting your emotions and understanding them on a deeper level. You may also benefit from guided meditations to achieve better inner awareness. The main focus of these meditations is grounding yourself in the present moment and maintaining awareness of your thoughts without judgment. This helps you develop a more balanced and mindful approach to your emotions.

It is easier to see how anxious attachment can manifest in your life if we look at a few personal stories I have heard. Consider Emma, who has an anxious attachment style and, in the past, has experienced consistent anxiety in her relationships. She was constantly craving reassurance and feared that her partners would leave her, and, unfortunately, this often ended with her partners feeling pushed away and frustrated. Emma started to help herself with self-examination and therapy. These assisted her in realizing that she had an anxious attachment style, and she began to work on increasing her confidence and trust in relationships.

We see a similar story with John, who struggled with relationship trust issues. He frequently had difficulty believing that his partner had genuine affection and loyalty toward him. As a result of this lack of trust, John experienced anxiety, emotional distress, and constant arguing with his partner. It was through acknowledging that he had an anxious attachment style and getting the right kind of help that John eventually was able to feel more secure in his relationships, helping them become a healthier couple.

Do not consider recognizing your attachment style as labeling yourself. Identifying and understanding your attachment style and how it manifests in your life is essential to achieving greater insight and having healthier, more fulfilling relationships.

When you have an anxious attachment style, you often feel like there is a constant conflict between craving closeness and fearing loss. Using self-assessment tools, reflecting on personal stories, and doing reflective exercises can help you begin to understand and disengage from anxious attachment patterns. With this awareness, you will be much better able to take actionable steps, manage your attachment-related anxiety, and build lasting, more secure relationships.

PERSONAL ATTACHMENT HISTORY: MAPPING YOUR PAST

Another tool I have found helpful is to create an attachment timeline to give you crucial insights into how your past shapes how you feel and behave in the present. Begin by thinking about the significant events and relationships in your life. Think back to your earliest memories of connection and disconnection. Did you feel secure and loved at those times, or do you remember some neglect or inconsistency? When you pinpoint these events, it will be easier to see the big picture. Reflect on pivotal moments. These could be moving to a new city, your parents divorcing, or a new sibling being born. Each of these events can influence your sense of stability and security. Think about how you felt during events like this, and analyze the reasons for your feelings. You will understand how your attachment style developed when you map out your past like this.

Remember what I discussed earlier about how your childhood experiences with your caregivers enormously impact your future attachment style. Spend time contemplating your relationships with your parents or primary caregivers. Did they make you anxious or uncertain, or were they dependable and consistent? You also need to consider family dynamics. If you had an unpredictable or chaotic family environment, you may have high anxiety and hypervigilance today. Remember that early experiences affect how we feel and act in our relationships.

It is also crucial to analyze your past relationships. Consider your previous romantic and platonic relationships. What were your feelings and emotional state in those relationships? Did you have anxiety about abandonment and not being good enough? Keep an eye out for common themes and behaviors. You might notice a tendency to become overly dependent on your partners. You might also realize that you get jealous and insecure frequently. Patterns in the way you respond emotionally are essential to examine. When you have to face conflict, do you have an anxious reaction? Or do you usually withdraw and just shut down? By understanding these patterns, you will find it easier to understand what caused your anxious attachment.

You need to do a lot of introspection to heal from the attachment-related wounds of the past. CBT and other therapeutic approaches, such as EMDR (eye movement desensitization and reprocessing), can be incredibly effective. Using these kinds of therapies will support you in processing and reframing traumatic experiences. This will cut down on how much they impact your current life. You should also do self-compassion exercises. Be kind and compassionate in how you speak to yourself, especially when you are dealing with anxiety. This change in your self-talk can be transformational for your emotional well-being and self-esteem. I have also benefited from rewriting my narratives. Try not to see yourself as a victim of your past. Instead, think of yourself as a survivor who has used their experiences to learn and grow. Make this change in your perspective and empower yourself with confidence. This will make you more resilient.

EMOTIONAL TRIGGERS: IDENTIFYING AND UNDERSTANDING THEM

Thinking deeply about your experiences and reactions can help uncover the hidden emotional patterns of your anxious attachment style, increasing your self-awareness. It will also help you learn about the factors that trigger you in relationships.

An emotional trigger is something that leads to an intense emotional reaction. For example, you may see specific situations that cause insecurity or anxiety. It could also be a memory or event. If you have an anxious attachment, you will probably have triggers that cause you to feel insecure or fearful. If you have an anxious attachment, your triggers may be perceived rejection, criticism, or even minor instances of neglect. For example, if your partner seems distracted during a conversation, you might immediately fear that they are losing interest. These triggers can lead to heightened emotional responses such as anxiety, anger, or sadness, often out of proportion to the actual event. It is crucial to understand your triggers to know how they affect your emotional well-being and relationship dynamics.

There is an easy way you can begin to identify your triggers—by keeping a trigger journal. Every time you have a strong emotional reaction, write down the situation that caused it. Note the specifics, including what was said, where you were, and who was involved. Reflect on your past emotional reactions. Consider situations in which you experienced intense anxiety or fear. What was happening at the time? What thoughts were running through your mind? Also, attend to the physical and emotional responses you experience when exposed to these triggers. Know about the physical cues of being triggered. These could be a knot in your stomach, a racing heart, or a sense of impending doom.

After you have found out what your triggers are, it is time to manage them. You could also do self-soothing activities, such as taking a warm bath or listening to your favorite music. Doing mindfulness exercises can be helpful, as can doing relaxation exercises such as deep breathing, progressive muscle relaxation, and mindfulness meditation. These exercises can calm your nervous system and reduce the intensity of your emotional reactions. I also recommend using cognitive reframing techniques. This means that you change how you interpret the event that triggers you. If you get triggered because your partner does not immediately respond to a text, you can reframe your thought that they are ignoring you because they do not care, instead thinking they are probably too busy to respond. It is equally essential to develop effective coping mechanisms. For example, you could seek support from a trusted friend or start a new hobby. (The next chapter will review these strategies and techniques more thoroughly.)

Let's take a look at a specific example with Sarah, who tended to feel intense anxiety when her partner, Tom, did not immediately respond to her messages. It was because she kept a trigger journal that she was able to identify her anxiety getting out of control whenever Tom was busy with his work or out with his friends. When thinking about her childhood, she realized that her father's unavailability was the root cause of her anxious attachment style. She began using cognitive reframing. She told herself that Tom was not rejecting her when there was a delay in his response. Also, she made mindfulness practice part of her routine, which was vital to keeping her grounded. Her anxiety eventually decreased, and she felt safe and secure in her connection with her partner.

So, to begin with, let us set aside some time every day to reflect on your triggers and how you respond emotionally. Make a note of situations that gave rise to a strong emotional reaction, and consider why they may have had this effect.

CHAPTER 3
MANAGING ANXIETY AND EMOTIONAL REGULATION

THERE HAVE BEEN TIMES I HAVE WOKEN UP IN THE MIDDLE OF THE night, my heart pounding and thoughts racing. Before I knew how to deal with this, my worry would not disappear when I tried to calm myself. Do you ever have moments like this? Many of us have endured intense anxiety triggered by the fears of abandonment that come with feelings of insecurity in relationships.

Practical strategies for managing anxiety are a lifeline at times like these. In this next chapter, we will discuss tools that you can use to relieve your stress and regulate your emotions. We will then look at some more long-term maintenance and planning for emotional balance and create a daily anxiety management routine.

STRATEGIES AND TOOLS FOR ANXIETY RELIEF AND EMOTIONAL REGULATION

Think of this section as a toolkit to reach into when you have moments like the one mentioned above. We will review several techniques you can harness to help relieve your anxiety and regulate your emotions.

Self-Soothing Techniques for Immediate Relief

Self-soothing is comforting yourself when you are feeling stressed or anxious. This is a crucial skill for all of us, but it is especially essential if you have anxiety and an anxious attachment style. Self-soothing techniques will help regulate your emotions, reduce stress, and return you to calm.

When you self-soothe, you make yourself feel safe and secure within yourself. Self-soothing is finding ways to calm yourself mentally and physically when you cannot find any external reassurance. It plays a vital role in emotional regulation. You will not need constant reassurance from other people because you will be able to control your emotional responses. This feeling of independence will empower you and allow you to enjoy more stability and fulfillment in your relationships.

If you have an anxious attachment, there are many situations in which you need self-soothing. One example might be feeling anxious after disagreeing with your partner, and you can use self-soothing to help you calm down and achieve clarity of thought. If you have anxiety in social settings or when in uncertain circumstances, you can also use self-soothing techniques to get immediate relief and help you navigate those kinds of situations.

Here are some practical physical self-soothing strategies that you can try:

1. **Weighted Blankets**: These have become popular lately, and many people find them comforting. The blanket gives gentle pressure that mimics a comforting hug, promoting safety and calm. It is beneficial during moments of intense anxiety or when you are having trouble falling asleep.
2. **Warm Bath**: A warm bath is another fantastic way to soothe your body and mind. The warmth of the water can reduce your anxiety and relax your muscles. You could add a calming scent (lavender is a good choice) to your bath, making it even more relaxing.
3. **Light Exercise**: Another self-soothing method is light physical exercise, such as walking or gentle yoga. Exercise helps because it releases endorphins, which are natural mood lifters. Plus, it helps distract your mind from thoughts that are making you anxious.

Along with physical techniques, you can also use emotional self-soothing methods:

1. **Listening to Music**: One example is listening to some tranquil music. I find that this quickly transforms my mood to a more peaceful state, reducing anxiety and promoting relaxation. Make a playlist of calming songs and use it during stressful moments.

2. **Positive Affirmations**: I also recommend doing positive affirmations. When you use affirmations, you challenge negative thoughts and promote a more balanced perspective. Some helpful affirmations are "I am safe and loved," "I am capable of handling this," and "I trust the process of life." By repeating these affirmations, you will positively change your mindset and cut down on your anxiety.

3. **Creative Activities**: You can also try participating in creative activities such as drawing, painting, or writing. These activities are a healthy and productive outlet for emotional expression and can be a type of mindfulness practice, improving your focus.

I have found it helpful to have a personal self-soothing toolkit. It has made making self-soothing a part of my daily life much easier. Include items that make you feel happy and comforted, such as a journal, a blanket, or a book. I always keep my self-soothing toolkit nearby to use whenever I need to. Making time every day to do self-soothing activities can help to prevent anxiety before it starts. This could be a bit of deep breathing every morning or a relaxing bath at night.

As we see, self-soothing is helpful for people who suffer from the anxiety of anxious attachment. Knowing how to soothe yourself without needing help from anyone else can create calmer and more stable relationships.

Grounding Exercises for Anxiety and Emotional Stability

I have discovered that grounding exercises are practical for anxiety and emotion stabilization. Do grounding exercises to keep your mind in the present and connected to the here and now. Grounding has been able to anchor me when I have been otherwise overwhelmed by anxiety. When you ground yourself, you use your senses to secure your focus in the present. I know from experience that this can be an enormously helpful tool when you are anxious. Bring your focus to tangible, sensory experiences, and you will find that it helps you disrupt the cycle of worry, establishing better control over your emotional state.

Grounding has many benefits. One is that it reduces the immediate sense of panic, creating a sense of calm. Grounding can also be a mental and emotional reset button, letting you break free from the grip of anxious thoughts. Try grounding before situations that make you nervous, such as a big presentation at work or during an emotionally wrought conversation.

Here is one effective physical grounding technique: it is called the 5-4-3-2-1 technique. It engages all of your senses and makes you reconnect with your surroundings. You can practice it by identifying five things you can see around you. Next, focus on four things you can touch, followed by three things you can hear. After that, focus on two things you can smell and one thing you can taste. When you do this exercise, it helps to redirect your attention away from anxious thoughts and back to the present moment. Another surprisingly effective technique is holding an ice cube or other cold object. The intense sensation of cold can snap you out of an anxious state by forcing your focus on the physical sensation. Another way to ground yourself is to walk barefoot on grass. You will benefit from the soothing texture and coolness of the grass and feel more connected to the earth.

You could also try mental grounding techniques. One I often use is counting backward from 100. It requires focus and concentration, helping to distract your mind from anxiety. You can also try creating a detailed description of an object to help ground your thinking. Choose an object nearby and describe its size, shape, color, and texture. Doing this means you have to focus on something specific and tangible, and you will be pulled away from your anxious thoughts. Another approach is reciting a favorite poem or song. The rhythm and familiarity of the words can be calming, and as you focus on the recitation, you shift your attention away from the anxiety.

I recommend creating a grounding routine for yourself. It can help you make grounding exercises a part of your daily life. Decide on the specific times of each day when you will do grounding. This could be in the morning as you begin your day or in the evening when you want to relax. I recommend bringing together grounding techniques with other strategies for anxiety management. Here is an example. You could begin with a grounding exercise and follow it up with a mindfulness meditation or a breathing exercise. Doing grounding exercises in various environments to improve your adaptability is also helpful. I make sure that I have a repertoire of grounding techniques that can make it easier to manage anxiety wherever you find yourself.

As shown here, grounding techniques will help you manage your emotions when you have an anxious attachment style. If you understand how important it is to stay grounded and use mental and physical grounding exercises in your routine, you will create a better feeling of stability. This will help you stay calm when your anxiety starts to rise. I recommend developing a consistent grounding routine, empowering you to deal with your anxious attachment more effectively.

Visualization Practices to Calm the Mind

Visualization is also a great idea, as it is a powerful tool for managing anxiety. It gives you psychological and physiological benefits that may dramatically alleviate your stress. Engaging in visualization means you use your mind to create calming and peaceful images that help to reduce your heart rate and muscle tension. There is science behind this technique. It is based on how visualization can activate the same neural pathways as real experiences. When you vividly imagine a peaceful scene, you get a brain response similar to being in that environment. This means that calm neurotransmitters like dopamine and serotonin are released. Visualization is an incredibly fantastic tool when you are in a high-stress situation. This could be before a big meeting, during a confrontation, or even when you feel overwhelmed by daily tasks. You will have a mental escape, allowing you to regain control over your emotions and thoughts.

The most important part of visualization is guided imagery exercises. One of the most effective exercises is to visualize a peaceful place. Close your eyes and picture a comfortable, quiet place encouraging a tranquil mind. This could be a beach, a forest, or a cozy room. Take the time to imagine and picture all the details. Imagine all the sensory input you would experience if you visualized the beach. This includes the sound of waves crashing and the feel of the sand under your feet. This can become a mental sanctuary to which you can retreat whenever you get anxious. Another helpful exercise you can try when you are feeling anxiety is imagining a positive outcome to whatever stressful situation you may be in. Are you worried about giving a presentation at work? Visualize yourself speaking confidently and receiving positive feedback, as well as the feeling of being accomplished. Using this positive imagery can have an enormous impact on reducing anxiety and building confidence. You can also create a mental sanctuary for relaxation. Design a space in your mind where you can retreat whenever anxiety strikes. You can imagine a range of comforting objects in it, such as soft pillows, calming colors, and soothing sounds.

You can integrate practical visualization techniques into your daily life with ease. I find the "safe place" visualization highly effective in many situations. Whenever you feel anxious, close your eyes and picture a place where you feel completely safe and secure. Examples could be a childhood home, a favorite vacation spot, or even an imaginary world. It is also good to visualize success in challenging situations. Whenever you need to face a difficult task, visualize yourself achieving success for a few moments. Picture yourself meeting the challenge head-on, succeeding, getting praise, and feeling proud. In my experience, this technique is great for boosting confidence and reducing anxiety. Also, mindful visualization is something you can try, especially when you are doing everyday activities. For example, while washing your dishes, imagine the water washing away your stress. Or perhaps while walking, you could visualize each step grounding you and bringing you closer to a calm state.

Think about using visualization apps and tools. Some out there provide guided exercises, which are great for reminding you to practice regularly. Many apps or videos with guided visualizations can be highly effective. They offer a variety of guided visualizations tailored to different needs. I recommend combining visualization with other relaxation techniques to make it even more effective. For instance, I usually begin with deep breathing to relax before I start my visualization.

With the proper visualization practices, you have a robust and accessible way to manage your anxiety. By understanding the benefits and science behind visualization, engaging in guided imagery exercises, and incorporating practical techniques into your daily routine, you can create a mental toolkit for reducing stress and enhancing emotional well-being. With visualization, you can make a mental sanctuary, a place where you can find peace and calm amid the chaos of daily life, helping you navigate challenges with greater ease and confidence.

Breathing Exercises for Reducing Stress and Emotional Regulation

Do breathing exercises to manage your stress and anxiety. Breathing is so powerful because it affects your body's physiological responses. Deep breathing techniques, for example, can activate your parasympathetic nervous system, helping to calm your body and reduce the fight-or-flight response. Controlled breathing can lower your heart rate, ease muscle tension, and promote relaxation. Breathing techniques are also helpful for emotional regulation in general.

1. **Diaphragmatic Breathing**: Also known as belly breathing, this is a simple yet effective method of calming one's mind. Breathing deeply into one's diaphragm activates the parasympathetic nervous system, encouraging relaxation. This technique can help reduce anxiety, lower stress levels, and bring a sense of calm. Begin by sitting or lying down in a comfortable position. Put one hand on your chest and the other on your belly. Take a deep breath through your nose so your belly rises as air fills your lungs. Your chest should remain relatively still. Do a slow exhale through your mouth, allowing your belly to fall. Repeat these steps several times over several minutes, focusing on the rise and fall of your belly. This technique helps deepen your breath and promote relaxation.

2. **Resonant Breathing**: Also referred to as coherent breathing, this technique involves breathing at a rate that maximizes your heart rate variability, which may promote relaxation and emotional stability. When you want to practice resonant breathing, sit or lie comfortably, slowly inhale through your nose for a few seconds, and then slowly exhale through your nose. Aim to maintain a steady, even rhythm, breathing at about five deep, slow breaths per minute. This technique tends to be effective for synchronizing your heart rate and breathing, reducing stress and anxiety.

3. **4-7-4 Breathing**: This is another powerful breathing technique to reduce anxiety. Start by sitting or lying down

and getting yourself comfortable. Close your eyes, and then inhale quietly through your nose. Hold for a few seconds. After that, exhale completely through your mouth for a count of eight. This extended exhalation helps you expel more air from your lungs, promoting a sense of calm. Repeat this cycle three to four times, allowing yourself to relax with each breath.

4. **Box Breathing**: Also known as square breathing, this is a technique that Navy SEALs use to stay calm and focused even in the most high-pressure situations. Here is how to practice box breathing. Sit comfortably with your back straight, and then close your eyes. Inhale slowly through your nose. Try to hold your breath for a count of four. Exhale slowly through your mouth. Finally, try to hold your breath again for a count of four. Repeat this cycle four to five times, maintaining a steady rhythm. Using this technique may help you get control over your breathing, reducing anxiety.

5. **Alternate Nostril Breathing**: Try this advanced breathing technique to achieve a deeper level of relaxation. Alternate nostril breathing, also called *Anulom Vilom*, is a practice yoga practitioners use to balance the mind and body. Sit in a comfortable position, keeping your spine straight. Using your right thumb, close your right nostril and inhale deeply through the left. Then, close your left nostril with your ring finger and release the right one, exhaling fully through the right. Inhale through the right nostril, close it with your thumb, then exhale through the left nostril. Keep repeating this pattern for several minutes, focusing on

your breath. This technique can make me feel more balanced and calmer.

6. **Breath-Counting Meditations**: I also like doing a combination of breathwork and meditation. It is another advanced technique that combines mindfulness and controlled breathing. Start sitting comfortably with a straight back, then close your eyes. Take a few deep breaths and take your time settling in. After that, breathe naturally and start counting each exhale. Count "one" on the first exhale, "two" on the next, and so on. Keep going until you get to five. After reaching five, start over at one. If your mind wanders, gently bring your focus back to your breath and the counting. With this technique, you will stay present and centered, alleviating your anxious thoughts.

Breathing exercises can significantly reduce stress and anxiety in daily life. Therefore, creating reminders to practice breathing exercises at different points of the day can be beneficial. For example, you could do your breathing exercises in the morning, during your lunch break, or before bed. Combining your breathing exercises with mindfulness and meditation will make them even more centering and calming. For instance, you could begin with a breathing exercise to calm your mind, and after that, you could do a mindfulness meditation to keep yourself in the present moment. Remember that once you know how to do breathing exercises, you can do them in various situations, such as at home, work, or public places. When you have a repertoire of breathing techniques, they can empower you to manage anxiety wherever you are.

Cognitive-Behavioral Techniques for Anxiety Management

CBT is established to be one of the best methods of anxiety management. With CBT, you focus on noticing and changing your negative thought patterns that cause you anxiety and distress. It is based on interconnectedness regarding your feelings, thoughts, and behaviors. Addressing irrational and unhelpful thinking patterns can positively influence your emotions and behavior. CBT is especially beneficial for people with anxious attachment, as it offers practical methods for challenging your worried thoughts, giving you a way to reframe them. By taking part in CBT therapy, you get empowered to get the control you need over your anxiety. This gives you a way to improve your psychological health and the health of your relationships.

When you do CBT, one of the first steps you will take is identifying your negative thought patterns. In CBT, these patterns are called cognitive distortions. They include common pitfalls, such as catastrophizing. That is when you imagine the worst possible outcome or engage in black-and-white thinking, where you see situations in extremes without understanding that there are gray areas and middle ground. You could write in a thought diary, a powerful tool for this purpose; every time you start feeling anxious, write down the situation, what you think about it, and the emotions resulting from your thoughts. There are specific questions you can ask yourself for reflection. For example, ask yourself, "What evidence do I have for this thought?" or "Is there another way to interpret this situation?" When you ask yourself to answer these questions, you are encouraged to think critically about how you tend to react.

After you have noticed your negative thoughts, you need to do cognitive restructuring. Doing this process means that you challenge and change your negative thoughts. Begin by contemplating the evidence for and against your anxious thoughts. An example could be if you think, "My partner did not call me, so they must be losing interest," seek evidence that contradicts this thought, such as when your partner has shown you care and affection. You should also try positively reframing your thoughts. For instance, instead of thinking, "They did not call because they do not care," you might reframe this thought as "They are likely busy but will call when they can." By practicing using alternative, balanced thinking, you get practice consistently applying your new, more rational thoughts so much that they will eventually become second nature.

CBT involves a combination of behavioral techniques and cognitive strategies. Exposure exercises allow you to face your fears with a controlled and gradual approach. Do you fear being alone? You might begin by spending short periods alone, gradually stepping up the time as you become more comfortable. You can even try to do behavioral experiments to help you test the validity of your negative thoughts. Let's take a look at an example. Say that you believe asking for reassurance would annoy your partner; try asking them about this calmly and carefully and see what reaction you get. Doing this can give you real-life evidence that contradicts your fears. This kind of exercise provides gradual desensitization, which means slowly exposing yourself to situations that cause anxiety to cut down on your sensitivity over time. Do social situations cause stress for you?

Begin by attending small gatherings and gradually working up to more significant events.

LONG-TERM MAINTENANCE FOR EMOTIONAL REGULATION AND BALANCE

Life can be overwhelming for anyone, but it tends to be even more distressing for people with anxious attachments. That is why self-awareness and emotional regulation are so vitally important. Emotional regulation is managing and healthily responding to one's emotional experiences. It is an essential tool for navigating life's ups and downs with greater ease and resilience.

You need solid emotional regulation for good mental health and healthy relationships. Effective emotional dysregulation means regulating your emotions even in the most distressing conditions. This is crucial, as emotional dysregulation can lead to impulsive actions, strained relationships, and mental health issues. Emotional dysregulation occurs when you have intense emotional responses disproportionate to the situation—for example, feeling overwhelming anger over a minor inconvenience or experiencing deep sadness from a slight criticism.

These intense emotional reactions can disrupt your life, making it hard to maintain stable relationships and a sense of well-being. Regularly developing better emotional regulation skills can enhance your emotional intelligence, improve your relationships, and foster a sense of inner peace.

Regular Mindfulness and Breathing Practices for Self-Awareness

When you are mindful, you are fully present in the moment and aware of your thoughts, feelings, and surroundings without judgment. It is about paying attention to the here and now rather than getting lost in past regrets or future worries. You will enhance your self-awareness by improving your mindfulness, as it helps you notice your emotional and physical reactions as they happen. This awareness can improve emotional regulation, stress reduction, and mental health. Practicing mindfulness regularly can help you develop a deeper understanding of your inner world, making it easier to manage your emotions and respond to life's challenges with greater clarity and calm.

Practicing mindfulness regularly has many other benefits, including reducing anxiety and stress. When you practice mindfulness, you create a space between yourself and your reactions, letting you observe your thoughts and emotions without them overwhelming you. This detachment can help you respond more thoughtfully rather than react impulsively. Mindfulness can also improve focus and concentration, enhance self-compassion, and promote inner peace. Examples of mindfulness practices include mindful breathing, body scan meditation, and mindful observation of daily activities. Each of these practices offers a unique way to cultivate awareness and presence.

Mindful breathing exercises are a cornerstone of mindfulness practice. As we discussed earlier, focused breathing techniques involve paying close attention to your breath, feeling the air fill your lungs, and noticing the rise and fall of your chest. If your mind wanders, gently bring your attention back to your breath. Counting breaths can also enhance mindfulness. Inhale deeply and count "one," then exhale and count "two." Continue counting with each breath until you reach ten, then start over. This simple exercise can help anchor your mind and increase your awareness of the present moment.

Breathing with body awareness takes mindful breathing a step further by focusing on physical sensations. As you breathe in, notice how the air feels as it enters your nose, travels down your throat, and fills your lungs. Pay attention to the subtle movements in your body as you breathe, such as the expansion of your rib cage and the gentle rise of your abdomen. On the exhale, notice the sensation of the breath leaving your body and the slight relaxation that follows. With this practice, you will connect more deeply with your body. It can be exceptionally grounding and calming.

Another tool to use for self-awareness is body scan meditation. This practice involves mentally scanning your body from head to toe, paying attention to any sensations you notice. The first step is to find a comfortable position and close your eyes. Begin to relax by taking a few deep breaths. Start by focusing on the top of your head and slowly move your attention down your body. Notice any areas of tension, discomfort, or relaxation. Observe your feelings rather than trying to change anything. For example, you might feel tightness in your shoulders or warmth in your hands. Reflecting on these physical sensations can help you become more attuned to your body and its signals. A guided body scan meditation script can further assist in this practice, providing step-by-step instructions to help you stay focused and present.

Use mindful observation to understand your surroundings and internal states without judgment. Observe each thought and emotion as it arises, refraining from labeling it good or bad. For instance, if you notice a feeling of sadness, acknowledge it by saying to yourself, "I am feeling sad," without trying to push it away or analyze it. This non-judgmental awareness can help you develop a more accepting and compassionate relationship with yourself. Mindful observation can also be applied to daily activities. Whether you are washing dishes, walking, or eating, try to engage in the experience fully. Notice the sights, sounds, smells, and sensations involved in the activity. This practice can transform mundane tasks into opportunities for mindfulness and presence.

Reflective questions can further enhance your practice of mindful observation. Ask yourself, "What thoughts and emotions am I experiencing right now?" or "How do my surroundings affect my mood?" These questions encourage you to explore your inner world and deepen your self-awareness. Regular practice of mindful observation lets you develop a greater sense of presence and clarity, making it easier to navigate life's challenges with a calm and balanced mind.

Self-Compassion Exercises

Self-compassion is a necessary part of emotional regulation and overall well-being. It means you treat yourself with the kindness and understanding you would offer a close friend. It involves acknowledging your suffering without judgment and recognizing that imperfection is a shared human experience. There are profound benefits to showing yourself compassion. It can reduce your anxiety, increase resilience, and improve your overall mental health. Let's take a look at an example. Imagine you have made a mistake at work. Instead of criticizing yourself, you might acknowledge that everyone makes mistakes and use them as learning opportunities. This shift in perspective can lead to better emotional balance and greater self-acceptance.

I like taking self-compassion breaks. They are a practical way to incorporate this practice into your daily life. When you notice stress or self-criticism, pause and give yourself a moment of kindness. Start by acknowledging your suffering. You might say, "This is hard right now." Next, remind yourself that suffering is a part of life, saying, "I am not alone; others feel this way too." Finally, offer yourself a kind gesture, such as placing a hand over your heart and saying, "May I be kind to myself." Reflecting on your need for self-compassion can help you recognize when you are being too harsh with yourself. Practice scenarios for self-compassion breaks could include moments of failure, rejection, or intense pressure. Take regular self-compassion breaks to create a more compassionate relationship with yourself.

Self-compassionate journaling is another effective tool. Start by using journaling prompts focused on self-compassion. For example, write about a time when you struggled and how you responded to yourself. Reflect on whether you were kind or critical. Another prompt might be to list ways to be more compassionate with yourself in the future. It is equally important to reflect on your self-critical thoughts. Notice when you are being harsh with yourself and challenge these thoughts. For instance, if you think, "I am not good enough," ask yourself if this is accurate and what evidence you have to support it. Writing letters to yourself with compassion can also be powerful. Treat yourself like you would a dear friend, providing words of kindness and encouragement. This exercise can help shift your inner dialogue from critical to supportive.

Another technique I like to use is compassionate imagery. In this approach, you visualize a compassionate figure offering kindness and support. Begin by finding a quiet place to sit comfortably. Close your eyes and take a few deep breaths. Visualize a person who embodies compassion. This could be someone you know, a historical figure, or even an imagined being. Imagine this person offering you warmth and kindness. Imagine them saying words of comfort and understanding. Reflect on the feelings evoked by this imagery. You might feel a sense of relief, warmth, or connection. Compassionate imagery can support you during stressful times, offering a mental refuge of kindness and empathy.

Make self-compassion exercises part of your daily life so that you will foster a more nurturing and supportive relationship with yourself. Whether taking self-compassion breaks, journaling, or using compassionate imagery, each practice offers a way to cultivate kindness and understanding. Shifting your perspective in this way can bring you better emotional balance, resilience, and overall well-being. Self-compassion allows you to transform your inner dialogue and create a foundation of support and kindness that enhances every aspect of your life.

Cognitive Reappraisal and Emotional Labeling

Cognitive reappraisal is a technique that involves changing the way you interpret and respond to situations. You can change your emotional response when you reinterpret a problem from a different perspective. The steps for cognitive reappraisal include identifying the negative thought, challenging its validity, and replacing it with a more balanced perspective. For example, if you receive critical feedback at work, your initial reaction might be to feel hurt and defensive. By practicing cognitive reappraisal, you can reframe the feedback as an opportunity for growth and improvement. By making this kind of shift in perspective, you can reduce negative emotions and promote a more positive outlook.

You can practice this kind of cognitive reappraisal by doing reflective exercises. Begin by noting a recent situation that triggered a strong emotional response. Identify the specific negative thoughts you had about the problem. Present a challenge to these thoughts by asking yourself questions such as, "Is there evidence to support this thought?" or "Could there be another explanation?" Finally, reframe the situation with a more balanced perspective. For example, if you felt rejected because a friend canceled plans, you might reframe it by considering that they might have had a legitimate reason and still value your friendship. Regular cognitive reappraisal can help you develop a more resilient and balanced approach to life's challenges.

You can also become skilled in emotional labeling to achieve sound emotional regulation. This means that you learn how to recognize and name your emotions accurately. After all, you need to know your feelings before genuinely understanding and managing them. The importance of emotional labeling lies in its ability to provide clarity and reduce the intensity of negative emotions. When you accurately label your feelings, your prefrontal cortex is activated. This helps you regulate the emotional response generated by the amygdala. This process can create a sense of distance from the emotion, allowing you to respond more thoughtfully.

To practice emotional labeling, tune into your physical sensations and thoughts. Ask yourself, "What am I feeling right now?" and try to identify the specific emotion. It might be anger, sadness, fear, or frustration. Use precise words to describe the feeling, such as "annoyed" instead of "angry" or "disappointed" instead of "sad." Journaling prompts can also aid in emotional labeling. For instance, write about a recent event and describe the emotions you felt during and after the event. Reflect on how these emotions influenced your thoughts and actions. Regularly practicing emotional labeling can enhance your emotional awareness and regulation skills.

You should incorporate these techniques into your daily life to significantly improve your ability to regulate emotions. Whether you practice cognitive reappraisal or emotional labeling, each method is valuable for managing your emotional experiences. These skills can help you navigate the complexities of relationships and life with greater ease and resilience, fostering a sense of emotional balance and well-being.

Guided Meditations for Emotional Balance

Guided meditations are structured practices where a narrator, often in a soothing voice, leads you through a series of steps to achieve a specific mental state. These meditations help you focus your thoughts, calm your mind, and achieve emotional balance. You can use guided meditations to support your emotional regulation by giving you a framework for calming your thoughts and directing your attention inward. They can reduce stress, increase self-awareness, and promote peace. Examples of guided meditations include loving-kindness meditation, grounding meditation, and emotional release meditation. Each offers unique benefits, and you can tailor them to your needs.

Loving-kindness meditation (*metta* meditation) fosters compassion for yourself and others. To do this practice, you need to silently repeat (in your mind or whispering) phrases that convey goodwill and kindness. To begin, find a quiet place to sit comfortably. Close your eyes and take a few deep breaths. Start by directing loving-kindness toward yourself. Silently repeat phrases such as, "May I be happy. May I be healthy. May I be safe. May I live with ease." Next, extend these wishes to someone you care about, repeating similar phrases. Gradually include a neutral person, someone you struggle with, and all living beings. Doing this meditation is excellent for softening your heart and building greater empathy. As you reflect on the experience, you will probably notice a warm, tender feeling that grows with each repetition. This will enhance your sense of connection and compassion.

Use grounding meditation to help you stay present and balanced, especially during stressful times. It involves visualizing yourself firmly rooted in the ground, much like a tree with deep roots. Start by sitting in a comfortable position and closing your eyes. Take a few deep breaths to relax. Imagine roots growing from the soles of your feet, traveling deep into the earth. Visualize these roots anchoring you, providing stability and strength. Feel the connection with the ground beneath you, supporting you entirely.

Practical applications of this meditation include using it before a stressful event, like a presentation or difficult conversation, to help you remain calm and centered. The visualization of being deeply rooted can provide stability and resilience.

Emotional release meditation is a technique for letting go of pent-up emotions. In this practice, you can release emotions in a safe and controlled way. Begin by finding a comfortable position and close your eyes. Take several deep breaths to center yourself. Identify the emotion you wish to release, such as anger, sadness, or frustration. Visualize this emotion as a physical object within your body, such as a dark cloud or a heavy stone. With each exhale, imagine this object slowly dissolving or being expelled from your body. Techniques for visualizing emotional release include seeing the emotion dissipate into the air or flow away like water. As you reflect on the experience, you may feel a sense of lightness and relief as the emotional burden lifts, leaving you with a clear and calmer mind.

Guided meditations provide a structured approach to achieving emotional balance, and each type is best for specific needs. Whether you are fostering compassion through loving-kindness, finding stability with grounding techniques, or releasing pent-up emotions, these practices can transform your emotional landscape. Make guided meditations part of your routine to improve your emotional well-being and cultivate a more profound sense of inner peace.

The Role of Self-Care in Emotional Regulation

Self-care is taking deliberate actions to maintain and improve your physical, emotional, and mental well-being. It is about recognizing and meeting your needs, even when your life is busiest. Prioritizing self-care gives you a foundation for better emotional regulation. This means you are better equipped to handle stress, anxiety, and other emotional challenges. Think of self-care as recharging your internal batteries. Without it, you may run on empty, making you more likely to end up with emotional dysregulation and burnout.

Self-care offers many benefits when it comes to emotional regulation. Doing regular self-care will reduce your stress, improve your mood, and increase your resilience. For instance, engaging in activities that bring you joy, such as reading a book, walking in nature, or spending time with loved ones, can boost your mood and buffer against stress. Physical self-care activities, such as regular exercise, adequate sleep, and a balanced diet, can also profoundly affect your emotional well-being. When your body feels good, your mind often follows. Emotional self-care, like journaling, talking to a friend, or practicing gratitude, helps you process and manage your feelings. Mental self-care, such as setting boundaries, taking breaks, and engaging in hobbies, ensures you have the mental space to think clearly and make thoughtful decisions.

Creating a self-care plan begins with identifying your self-care needs and preferences. Everyone has different needs, so reflecting on what activities help you feel more balanced and rejuvenated is essential. Start by listing activities that you enjoy and that help you achieve a sense of inner peace. These could be simple activities such as having a hot bath, doing yoga, and listening to your favorite music. After that, think about balancing different types of self-care. Physical self-care might include regular exercise, a healthy diet, and sufficient sleep. Emotional self-care could involve talking to a therapist, journaling, or practicing mindfulness. Mental self-care might encompass setting boundaries, taking mental health days, and engaging in creative hobbies. Make sure that you set realistic self-care goals. Aim for small, achievable goals that fit into your daily routine. For example, you might set a goal to take a ten-minute walk daily or spend fifteen minutes journaling each evening.

It takes intentionality and planning to make self-care part of your daily life. Start by scheduling your self-care activities like you would an appointment. For instance, you might block time in your calendar for a weekly yoga class or a daily meditation session. Combining self-care with other daily tasks can make it more manageable. You might practice deep breathing exercises while commuting, listen to calming music while cooking, or take a walk during your lunch break. Making self-care a nonnegotiable priority is essential. This means committing to your self-care activities even when life gets busy. It might help to remind yourself that taking care of your needs allows you to be more present and effective in other areas of your life.

You should evaluate your self-care practices continually, making adjustments when you need to do so to keep them aligned with your needs. I like keeping a self-care journal. It is perfect for tracking my self-care activities and reflecting on how they make me feel. I recommend that you keep a self-care journal, too. You can write down your reflections on how different self-care activities affect you to determine which ones work best. For instance, note any changes in your mood or energy levels after a week of regular exercise. Adjustments based on personal needs and feedback are a continuous process. Your self-care needs will change and evolve as your life circumstances change. So, take the time to reassess your self-care plan regularly and be flexible in adapting it to your current situation. This might mean trying new activities, increasing the frequency of specific practices, or letting go of activities that no longer serve you.

Self-care is a dynamic and ongoing practice critical to emotional regulation and well-being. By understanding your self-care needs, creating a balanced plan, integrating it into your daily life, and regularly evaluating its effectiveness, you can build a sustainable self-care routine that supports your emotional health and resilience.

Managing Emotional Volatility and Handling Emotional Triggers in Relationships

Emotional volatility can feel like riding a roller coaster with unpredictable highs and lows. It affects your well-being and relationships, leaving you exhausted and overwhelmed. Emotional volatility is characterized by intense and frequent emotional shifts that various factors can trigger. These triggers might include stress, unresolved trauma, relationship conflicts, or even minor daily inconveniences. For instance, a slight disagreement with a partner might escalate into a full-blown argument, or an offhand comment from a colleague could lead to a day of feeling upset and distracted. In daily life, emotional volatility tends to create significant problems with maintaining stable relationships, not to mention a sense of inner peace.

Building emotional resilience is critical to handling emotional volatility more effectively. Begin by recognizing areas where you can build resilience, such as stress management, self-care improvement, and relationships. Reflective exercises can help you develop resilience. For instance, keep a journal to document challenging situations and how you responded. Reflect on what worked well and what did not, and think about how you can apply these lessons in the future. Examples of resilient behaviors include maintaining a positive outlook, seeking solutions rather than dwelling on problems, and staying flexible in the face of change. Developing these habits can make you more adaptable and better equipped to handle and reduce emotional volatility.

As we saw at the end of Chapter 2, emotional triggers can significantly impact those with anxious attachment styles, often leading to heightened feelings of insecurity and fear of abandonment in relationships. Understanding and managing these triggers is crucial for recovery and fostering healthier connections. Here is a quick checklist summarizing critical points we have discussed in this chapter that will help you handle both emotional volatility and emotional triggers:

1. **Self-Awareness**: The first step in managing emotional volatility and triggers is recognizing them. You should take the time to identify specific situations, behaviors, or comments that evoke intense emotions. Journaling or

reflecting on past experiences can help you better understand your triggers and associated feelings.

2. **Grounding Techniques**: When faced with emotional volatility or triggers, grounding techniques can be incredibly effective in managing anxiety. These include deep breathing exercises, mindfulness practices, or physical activities that help redirect focus away from overwhelming emotions. Such techniques can create a sense of calm and help regain control over emotional responses.

3. **Coping Strategies**: Establishing coping strategies tailored to your needs is crucial. This process of self-discovery and self-care empowers individuals, giving them a sense of control over their emotional responses. This may include self-soothing techniques, affirmations, or engaging in hobbies that bring joy and comfort. Having a toolkit of coping strategies can empower us and reduce the impact of emotional triggers when they arise.

4. **Reframing Negative Thoughts**: Many with an anxious attachment may fall into patterns of negative thinking when confronted with triggers. Practicing cognitive restructuring, like CBT and cognitive reappraisal, can help shift perspective and diminish anxiety. Take time to challenge and reframe negative thoughts with more balanced thinking. Focusing on the positive aspects of our relationships can counteract fear and doubt and alter your emotional response, reducing the intensity of your reactions.

5. **Partner Communication**: After triggers are identified, it is vital to communicate openly with partners. Sharing what

triggers feelings of anxiety or insecurity can create a mutually supportive environment where both partners can work together to mitigate these triggers. This open dialogue fosters trust and understanding, which are essential to any healthy relationship. We will discuss the best communication techniques with our partners in Chapters 6 and 7.

6. **Gradual Exposure**: For triggers that frequently arise within specific scenarios, gradually exposing oneself to these situations can build resilience. This incremental approach allows us to face our fears in a controlled manner, helping to reduce anxiety over time and strengthen emotional responses.

7. **Support Systems**: These play a crucial role in managing emotional volatility. Identifying and contacting a support network can give you the emotional backing you need. This network might include friends, family, or support groups. Regular check-ins with people you trust can offer a space to express your feelings and gain perspective. An example could be having a weekly coffee date with a close friend or attending a weekly support meeting.

8. **Professional Support**: Make sure that you get professional help if you need it. Experienced counselors can be a game-changer for those struggling to manage emotional triggers. Therapy is a safe space to explore underlying issues associated with anxious attachment and develop specific coping strategies. A therapist can help us understand our triggers and foster healthier relational dynamics. They can also offer strategies tailored to your

needs and help you navigate particularly challenging periods of emotional volatility.

By employing these strategies, those of us with anxious attachment can begin to navigate our emotional volatility and triggers more effectively, facilitating recovery and promoting healthier, more secure relationships. Using the proper strategies to stabilize your emotions, build resilience, and leverage support systems can create more balance and peace in your emotional life. These strategies improve your well-being, making connecting with others in meaningful ways easier.

As you continue to explore these techniques, you will find that managing emotional triggers and volatility becomes more intuitive and less daunting, paving the way for deeper self-awareness and emotional stability. Emphasizing the need for self-compassion and patience throughout this journey is essential. It is important to remember that healing and growth take time, and being patient with yourself is okay as you work through these strategies.

Developing a Daily Anxiety Management Routine

It is best to have a structured anxiety management routine. When you have a routine, it helps to provide stability and predictability. This gives you comfort when you are feeling overwhelmed. When you know precisely what you will do each day to manage your anxiety, you gain a sense of certainty. This is important, as uncertainty is one of the primary triggers of anxiety. When you achieve consistency in your activities, your mind and body will more easily find a rhythm, making it easier to cope with stress. To create a positive tone, many people find it helpful to start their day with a set morning routine that includes mindfulness exercises. Ending each day with a calming routine that encourages sound sleep and overall well-being can also be helpful.

To create a personalized anxiety management routine, you must identify critical activities and exercises you feel will be most effective. You can start by listing the techniques you think will be most helpful, such as grounding, breathing, or cognitive restructuring. Once you have done that, think about your daily schedule and identify pockets of time you can most easily incorporate these activities. Remember the importance of balance. It is vital to make your routine flexible enough to accommodate unexpected daily changes. That way, you will not feel stressed if you need to make some adjustments or miss one of your sessions.

It is best to integrate a variety of anxiety management techniques into your routine to achieve a holistic approach that addresses multiple aspects of anxiety. For example, begin your morning by centering yourself with a grounding exercise. After that, do cognitive restructuring exercises to challenge negative thoughts. Throughout the day, use self-soothing techniques whenever you have feelings of anxiety, incorporating visualization practices to maintain a calm mindset.

To achieve long-term success, you must keep track of your routine, adjusting it whenever needed. Maintain a routine diary in which you track your activities and write down how they affect your anxiety levels. Use this record to think about what works well for you and what does not in reducing your anxiety—that way, you know what kinds of adjustments to make. If you discover a less effective technique, try using a different one. Review your routine regularly so you can make changes that keep your practices tailored to your needs. With this ongoing evaluation, staying engaged and motivated to keep up your routine for the long term is more manageable.

Create a well-rounded routine, including grounding, breathing, cognitive, and visualization techniques. That will give you the tools and stability to deal with everyday stressors. You will be empowered to take control of your anxiety, fostering greater emotional resilience and well-being. I also recommend combining cognitive and behavioral techniques to help you create a robust anxiety management framework. Identifying and restructuring negative thoughts and using behavioral strategies to reinforce positive changes can help you develop a more balanced and less anxious mindset. If you use this approach, you will probably find that it enables you to manage your anxiety immediately and builds long-term resilience and emotional stability.

Building Self-Trust

I want to end this chapter by mentioning that cultivating self-trust is a foundational element in recovering from anxious attachment. This involves recognizing and affirming one's capabilities and judgments, which can often feel compromised by the uncertainties accompanying anxious attachment patterns.

To build self-trust, start by acknowledging your emotions and instincts as valid. Rather than dismissing your feelings as irrational or unfounded, permit yourself to explore and understand them. Keep a journal to document your thoughts and emotional responses. This practice allows you to reflect on your experiences, validate your feelings, and track your growth over time. By seeing your emotions in writing, you may also realize patterns in your thinking that you can address more effectively.

Another crucial step is setting realistic expectations for yourself. Understand that recovery is not a destination but a journey. This understanding will help you be patient and kind to yourself, allowing you to make mistakes and learn from them. Celebrating your small victories is essential, as these moments build a reservoir of trust in your capabilities.

Self-care is also integral to building trust. Engaging in activities improves your physical, emotional, and mental well-being. These can be anything from exercise and meditation to pursuing hobbies you love. When you prioritize your needs, you tell yourself you are worthy of attention and care, further strengthening your self-trust.

Finally, practice positive self-talk. Challenge negative internal dialogues that undermine your confidence by identifying them when they occur and consciously replacing them with positive affirmations. Focus on your strengths and past successes instead of what could go wrong or what you fear. Positive affirmations can be powerful tools to reshape your self-perception and reinforce your belief in your abilities.

By consciously cultivating self-trust through these practices, you mitigate the effects of anxious attachment and empower yourself to engage more deeply and authentically in your relationships. It is a gradual process, but each step you take toward trusting yourself lays the groundwork for healthier connections with others, giving you a sense of control and confidence.

CHAPTER 4
INNER CHILD HEALING

IMAGINE YOURSELF AS A FIVE-YEAR-OLD CHILD, AND THERE IS A SCARY thunderstorm outside, and you are clutching a beloved stuffed animal for comfort. You feel small, scared, and craving reassurance. Now, imagine that this child exists within you, carrying the emotional weight of traumatic childhood experiences into your adult life. This is the essence of the inner child—the part of you that holds your childhood memories, emotions, and unmet needs.

INTRODUCTION TO INNER CHILD WORK

The concept of the inner child is a powerful representation of one's childhood self. It encompasses the feelings, memories, and experiences from your early years that continue to influence your adult behaviors and emotions. Much more than just a metaphor, your inner child is a fundamental part of your psyche that holds the emotional imprints of your formative years. These emotional memories can be both positive and negative, shaping how you interact with the world around you. During adulthood, when your inner child feels scared or unheard, its old wounds can resurface. This can impact your relationships and sense of self-worth.

If you have an anxious attachment, you need to address your inner child. Your insecurities and fears as an adult are often rooted in unresolved childhood traumas. When you work on reconnecting with your inner child, you will start to comprehend and heal childhood wounds. In this process, you recognize that you have had unmet needs and pain in the past, which lets you address them and show self-compassion. Healing your inner child means creating a more stable and loving inner world, which can transform your relationships today.

The inner child concept has its roots in Gestalt therapy and other therapeutic approaches in psychology. In Gestalt therapy, we see an emphasis on how our past experiences impact our present self. Inner child work became popular in the 1980s when John Bradshaw, an expert in the field, discussed it. In Bradshaw's work, there was a focus on the ways that childhood abuse, neglect, and abandonment manifest in adult behaviors, including addiction and codependency. He believed healing these childhood wounds was essential for personal growth and emotional well-being.

John Bradshaw emphasized how unresolved childhood traumas can lead to adult problems. He did research and held workshops that assisted many people in confronting their past and beginning the healing process. To address these deep-rooted issues, his approach combines different therapeutic approaches, including CBT and DBT (dialectical behavior therapy). His work has inspired many therapists to make inner child healing part of their practice, recognizing its importance in addressing the root causes of emotional distress.

Many people misunderstand inner child work. One of the most common misconceptions is that it is only for those with severe trauma. However, everyone has an inner child, and everyone can benefit from this healing process. Whether your childhood experiences were mildly unsettling or deeply traumatic, you can get profound insights and emotional healing from reconnecting with your inner child. You might also believe inner child work is too painful or difficult to engage with. While it can be challenging, the rewards far outweigh the discomfort. Confronting and healing your past can lead to profound personal growth and healthier relationships.

Another misconception is that inner child work is not scientifically supported. However, many studies and therapeutic practices validate its effectiveness. Research in psychology and neuroscience shows that early experiences shape our brain development and emotional responses. Addressing these foundational experiences can rewire your brain and create new, healthier behavior patterns. Techniques such as visualization, journaling, and therapeutic dialogue with the inner child are grounded in evidence-based practices and have demonstrated effective emotional healing.

When you do inner child work, you embark on self-discovery and healing. It is time to understand the concept of the inner child and its significance so you can begin to address unresolved traumas, reconnect with lost parts of yourself, and build a foundation for emotional security.

CONNECTING WITH YOUR INNER CHILD

Several techniques help you establish a connection with your inner child. First, creating a safe space for inner child work is essential. Start by setting up a comfortable physical space to relax and focus. For example, you could set up a cozy corner of your home with soft lighting, comfortable seating, and calming objects like candles, plants, or favorite books. Using calming and comforting objects can enhance the sense of safety. Consider including items that remind you of your childhood, such as a favorite toy or a blanket. Mindfulness is also crucial to establishing emotional safety. Practice mindfulness techniques to stay present and grounded. Deep breathing exercises, body scans, or gentle yoga can help create a calm and nurturing environment for working on your inner child.

Set intentions when you start connecting with your inner child. It is crucial to set intentions. Decide what you want to achieve from encountering your inner child, whether understanding a specific emotion, addressing an experience, or simply offering comfort. Use guided visualization as a tool for this initial meeting. Close your eyes and imagine a safe and welcoming place. This is where you should visualize and gently approach your younger self. Take note of their appearance, expressions, and emotions. Reflect on this experience and how you felt during the process. After you have finished your visualization, record your thoughts and feelings in a notebook or journal. Include what you observed and how your inner child responded. This reflection lets you better process the encounter and plan your next steps.

Visualization exercises can also be beneficial here. Imagine yourself as a child, perhaps in a place where you felt safe and happy. Picture every detail vividly—the colors, the sounds, the smells. Visualize your younger self and approach them with kindness and curiosity. Another technique is dialoguing with your inner child. This involves having a mental or written conversation with your younger self. Ask questions like, "How are you feeling?" or "What do you need?" Listen to the responses with empathy and understanding. Creative activities such as drawing or writing letters to your inner child can also be powerful. These activities allow you to tangibly express your emotions and thoughts, fostering a deeper connection.

You must do regular check-ins to create a trusting and loving relationship with your inner child. Set a daily habit of connecting with your inner child. This could be through a quick mental check-in, a short journal entry, or a brief visualization exercise. It is essential to acknowledge and validate the emotions of your inner child. When your inner child expresses fear, sadness, or joy, accept these emotions without judgment. Tell your inner child that you recognize their feelings, acknowledging their validity. Showing love and compassion toward your inner child can take many forms. Speak kindly to your inner child, offer words of comfort, and reassure them that they are loved and safe. This ongoing nurturing helps build a strong and secure relationship, allowing your inner child to heal and thrive.

IDENTIFYING CHILDHOOD TRAUMAS

Identifying childhood traumas is a crucial step in the healing process. Reflecting on significant childhood events can help you pinpoint moments that left a lasting impact. However, it is best to have support systems when you are trying to heal childhood traumas. Seeking professional help from therapists can provide the structured support you may need. Therapists trained in trauma-informed care can guide you through the healing process with empathy and expertise.

You could also benefit from joining support groups. These groups offer a sense of community and understanding, allowing you to share your experiences and learn from others facing similar challenges. It is helpful if you can lean on trusted friends and family. You may get emotional support and validation by sharing your journey with loved ones. If they give you support, it can help you feel less isolated and more connected.

To begin with, think about times when you felt scared, lonely, or unsupported. These could be moments when you were bullied at school, felt neglected by a caregiver, or experienced a family breakup. It is also crucial to recognize signs of unresolved trauma. Potential symptoms include recurring nightmares, intense emotional reactions to specific triggers, and persistent feelings of insecurity. An excellent way to further explore these memories is to write journaling prompts, such as "What is my earliest memory of feeling afraid or alone?" or "What events from my childhood still affect me today?" You will find that writing about these experiences can help you achieve clarity and understand their influence on how you currently feel and behave.

Specific therapeutic approaches can help you in healing childhood traumas. EMDR is one of these methods. In this therapy, you recall distressing memories while engaging in bilateral stimulation, such as moving your eyes from side to side or tapping. This process helps you reframe traumatic memories so that they become less overwhelming. Somatic experiencing focuses on the body's physical responses to trauma. It lets you use gentle movements and awareness of bodily sensations to help you release stored tension and trauma. Cognitive-behavioral techniques are also effective. They involve identifying and challenging negative thought patterns that stem from childhood experiences, replacing them with healthier, more balanced perspectives.

You can make these strategies part of your life to help you identify childhood traumas and foster healing and a sense of self-compassion and emotional security. Build a support system by seeking professional help, joining support groups, and leaning on trusted friends and family. Reflect on significant childhood events, recognize signs of unresolved trauma, and use journaling to explore your memories. Look into therapeutic approaches like EMDR, somatic experiencing, and cognitive-behavioral techniques and how these techniques may help you. Following these steps gives you the best chance to work toward healing and creating a healthier, more fulfilling life.

EXERCISES FOR INNER CHILD HEALING

Creative expression is often a powerful way to heal your inner child. For example, you could try drawing or painting childhood memories. It lets you visually explore and process past experiences. You do not need to be an artist to benefit from this exercise. Simply sketching scenes from your childhood can bring buried emotions to the surface. Consider creating a collage of images representing your childhood using magazines, photos, and other materials. This artistic process helps reconnect you with your younger self so you can understand the emotions tied to those memories.

Try writing letters to your inner child. Start by addressing your younger self and acknowledging their feelings and experiences. Write as if you are speaking to a dear friend, providing comfort and understanding. You might begin with, "Dear [Your Name], I remember how you felt when..." With this exercise, you validate your inner child's emotions and provide the reassurance they needed back then. Creating a scrapbook of positive childhood experiences can also be a healing practice. Gather photos and mementos, and write down happy memories. This scrapbook serves as a reminder of the joy and love you experienced, helping to balance the painful memories.

You can also find guided meditations that connect you with your inner child and provide comfort. These meditations often begin with a relaxation phase, helping you to calm your mind and body. A meditation script might guide you to visualize a safe, peaceful place where you can meet your inner child. Imagine holding their hand, offering words of reassurance, and listening to their concerns. Many people find it soothing to visualize comforting and nurturing your inner child. Picture yourself wrapping them in a warm blanket or reading them a bedtime story. Audio resources for guided meditations are widely available and valuable in your healing practice.

Role-playing scenarios can be another effective way to re-enact and heal past experiences. Make sure that you have a trusted partner for these kinds of exercises. They let you revisit specific events from your childhood in a safe and supportive environment. For example, you might role-play a conversation with a parent or teacher, expressing feelings you could not articulate at the time. You could also try therapeutic role-playing in a group setting. This might allow you to share your experiences with others with similar traumas, providing a sense of solidarity and understanding. Using role-playing to practice new responses to old triggers can help you develop healthier coping mechanisms. You get to rehearse new behaviors, making it easier for you to integrate them into your daily life, reducing the impact of past traumas.

Daily affirmations are yet another powerful tool for reinforcing inner child healing. Writing personalized affirmations that address your inner child's needs and fears can be healing. Does your inner child feel unworthy? You could use the affirmation, "I deserve love and respect." When you incorporate the right affirmations into your daily routine, they can help solidify new positive beliefs. Repeat them in the morning, before bed, or during moments of stress. Over the long term, your daily affirmations can be a transformational tool for healing. Keep a journal to note changes in your feelings and behaviors, celebrating the small victories.

Ultimately, you must practice self-compassion and forgiveness for a successful healing process. Self-compassion exercises can help you treat yourself with the kindness and understanding you would offer a friend. For example, when you notice self-critical thoughts, use compassionate language in reframing.

Another powerful tool is guided meditation for self-forgiveness. These meditations guide you through visualizing forgiveness, helping you release guilt and shame associated with past events. Writing forgiveness letters to yourself is another effective technique. In these letters, acknowledge the pain you have experienced and give yourself forgiveness and understanding. This act of self-compassion can be incredibly liberating and healing.

By making inner child exercises part of your life, you can connect profoundly with your inner child and begin to heal. Whether through creative expression, writing, guided meditations, role-playing, daily affirmations, or self-compassion, each activity offers a unique way to address and heal past wounds. These exercises will help nurture your inner child, creating a more secure and loving inner world and positively impacting your relationships and overall well-being.

HOW TO INTEGRATE INNER CHILD WORK INTO YOUR LIFE

I find doing daily inner child practices grounding and transformative. Begin each morning with a simple check-in. When you wake up each morning, close your eyes briefly and visualize your inner child. Ask them how they are feeling and what they need today. This brief mental connection sets a nurturing tone for your day. Also, before you go to bed every night, reflect on your day and your inner child's emotions at different points. If they need reassurance, provide it. These practices can help you maintain a solid emotional connection with your inner child.

Mindfulness is crucial for integrating inner child work into your daily life. With simple mindfulness practices, staying present and maintaining the proper emotional connection is much easier. I recommend doing mindful breathing exercises, as they can center you in the present moment. Take a few minutes to focus on your breath, inhaling deeply and exhaling slowly. This practice calms your mind, allowing you to tune into your inner child's emotions. Practicing presence in everyday activities can also help you. Try to be mindful in daily activities, such as eating, walking, and working. Notice the sights, sounds, and sensations around you. This mindfulness is critical to staying grounded and aware of your inner child's needs and emotions.

Daily rituals can also honor the presence of your inner child. These rituals do not have to be elaborate. Simple acts like enjoying a favorite childhood snack, listening to music that brings back happy memories, or spending time on a beloved hobby can be meaningful. These activities are helpful reminders for nurturing and caring for your inner child, integrating their needs into your daily life. You can gain much insight by journaling your interactions with your inner child. Document these moments to track your progress and understand the evolving relationship with your inner self.

Maintain a balance between your inner child's needs and your adult responsibilities. You achieve this through thoughtful boundary-setting. Set times for your inner child work, ensuring it does not interfere with your daily tasks. For instance, you might set aside fifteen minutes in the morning and evening for this practice. Prioritizing self-care without neglecting your responsibilities is critical. Ensure you meet your basic needs, such as proper nutrition, sleep, and exercise. Taking care of yourself is one way to care for your inner child. Creating a harmonious relationship between your inner child and adult self involves recognizing that both aspects of you need attention. Allow your inner child to influence your choices in ways that bring joy and creativity while your adult self manages responsibilities and decision-making.

Tracking my progress and reflecting on my inner child healing journey is immensely helpful for growth. Keep a progress journal to document your experiences, emotions, and insights. Reflective questions can guide your journaling, helping you assess your growth. Ask yourself, "How have my interactions with my inner child changed over time?" or "What new insights have I gained about my childhood experiences?" Answering questions like these means you do deep reflection and achieve better self-awareness. Remember to celebrate your milestones and achievements. Acknowledge small victories, like comforting your inner child during a moment of distress or gaining a new understanding of an experience. These celebrations reinforce your progress and motivate you to continue doing the necessary work to heal.

Case Studies in Inner Child Healing

In my journey, I have found looking at success stories to be a great source of inspiration. So, let's take a look at Emily's journey. Emily had always struggled with intense fear of abandonment, stemming from her parents' tumultuous divorce when she was just seven. She felt responsible for the split and carried this guilt into her adult relationships, always craving validation. Through inner child work, Emily began visualizing herself as that scared little girl, offering comfort and reassurance. She wrote letters to her younger self, expressing the love and support she had longed for. Over time, Emily's fear transformed into confidence, and she learned to trust herself and her relationships.

James's story is another powerful example. Growing up, James experienced frequent criticism from his father, leaving him deep-seated feelings of inadequacy. The result was struggling with self-compassion as an adult. He frequently criticized himself for even the most minor mistakes. Fortunately, James started to do guided meditations and self-compassion exercises, and in doing so, he began to reconnect with his inner child. He visualized holding his younger self, offering words of kindness and understanding. This practice helped James develop a sense of self-worth and self-love. He learned to practice self-forgiveness for past mistakes and embrace his imperfections. James's path to self-compassion transformed his relationships, making them more authentic and fulfilling.

Reflect on these stories and consider how they may resonate with your experiences. Ask yourself, "What childhood events have shaped my current behaviors?" or "How can I offer my inner child the support they need?" These reflective questions can help you see similarities between your journey and those of Emily and James. This can give you more insight into the whole process and how to proceed. Remember that you are never alone as you navigate your inner child healing journey. Countless other people have walked this path and achieved healing and transformation.

REPARENTING YOURSELF: STEPS AND STRATEGIES

The whole process of healing your inner child can be summed up around "reparenting yourself." It is a transformative approach to healing anxious attachment and fostering healthier relationships. This process involves nurturing and caring for your inner child— the part of you that may feel neglected, anxious, or unworthy due to past experiences. By actively reparenting, you can develop a secure attachment style, rebuild trust, and cultivate lasting love.

Steps to Reparent Yourself:

1. **Understand Your Inner Child**: To begin your reparenting journey, you must recognize and understand your inner child. This part of you carries the emotional imprints of joyful and painful childhood experiences. Anxious attachment often stems from unmet needs during our formative years, such as a lack of emotional support or inconsistent caregiving. By acknowledging the presence of your inner child, you can start to address the fears and insecurities that arise in adult relationships.

2. **Be Aware of and Acknowledge Emotions**: Begin by understanding your feelings and behaviors related to anxious attachment. Journaling can be an effective tool here. Write about moments when you feel uneasy in relationships and explore the triggers behind these feelings. Acknowledge your inner child's emotions and needs without judgment.

3. **Create a Safe Space**: Establish a mental or physical environment that feels safe and nurturing. It could be a cozy corner in your home or a visualization of a comforting place. When you feel anxious, retreat to this space, inviting your inner child to join you. Use this safe space to reflect, breathe, and ground yourself. Guided visualizations, where we create a safe space for their inner child, can offer comfort and reassurance.

4. **Engage in Dialogue**: Interacting with your inner child through dialogue is a powerful tool for reparenting. Set aside time to write letters to your inner child, expressing love and reassurance. You can also ask your inner child questions—encouraging them to share their fears and desires. Respond to their needs with compassion and understanding, reinforcing a sense of security. Additionally, rewriting personal narratives to reframe past experiences can help transform how we perceive ourselves and our relationships. These healing steps can significantly reduce the impact of adverse childhood experiences on attachment styles, offering a hopeful path for the future.

5. **Nurture Your Needs**: Identify and meet your emotional and physical needs as a caring parent would, including setting boundaries, prioritizing self-care, and engaging in activities that bring you joy and fulfillment. You might also explore mindfulness practices to stay present and calm during anxiety-provoking moments.

6. **Practice Self-Compassion**: Treat yourself with the kindness and empathy you would offer a frightened child. When you encounter feelings of anxiety, remind yourself

that it is okay to feel this way. Use affirmations to foster self-acceptance: "I am worthy of love" or "It is safe for me to open my heart." Regularly reaffirming your values and needs helps build a more supportive inner dialogue.

7. **Seek Support**: Reparenting can be challenging, and you may benefit from additional support. Consider working with a therapist specializing in attachment theory to guide you through this process. A therapist can help us explore how past experiences shape our current behaviors and relationships. They can provide valuable tools and perspectives to help you navigate your journey toward healing wounds. This process of gaining awareness and processing painful memories in a safe environment can lead to healthier attachment patterns.

8. **Reflect on Your Healing Journey**: Personal reflection is essential for growth. Think about keeping a reflection journal where you document your experiences, insights, and emotions. You can write on questions such as "What progress have I made in connecting with my inner child?" or "How have my relationships changed due to this work?" Additionally, you can share your reflections in support groups. Doing this can provide additional perspectives and encouragement. The community aspect of healing is vital. Sharing your experiences creates a space for mutual understanding and support, fostering a sense of belonging and solidarity.

Cultivating Lasting Self-Love

As you engage in reparenting, you are healing the wounds of your past and setting the foundation for more secure and fulfilling relationships. By addressing your anxious attachment, you can cultivate a deep sense of self-love, which ultimately paves the way for nurturing connections with others. Taking these healing steps can significantly reduce the impact of adverse childhood experiences on attachment styles.

Finally, reparenting yourself is an ongoing process that requires patience and dedication. The more you understand and care for your inner child, the more you will reclaim your sense of worth and the ability to love and be loved without fear. The journey may be challenging, but the growth and healing that await will empower you to build the solid and lasting relationships you genuinely deserve.

CHAPTER 5
BUILDING TRUST AND EMOTIONAL SECURITY IN YOUR RELATIONSHIPS

IMAGINE HOW YOU WOULD FEEL STANDING NEAR THE EDGE OF A CLIFF, looking down at the vast, unknown expanse below. Your heart races, your palms sweat, and you feel overwhelmed by the fear of falling. You might have this emotion when trust is broken in a relationship, and it illustrates how deeper trust is essential for building better emotional security and ensuring healthy and long-lasting relationships.

UNDERSTANDING AND REBUILDING TRUST

Our first step is understanding the full importance of trust—the foundation of emotional security. It is crucial for keeping relationships together. With the right level of trust, you have a feeling of safety and being valued and understood. You will be able to share your deepest fears and dreams without being afraid of judgment or betrayal. Building better trust also profoundly improves relationship satisfaction. You will enjoy more open communication and a stronger feeling of partnership and mutual respect. When you lack trust, your relationship can become unstable and filled with doubt and insecurity. Successful relationships, whether romantic, familial, or platonic, have a solid foundation of trust. When you look at couples who have weathered storms together, their bond has often become more robust because they trust each other's intentions and actions.

Make sure that you identify any trust issues in your relationship. There are different signs of broken trust you should look out for. For example, do you frequently desire to check your partner's phone, question their whereabouts, or doubt what they say? This kind of behavior indicates that there are probably underlying trust issues. You can also do reflective exercises to help you pinpoint these issues. Take the time to think about the root reasons for feelings of distrust. Did one specific incident shatter your trust? Or has there been a gradual buildup of distrust because you have been constantly let down?

It is best to take a structured approach to rebuilding trust. You first need to acknowledge the breach of trust and take steps to address it. For the problem to be resolved, both partners must recognize the issue and commit to making the necessary changes. It is crucial to have consistent and transparent communication. Openly share your emotions and practice active listening when considering your partner's concerns without judgment. You will find that transparency on both sides builds trust over time. Remember to demonstrate your reliability and dependability. Stay faithful to your promises, showing that you follow through. This includes even promises that seem small or relatively insignificant. If you say you will be home by seven, ensure you are. By taking this action course, you demonstrate to your partner that they can count on you. This will eventually help them rebuild their trust in you.

Be persistent in monitoring how you progress in rebuilding the trust in your relationship. I have found it helpful to keep a trust journal. That is where you will write down your thoughts and feelings and any significant interactions related to trust. By doing this, you will find it easier to keep track of how you progress and notice areas in need of improvement. You should set short-term and long-term goals. Examples of short-term goals can be daily acts of transparency, such as sharing your schedule. A long-term goal is rebuilding emotional intimacy. It is essential to check in regularly with your partner. Set aside time each week to talk about your progress and feelings and make the adjustments you find you need to make. With these conversations, you can help foster a stronger sense of partnership and mutual commitment to rebuilding trust.

You can get valuable insights from contemplating the steps you have taken and how much progress you have made. In this process, you might see that while some actions have helped you make great strides in rebuilding trust, others have not been as successful. Remember that the path toward rebuilding trust is not linear. There will be setbacks, but each step forward strengthens your relationship's foundation.

COMMUNICATION TECHNIQUES FOR TRUST-BUILDING

Trust-building is impossible without effective communication. Good communication can create a foundation of understanding and respect, which is essential to any healthy relationship. Active listening is a crucial part of that. With active listening, you focus entirely on what your partner is saying, ensuring you understand what they are communicating. Ensure you do not interrupt, and show engagement by nodding and with verbal cues, such as "I understand" or "Tell me more." Active listening shows your partner you value their feelings and perspective, creating a safe space for meaningful conversations. Open and honest dialogue is another vital principle. Seek transparency about how you feel and what you think, which will help foster trust. Non-verbal communication cues also play a significant role. Your body language, facial expressions, and tone of voice can communicate more than words. Be mindful of your non-verbal cues and be attentive to your partner's. Ensure that your non-verbal cues are aligned with your verbal messages when demonstrating engagement and concern.

You will find specific techniques helpful in maintaining transparency in communication. The "I" statement technique is particularly effective. You express your feelings and needs by starting sentences with "I," so you do not give the impression of placing blame. Here is an example. Instead of saying, "You never listen to me," you could say, "I feel unheard when we do not discuss things openly." By using this approach, you cut down on the chance of defensiveness, creating the conditions for a more open dialogue. It is an excellent idea to do reflective listening exercises to help maintain transparency. After your partner speaks, tell them what you heard and how you interpreted their statement to ensure you understood their intended meaning. For instance, say, "What I hear you saying is that you feel neglected when I work late." When you do this kind of active listening, you validate your partner's feelings and clarify any potential misunderstandings. You should also do regular relationship check-ins. Set aside time each week to discuss your relationship, share your feelings, and address any concerns. You create regular, open, honest communication opportunities by doing check-ins like these, reinforcing trust over time.

Seek to resolve your conflicts in a way that builds trust and requires you to remain calm and composed. Avoid engaging when emotions are high; when people do, they tend to say things they do not mean, and the situation can escalate. Breathe deeply and keep your focus on staying calm. You can also try collaborative problem-solving techniques. Adopt the spirit of teamwork in how you approach conflict, working to find solutions that satisfy both partners. For example, you could brainstorm ideas, weigh pros and cons, compromise, and negotiate. Compromise and negotiation are crucial in this process. Recognize that you might not get everything you want, but finding a middle ground can strengthen your relationship. Just say you and your partner disagree on how you want to spend a weekend. Try finding a way to incorporate both of your preferences. By adopting this collaborative approach, you foster mutual respect and trust.

You need strong communication to build emotional intimacy, which has a strong link with trust. You can deepen your connection by sharing personal stories and vulnerabilities. You invite your partner to do the same when you open up about your fears, dreams, and past experiences. This creates a mutual vulnerability that fosters trust and emotional closeness. Another way to improve emotional intimacy is by expressing appreciation and gratitude. Regularly tell your partner what you appreciate about them and your relationship. This positive reinforcement fosters a stronger bond and makes your partner feel valued. Engaging in meaningful conversations is equally essential. Talk about topics that matter to you both. Examples might be your personal goals and shared interests. These conversations foster a deeper understanding of each other, strengthening your emotional connection.

Practicing these communication techniques allows you to gradually rebuild and strengthen the trust between you and your partner. You will have to be patient and consistent with this process. Through this process, you can create a relationship in which trust and emotional security flourish.

CREATING A SECURE BASE: FOUNDATIONS OF EMOTIONAL SECURITY

For any relationship to have emotional security, it needs a secure base. Picture a child venturing out to explore a playground, constantly looking back to ensure their caregiver is there so that they can feel safe. As I discussed earlier, this concept from attachment theory extends to our relationships in adulthood. With a secure base, you feel stability and reassurance, letting you explore the world and take emotional risks, knowing you have a dependable safety net. This plays a vital role in fostering emotional security. A secure base means that you can feel confident to express your true self, knowing your partner will be there to support you. A few examples of secure base behaviors include frequent check-ins, comfort during stressful times, and showing that you are a reliable presence in daily life.

Specific characteristics are necessary for a secure base in a relationship. Two of these are consistency and reliability. Predictability in your partner's actions and responses is critical to building trust. You can feel secure knowing they will be there when you need them. It is also crucial to have emotional availability and support. You must be emotionally and physically present when your partner needs you. You must engage in active listening, validate emotions, and provide comfort. Mutual respect and achieving a better understanding further strengthen a secure base. This means acknowledging each other's needs, boundaries, and perspectives. Also, you and your partner should appreciate the unique qualities each of you brings to the relationship.

You need to use intentional actions and practices in building a secure base. Create rituals of connection, as they can be a powerful way to strengthen your bond. Examples of these rituals might be daily check-ins and weekly date nights. They could even be simple acts, such as enjoying coffee together each morning. With these shared moments, you foster a feeling of togetherness and dependability. Another essential step is making sure that you are emotionally available. Being there for your partner is a top priority, especially when they are going through challenging times.

In many cases, this might involve setting distractions aside so that you can fully listen and provide a comforting presence when they feel stressed. It is also crucial to practice supportive behaviors consistently. This involves demonstrating empathy, offering help without your partner having to ask, and celebrating the successes each of you achieves.

You can do specific reflective exercises to assess and strengthen your secure base. Begin with ones that help you evaluate the current state of your relationship. Ask yourself questions such as, "Do I feel safe and supported by my partner?" or "Are there areas where I feel more vulnerable?" The next thing to do is identify areas where your relationship can improve. Maybe you realize that while your partner makes you feel emotionally supported, you see that daily interactions lack some consistency. Put changes into motion by setting specific goals.

An example might be agreeing to have a daily debrief. This is a time when each of you shares your highs and lows of the day. Remember to keep track of your progress. I like keeping a journal documenting how these changes impact your sense of security. You can think about what you notice there and discuss your observations with your partner regularly.

Strengthening a secure base is an ongoing process. You and your partner must show commitment to maintaining and improving the relationship. You will strengthen your relationship by regularly revisiting and assessing your efforts, ensuring both partners feel secure and valued. Focusing on these practices will help you build a resilient and supportive foundation that improves your connection and emotional security.

OVERCOMING MISTRUST: STRATEGIES AND EXERCISES

You need to understand the origin of your mistrust before you can effectively address it in your relationship. In many cases, past experiences and traumas lead to mistrust. Being betrayed in any relationship can leave deep scars. When you have scars like these, you will find it difficult to trust someone again fully. That is because you are constantly on guard, waiting for history to repeat itself. Your trust is eroded by someone who breaks promises and behaves inconsistently.

When someone says one thing but does another, it creates confusion and doubt. Over time, these inconsistencies can accumulate, and this can cause you to question whether the person you are dealing with is genuinely reliable. Other factors that can have an impact include external influences and pressures. Our views on trust and trustworthiness are affected by societal expectations, peer pressure, and cultural norms. Did you grow up in an environment that was full of mistrust? If so, you will likely find it challenging to free yourself from that way of thinking.

Fortunately, there are cognitive techniques that can help you challenge and change your mistrustful thoughts. Begin by noticing your negative thought patterns. Do you find that you always tend to assume the worst? Take a moment to recognize this pattern. Once you have identified a pattern like this, challenge these negative thoughts by asking yourself for evidence. If you keep imagining that your partner is untrustworthy, ask yourself if these fears are based on past experiences. Are there any objective reasons you should feel mistrustful? If not, challenge your thoughts and reframe them. With reframing, instead of thinking, "They are probably lying to me," try to reframe it to, "I have no reason to doubt their honesty right now." This will help you develop more balance in how you perceive and think about things. You will find it easier to see situations from a neutral standpoint. With this perspective, you can recognize that while there may be risks in trusting someone, you also get life-enhancing opportunities for deep, meaningful connections.

You should also consider using behavioral strategies to build trust. A great example of this is showing your reliability with your actions. Remember, actions speak louder than words. Ensure you follow through if you have said you will do something. When you show consistency in your actions, it helps build a stronger foundation of trust. You can also take part in trust-building activities. Examples of these activities include spending quality time together, working on joint projects, or simply being there for each other during tough times. When you consistently follow through on commitments, no matter how small, that reinforces trust. That is because it demonstrates that you are dependable and that your words match your actions.

You may find specific exercises helpful to overcome mistrust for couples. An excellent place to start is with trust-building conversations. Set aside time to discuss your fears and concerns openly. Use "I" statements to express how specific actions make you feel without placing blame. Joint goal-setting activities can also create more trust. Working together toward a common goal, whether planning a trip or saving for a house, fosters a sense of partnership and mutual reliance. It is also helpful to practice forgiveness and letting go. Holding onto past grievances only fuels mistrust. Learn to forgive and move forward, shifting your focus to building a positive future together.

Reflective exercises can help you and your partner work through mistrust. An example could be writing down three instances where you felt mistrustful and then discussing them together. Identify what triggered these emotions and tactics for addressing them moving forward. You can also integrate trust-building activities into your daily routine. Strengthen your bond with simple acts like sharing a distraction-free meal or relaxing and discussing your day. To practice forgiveness, you must recognize past hurts and consciously decide to let them go. This does not mean forgetting what happened. It just means choosing not to allow past pain to dictate your current relationship.

Both partners must commit to overcoming mistrust to improve the relationship. Focus on building new, positive experiences that counteract past hurts. As we have seen here, we can create a stronger, more resilient relationship when we understand the origins of mistrust, use cognitive and behavioral strategies, and participate in trust-building exercises. Be patient. Trust is never rebuilt overnight. Instead, it takes commitment and dedication.

TRUST-BUILDING ACTIVITIES FOR COUPLES

Doing joint activities is a highly effective way of building better trust in relationships. That is because shared experiences create a bond that cannot be achieved with words alone. When you engage in activities together, you can show dependability and consistency. This is especially true in settings that require teamwork and mutual support. For example, going on a challenging hike together brings you closer physically and emotionally. You build a sense of partnership and mutual reliance as you navigate the trail together. Completing such activities strengthens the emotional connection, reinforcing that you can depend on each other in various situations.

There are many types of joint activities, each with its unique way of building trust. Try adventure-based activities if you want something requiring you to depend on each other and bond more closely. Examples are hiking and team sports. For instance, navigating a problematic trail together or competing in a friendly game fosters a sense of teamwork and partnership. Another great choice of trust-building activity is a collaborative project, such as a home improvement task or trip planning. These projects require you and your partner to develop better coordination, communication, and shared responsibility—all critical components of trust. Intimacy-building activities like couple's yoga or dance classes offer another layer. These activities require you to be present and connected, both physically and emotionally. In this way, they enhance your bond and trust.

There are specific guidelines to remember when planning and doing trust-building activities. First, ensuring that you and your partner are interested in the activity and fully willing to participate is vital. Do not pressure your partner to participate in something they do not want. When both are interested in an activity, you have an equal chance of enjoying yourself and getting meaning from the experience. Next, set clear expectations and goals. Before you start the activity, talk about what you hope to achieve and any boundaries or limitations. Clear communication from the outset helps to prevent misunderstandings and ensures that both partners are on the same page. You should also reflect on the experiences you had during the activity afterward. Discuss what you enjoyed, what you found challenging, and how the activity affected your relationship. This reflection will help solidify the activity's positive effects and reinforce trust.

Let's take a look at Mark and Lisa. They decided to take up adventure sports to build trust and reconnect. Their first activity was rock climbing, something neither had done before. The experience required them to rely on each other for safety and encouragement. They faced challenges and fears initially but gave each other the needed support. They felt renewed trust and partnership when the climb was finished. I recommend thinking about some reflective questions after an experience like this. You could ask yourself questions such as, "How did this activity make me feel about my partner?" or "What did I learn about our ability to work together?" These questions encourage you to reflect deeply to understand how the activity impacts your relationship.

Many trust-building activities are available, and you can tailor them to resonate with you and your partner. The key is to engage in activities that require cooperation, communication, and mutual support. Whether it is adventure sports, collaborative projects, or intimacy-building exercises, these activities offer a hands-on way to strengthen your bond and build trust. By following the guidelines of mutual interest, clear expectations, and post-activity reflection, you can maximize the benefits of these experiences. Over time, these shared moments will create a stronger, more resilient foundation of trust in your relationship.

HOW TO HANDLE SETBACKS IN TRUST-BUILDING

You should know how to recognize common setbacks in the trust-building process. Relationships are complex, and setbacks are inevitable. For example, you might occasionally relapse into old behaviors, such as feeling unreasonably suspicious and overreacting to minor issues. You will feel frustrated, but it is all part of the process. You should also be prepared for potential miscommunications and misunderstandings. You might say something with one intention, but your partner interprets it differently. These misunderstandings can lead to unnecessary conflicts and feelings of distrust. External stressors, such as work pressure, financial strain, or family issues, can also impact your relationship. When stressed, we are more likely to misinterpret what our partners say, which can lead to further mistrust.

You will need to have open and honest discussions when setbacks occur. When there is a setback, discuss it openly with your partner. Acknowledge the issue without placing blame. Discuss what happened, how it made you feel, and how you can avoid similar setbacks in the future. Be open to reassessing and adjusting your trust-building plans. Do not be fearful about changing your strategy if it is not working. Flexibility is key. You should try different approaches to find what works best for you both. Seeking external support can also be beneficial. Sometimes, an outside perspective can provide valuable insights. For example, you could talk to a therapist or counselor specializing in relationships. They can offer guidance and strategies to help you navigate setbacks.

You need to maintain resilience and commitment in the trust-building process. Recognize the importance of maintaining your motivation even when challenges try to hold you back. Remind yourself why you are putting in the effort, and keep focusing on the positive changes you have already made. Be patient, and realize that trust is not rebuilt overnight. It takes time, and there will be ups and downs. Celebrate small victories and progress. No matter how small, each step forward is a sign of growth. Recognize and appreciate these moments. They can provide the motivation you need to keep going.

You have an opportunity for growth when you learn from setbacks. Reflect on what caused them, asking yourself what triggered the issue and how you responded. This reflection can help you understand the underlying patterns and behaviors that led to the setback. The next thing to do is identify the lessons you have learned. Think about what you could have done differently and what strategies might be more effective in the future. Implementing changes to prevent future setbacks is crucial. Make adjustments to your approach by contemplating the insights you gained during reflection. For example, if you realize that external stressors often lead to misunderstandings, find ways to manage stress more effectively. This proactive approach can help you avoid similar issues in the future.

You can navigate the trust-building process optimally by recognizing common setbacks, addressing them openly, maintaining resilience, and learning from each experience. Remember, setbacks are not failures. Instead, they are opportunities to learn and grow. Embrace them as part of your journey toward building a stronger, more trusting relationship.

CHAPTER 6
STRENGTHENING RELATIONSHIP SKILLS

COMMUNICATION STRATEGIES AND EXERCISES

THINK ABOUT A TIME WHEN YOU FELT UNHEARD IN A CONVERSATION. Maybe your words were bouncing off a brick wall of indifference. The frustration and isolation that followed stayed with you, making you wary of speaking up again. This experience is all too common, reminding us that communication is essential in relationships. Communication is the lifeblood of any relationship, and mastering it can transform your connections, turning misunderstandings into clarity and conflict into cooperation.

Active Listening Techniques

Imagine a conversation where you feel honestly heard and understood. The person you speak with is fully present, reflecting on your words and asking clarifying questions. This is the essence of active listening, a skill that can transform relationships by fostering understanding and trust. Active listening goes beyond merely hearing words; it involves engaging with the speaker on a deeper level. While passive listening might involve nodding without truly processing the message, active listening requires full attention and participation. This difference is crucial. Active listening can change the dynamics of a relationship, making interactions more meaningful and reducing misunderstandings.

One of the core components of active listening is paying full attention to the speaker. This means setting aside distractions, maintaining eye contact, and being present in the moment. When you give someone your undivided attention, you value their words and feelings. Reflecting on what you hear is another vital aspect. This involves paraphrasing or summarizing the speaker's message to ensure you understand correctly. For instance, if your partner says, "I have been feeling overwhelmed at work," you might respond, "So, you are feeling a lot of pressure right now?" This reflection not only clarifies the message but also shows empathy and understanding.

You should also ask clarifying questions whenever necessary. These questions help you gather more information and better understand the speaker's perspective. For example, you might ask, "Can you tell me more about what has been overwhelming?" or "How can I support you during this time?" Such questions demonstrate your engagement and genuine interest in the other person's experience. They also encourage the speaker to open up and share more, fostering a deeper connection.

Practicing active listening techniques can enhance your skills and improve your relationships. Paraphrasing and summarizing the speaker's message helps ensure you grasp their point. This practice can prevent misunderstandings and demonstrate that you are actively engaged in the conversation. Non-verbal cues, such as nodding, maintaining eye contact, and leaning slightly forward, can further show your engagement and interest. These cues signal to the speaker that you are fully present and invested in what they are saying.

Avoiding distractions and interruptions is crucial for active listening. Managing distractions, like putting away your phone or turning off the TV, allows you to focus entirely on the conversation. This level of attention and respect can significantly enhance the quality of your interactions. Avoid interrupting your partner, as it can disrupt the flow of their speech and make them feel unheard. Wait until they finish speaking before responding.

Active Listening Exercises for Improvement

You can do active listening exercises with a partner or friend. Choose a topic and take turns speaking and listening. After each turn, the listener should paraphrase what they heard and ask clarifying questions. Doing this exercise effectively develops your listening skills and encourages better mutual understanding. Reflective journaling on listening experiences is another valuable practice. After a conversation, take a few minutes to write about what went well and what could be improved. Reflect on your listening behaviors, such as how well you paid attention, reflected on the message, and asked clarifying questions. Use this self-reflection to gain new insight and guide your growth.

Practicing active listening in different scenarios can also enhance your skills. Try actively listening during everyday interactions, such as with colleagues at work, friends over coffee, or family members at home. Each situation offers a unique opportunity to apply and refine your listening techniques. When you consistently practice active listening, making it a natural part of your communication style is more effortless. This will lead to stronger relationships and more profound connections.

In-Depth Strategies for Effective Communication

As we saw in the previous chapter, there are certain vital principles we need to remember that are essential to effective communication. Clarity and conciseness are paramount. Aim to be clear and straightforward when expressing your thoughts and feelings. Avoid beating around the bush or using ambiguous language that can lead to misunderstandings. For instance, instead of saying, "I feel like you never listen to me," you might say, "I feel hurt when I talk, and you seem distracted." This makes your point more straightforward and reduces the likelihood of defensive reactions.

Remember the tip I provided in an earlier chapter about using "I" statements? This technique involves framing your feelings and thoughts from your perspective so that you avoid creating the impression of making accusations. For example, saying, "I feel upset when plans change without notice," is more effective than "You always change plans at the last minute." "I" statements help you take ownership of your feelings and reduce blame, fostering a more open and constructive dialogue.

Maintaining a respectful tone is equally important. Even when discussing complex subjects or expressing frustration, keep your tone calm and respectful. Avoid raising your voice, using sarcasm, or resorting to name-calling. When you communicate respectfully, you encourage your partner to listen and engage, not shut down or become defensive.

You need to know how to recognize and address defensive behaviors to overcome communication behaviors. Defense mechanisms like stonewalling, where one partner shuts down and refuses to communicate, can hinder effective communication. It is essential to address these behaviors calmly. Acknowledge the tension and suggest a break if emotions run too high. This can prevent escalation and allow for more productive discussions later.

It is essential to minimize distractions and maintain focus during conversations. Getting distracted by phones, emails, and other interruptions is too easy. Make a conscious effort to eliminate these distractions when having meaningful discussions. Put your phone on silent, turn off the TV, and find a quiet space to focus solely on the conversation. Giving your full attention to your partner shows that you value their words and are committed to understanding their perspective.

An excellent way to reduce the chance of miscommunication is to paraphrase and summarize what your partner says. This ensures that you have understood them correctly. For example, you might say, "So, what I hear you saying is that you felt ignored when I did not respond to your message. Is that correct?" This clarifies the message and shows you actively listen and engage in the conversation.

Non-verbal communication plays a significant role in how we convey and interpret messages. Reading body language and facial expressions can provide valuable context for spoken words. For instance, crossed arms and a stern expression might indicate defensiveness or discomfort, while maintaining eye contact and nodding can signal attentiveness and empathy. Understanding these cues can help you respond more appropriately and empathetically.

The tone and pitch of your voice also significantly impact how your message is received. A soft, calm tone can soothe and reassure, while a harsh or high-pitched tone can escalate tension and provoke defensive reactions. Being mindful of how you say something is just as important as what you say.

Using non-verbal cues to enhance verbal communication can strengthen your message. Simple gestures like a gentle touch on the arm, nodding in agreement, or maintaining eye contact can reinforce your words and convey sincerity and empathy. These small actions can significantly affect how your message is received and understood.

More Practice Exercises for Improving Communication Skills

Role-playing difficult conversations can be an effective way to practice and improve your communication skills. Find a trusted friend or partner and take turns role-playing various scenarios, such as discussing a sensitive issue or resolving a conflict. This practice can help you become more comfortable expressing your thoughts and feelings and develop strategies for handling challenging conversations.

Practicing active communication techniques with a partner involves setting aside time to focus solely on improving your communication. During these sessions, practice using "I" statements, maintaining a respectful tone, and employing paraphrasing and summarizing techniques. Reflect on your successes and areas for improvement, and encourage your partner to do the same. This mutual effort can enhance your communication skills and strengthen your relationship.

Reflect on your successes in communication with your partner and stay aware of areas for improvement so you can continue to grow. After a conversation, take a moment to reflect on what went well and what could be improved. Consider journaling your thoughts and feelings, noting any patterns or recurring issues. This reflection can provide valuable insights and guide you in making necessary adjustments to your communication style.

Focusing on these principles and strategies can transform your communication, fostering more profound understanding and connection in your relationships. Effective communication is a skill that you and your partner can develop and refine. With practice, it can become a powerful tool for building stronger, healthier connections.

Empathetic Responses in Relationships

Empathy is the ability to understand and share the feelings of another person. It goes beyond merely hearing words to genuinely grasping the emotions behind them. Empathy creates a bridge between people, which is essential for building deep and meaningful connections. Unlike sympathy, which often involves feeling pity for someone, empathy consists of putting yourself in their shoes and experiencing their emotions as if they were your own. In the context of a relationship, empathetic behaviors include truly listening when your partner talks about their day, comforting them when they are upset, and celebrating their successes as if they were your own. These actions demonstrate your care, helping fortify your relationship's bond.

You need to practice intentionally to develop better empathy. One strategy is called perspective-taking, and you do it by consciously trying to see a situation from another person's point of view. Imagine how they might feel and what they might be thinking. You will find it easier to respond more compassionately when you regularly do this exercise. Engaging in empathetic listening is another powerful tool. This involves entirely focusing on the speaker, reflecting on their emotions, and validating them. For example, if your partner tells you they are stressed about work, you might say, "It sounds like you are feeling overwhelmed right now. That must be tough." Another way to become more empathetic is to consider when someone shows empathy. How did it make you feel? What did they do that positively impacted you? Use these reflections to guide how you interact with others.

You can transform your relationships by expressing empathy effectively in your interactions. Verbal expressions of empathy involve acknowledging and validating the other person's feelings. Phrases like, "I can see that this hurts you" or "It sounds like you are feeling anxious" show that you are attuned to their emotional state. Non-verbal cues also play a significant role. For example, maintaining eye contact, nodding, and gentle touches can convey empathy even when you say nothing. These small gestures can make the other person feel seen and understood. Using empathetic language in challenging conversations can help de-escalate tension and foster a more constructive dialogue. Instead of saying, "You are always so negative," you might say, "I have noticed you have been feeling down lately. Can you tell me more about what's going on?" This approach shows concern and invites openness rather than defensiveness.

Empathy-Building Exercises

You can build better empathy skills by role-playing empathetic responses. Find a partner and share a recent experience while the other practices empathetic listening and responding. This exercise can help you become more comfortable expressing empathy and understanding how it feels to be on the receiving end. Another way to practice this is by doing community service or volunteer work. Helping others in need helps many people broaden their perspective and deepen their understanding of different life experiences. Make sure that you sometimes reflect on empathetic interactions and their impact. When you have conversations in which you practice empathy, take some time to journal about how it went. What did you say or do that felt empathetic? How did the other person respond? This reflection can help you identify what works well and areas for improvement.

Empathy is a powerful tool that can transform your relationships. By understanding empathy, developing it through practice, and expressing it effectively, you can create more profound, meaningful connections with the people around you. In addition to being beneficial in romantic relationships, they also enhance every other kind of connection and interaction. This includes your relationships with family, friends, colleagues, and acquaintances. Empathy means that you can understand and share the feelings of others, which fosters a sense of connection and community. Your relationships will be more resilient and emotionally fulfilling.

SETTING AND MAINTAINING HEALTHY BOUNDARIES

Understanding boundaries is crucial for fostering healthy relationships. Boundaries are like invisible lines defining where you end and others begin, ensuring your needs and limits are respected. There are various types of boundaries, including physical, emotional, and mental. Physical boundaries pertain to your personal space and physical touch, while emotional boundaries involve your feelings and personal information. Mental boundaries relate to your thoughts, values, and opinions. These boundaries maintain your integrity, protecting your sense of self and ensuring you do not lose yourself in your relationships. Healthy boundaries allow you to feel safe and respected, whereas unhealthy boundaries—either too rigid or too porous—can lead to discomfort and resentment. For instance, a healthy boundary might be setting aside time for yourself despite a busy schedule. In contrast, an unhealthy boundary might be always saying yes to others at the expense of your well-being.

Identifying your boundary needs starts with self-reflection. Reflective exercises can help you explore boundaries and understand what makes you comfortable or uncomfortable. Consider situations in the past where you felt your boundaries were violated. How did you react? What would you have preferred to happen? Recognizing these signs of boundary violations is critical to understanding your limits. Journaling can be beneficial in this process. Use prompts like, "When do I feel most respected?" or "What situations make me feel uncomfortable?" to set boundary intentions. Writing down your thoughts and feelings can clarify and guide you in establishing healthier boundaries.

To maintain your boundaries, you must communicate them to others. Use clear and assertive language to express your needs and limits. For example, instead of saying, "I do not like it when you are late," you could say, "I feel disrespected when plans are changed at the last minute. Can we agree to notify each other in advance?" This transparent communication helps others understand your boundaries without feeling attacked. Setting boundaries without guilt or fear is also essential. Remember, your boundaries are valid, and it is okay to prioritize your well-being. When you encounter pushback, stay firm and reiterate your boundaries calmly. For instance, if someone reacts negatively to your request for personal space, you might say, "I understand this is difficult, but I need this time to recharge. I appreciate your understanding."

Maintaining your boundaries consistently requires ongoing effort and reinforcement. Techniques for reinforcing boundaries include regular self-check-ins to meet your needs and adjust boundaries as necessary. To handle boundary violations calmly and assertively, you need to address the issue directly without aggression. For example, if a friend repeatedly interrupts you, you might say, "I value our conversations, but I need to finish my thoughts without interruption. Can we work on this?" Reflecting on boundary successes and challenges can also provide valuable insights. Keep a journal to document your experiences, noting what worked well and what needs improvement. This reflection helps you stay mindful of your boundaries and make necessary adjustments.

Boundary-setting is a dynamic process that evolves with your relationships and personal growth. Understanding, identifying, communicating, and maintaining your boundaries can create a foundation of respect and trust in your relationships. This practice enhances your well-being and fosters healthier, more fulfilling connections.

ADDRESSING ATTACHMENT CONFLICTS AND RESOLUTION STRATEGIES

Understanding Attachment Patterns and Triggers

Identifying attachment conflicts in relationships requires recognizing the deeper patterns beneath surface-level disagreements. These conflicts often manifest as recurring arguments over seemingly minor issues, accompanied by an underlying tension that refuses to dissipate. The most common pattern involves one partner becoming increasingly clingy as the other withdraws, creating a destructive cycle of pursuit and retreat. To understand these dynamics, partners must engage in honest self-reflection, asking questions like "What triggers my insecurity?" and "How do I react when my partner pulls away?"

These inquiries can reveal the fundamental fears and anxieties driving attachment conflicts.

Consider the illustrative case of Sarah and Tom, whose relationship struggled with attachment-related tensions. Sarah experienced intense anxiety whenever Tom didn't immediately respond to her messages, leading to frequent arguments where she accused him of insufficient care. At the same time, Tom felt overwhelmed by her constant need for reassurance. Through careful reflection, Sarah discovered that her anxiety stemmed from deep-seated abandonment fears rooted in past experiences. This crucial insight allowed the couple to address the core issue instead of treating its symptoms.

Maintaining Calm During Conflicts

The foundation of effective conflict resolution lies in maintaining composure, even when emotions run high. While challenging, this skill is essential for productive dialogue. Partners can employ deep breathing exercises, grounding practices, or simple counting methods to maintain composure. Using "I" statements proves particularly effective in expressing feelings and needs while reducing defensive reactions. For example, saying, "I feel hurt when you don't respond to my messages because it makes me feel unimportant," typically generates a more positive response than accusatory statements like "You never care about me." This approach empowers you to control your emotions and the conversation.

Creating a safe space for emotional expression requires both partners to practice validation and reassurance. Instead of dismissing or minimizing feelings, acknowledge them with statements like "I can see why you feel this way." This approach helps calm immediate emotional responses and builds a foundation of security within the relationship. Partners with anxious attachments may need extra reassurance during conflicts, making validation an essential component of the resolution process. This validation provides comfort and security, fostering a healthier relationship.

Implementing Effective Time-Out Strategies

De-escalation techniques are crucial in preventing conflicts from intensifying into significant arguments. Partners must recognize early warning signs of escalation, such as raised voices, frequent interruptions, or defensive body language. When these signs appear, implementing a structured time-out can prevent further deterioration of the conversation. However, you should never use these breaks as punishment or angry withdrawal. Instead, couples should agree on a specific duration for the time-out and set a precise time to resume the discussion.

During these intentional breaks, partners can engage in self-soothing activities and personal reflection. Deep breathing exercises, mindfulness practices, or simple grounding techniques can help restore emotional balance. The key is to use this time constructively, preparing to return to the conversation with renewed perspective and composure. Partners should also respect each other's different needs during these breaks. While some may need to process emotions alone, others might benefit from gentle reassurance about the relationship's stability.

Collaborative Problem-Solving Approaches

Shifting our views of conflicts as battles to seeing them as shared challenges can transform the resolution process. This collaborative approach emphasizes teamwork and mutual support, encouraging both partners to work together toward solutions. When discussing potential resolutions, remain open to compromise and creative solutions. For instance, Sarah and Tom developed a system where Tom would send quick acknowledgment messages when unable to fully respond while Sarah worked on managing her anxiety during these periods.

Clear communication of needs becomes fundamental in this process, particularly for those with anxious attachment styles who often harbor unexpressed expectations. Partners should engage in open discussions about their needs during and after conflicts. Understanding that one partner might need space to process while another might need immediate discussion can help establish protocols that respect both individuals' attachment styles and emotional requirements.

Post-Conflict Repair and Growth

After resolving conflicts, engaging in repair efforts helps restore emotional security and strengthen the relationship bond. These efforts might include small gestures of affection, written expressions of appreciation, or dedicated time for reconnection. Such actions demonstrate commitment to the relationship despite challenges and help rebuild emotional safety. Partners should also reflect on the conflict experience, talk about what worked well, and identify areas for improvement in their communication and resolution strategies.

Regular practice through role-playing exercises can help couples develop and refine their conflict-resolution skills. Working with hypothetical scenarios allows partners to experiment with different approaches in a low-pressure environment. For instance, partners can role-play situations where one partner feels neglected and the other feels overwhelmed, and then switch roles to understand each other's perspectives. This practice, combined with thoughtful reflection on past conflicts, builds confidence in handling future disagreements constructively.

Creating a Structured Resolution Plan

Developing a formal conflict resolution plan provides a reliable framework for addressing future disagreements. This plan should outline specific steps for approaching conflicts, including agreed-upon time-out procedures, methods for addressing triggers, and strategies for maintaining productive communication. Having such a structure helps reduce anxiety about future conflicts and provides clear guidance when emotions run high.

The plan should include regular review and adjustment periods, allowing couples to refine their approach based on experience and changing needs. This ongoing development process demonstrates a commitment to growth and mutual understanding within the relationship. Partners should also consider including preventive measures in their plan, such as regular check-ins about relationship satisfaction and scheduled times for discussing concerns before they escalate into conflicts.

While navigating attachment-related conflicts can be challenging, particularly for those with anxious attachment styles, implementing these strategies creates a foundation for healthy resolution and relationship growth. Success requires consistent effort, patience, and commitment from both partners. Through understanding attachment patterns, maintaining calm communication, using effective time-outs, engaging in collaborative problem-solving, and dedicating time to repair and reflection, couples can transform conflicts into opportunities for deepening their connection and building a more secure relationship bond.

BUILDING A SECURE ATTACHMENT WITH YOUR PARTNER

When you have a secure attachment, you enjoy a strong sense of safety and trust in your relationship. Both partners feel valued and respected. This attachment style contributes to high relationship satisfaction, fostering open communication, mutual support, and emotional intimacy. Critical behaviors of secure attachment include consistent emotional availability, genuine affection, and respect for boundaries. For example, a securely attached partner will reliably respond to emotional needs, provide comfort during distress, and offer support in pursuing personal goals. These behaviors create a stable and nurturing environment where both partners can thrive.

Behaving reliably and consistently is vital to building secure attachment in your relationship. Make a conscious effort to be dependable and predictable when interacting with your partner.

Show up when you say you will follow through on promises and be there for your partner when needed. Consistency builds trust so that you and your partner have a foundation of reliability. Emotional availability and responsiveness are also crucial. This means being present and attentive when your partner shares their feelings, ensuring you are actively listening and offering empathy and support. Did your partner have a tough day? Take the time to listen and comfort them, showing that you are emotionally attuned and responsive to their needs.

Creating rituals of connection strengthens the bond between partners. These rituals can be simple yet meaningful activities that you do regularly. An example could be setting a date night, when you spend quality time together, free from distractions. Or you could start a daily check-in routine in which you discuss your day and share your thoughts and feelings. These rituals reinforce your connection, providing consistent opportunities for bonding and intimacy. They are anchors in your relationship, reminding both partners of their commitment and lover.

Maintaining secure attachment over time requires ongoing effort and intentionality. Regular relationship check-ins are vital for assessing the health of your connection and addressing any issues that arise. Set aside time each week to discuss your relationship, discussing what is going well and what could be improved. This practice helps you stay attuned to each other's needs and prevents minor issues from escalating into more significant problems. I recommend practicing gratitude and appreciation as another powerful way to maintain a secure attachment in your relationship. Express gratitude for your partner and acknowledge their positive qualities and actions regularly. Simple gestures like saying "thank you" or writing a heartfelt note can go a long way in reinforcing your bond.

Addressing and resolving conflicts constructively is essential for maintaining secure attachment. When disputes arise, approach them with a collaborative and respectful mindset. Avoid blame and focus on finding solutions that work for both partners. Are you disagreeing about household chores? Discuss each other's perspectives and negotiate a fair plan for dividing responsibilities. This collaborative approach will help resolve the immediate issue and strengthen your partnership. That is because you are demonstrating your commitment to working together.

Finally, be sure to set continuous improvement goals so your relationship continues to grow and thrive, and identify areas where you want to strengthen your secure attachment and set actionable goals. For example, you aim to increase your emotional availability by practicing active listening or to enhance your connection by establishing new rituals. Regularly review and adjust these goals, celebrating your progress and making necessary changes. Building and maintaining secure attachment requires consistent effort, emotional availability, and intentional connection. Adopting these practices and reflecting on your attachment dynamics can create a resilient, nurturing, and deeply fulfilling relationship.

CHAPTER 7
ONGOING PERSONAL GROWTH AND DEVELOPMENT

PERSONAL GROWTH IS NOT A DESTINATION BUT A CONTINUOUS, intentional journey of self-discovery and transformation. For individuals recovering from anxious attachment, this journey represents more than a path to healing—it is a profound commitment to understanding oneself, breaking destructive patterns, and cultivating the emotional resilience necessary for healthy, secure relationships.

Recovery from anxious attachment is not about achieving a perfect state but developing a compassionate, curious approach to your inner world. Each step of growth is an act of courage—a willingness to look inward, challenge long-held beliefs, and create new, healthier ways of connecting with yourself and others. I designed this chapter as your companion and guide, offering practical strategies, insights, and tools to support your ongoing personal development.

Through self-reflection, continuous learning, professional support, and intentional lifestyle choices, you will discover that personal growth is a dynamic process of becoming. It is about learning to trust yourself, understanding your emotional landscape, and creating the conditions for lasting emotional security and meaningful relationships.

As you move through this chapter, approach each section with an open heart and a spirit of gentle curiosity. Your commitment to growth is a powerful testament to your strength, resilience, and capacity for transformation.

SELF-REFLECTION: A PATH TO EMOTIONAL AWARENESS

Self-reflection is a powerful mirror that offers a clear view of your inner world. Regularly examining your thoughts, emotions, and behaviors can enhance self-awareness and identify opportunities for personal growth. This practice is especially crucial for individuals dealing with anxiety attachment, as it empowers you to understand the roots of your emotional patterns and make conscious, intentional choices, putting you in control of your emotional well-being.

The Power of Journaling: A Tool for Self-Discovery

You will remember that I mentioned daily journaling as one of the most effective techniques for self-reflection. This transformative practice provides a safe, private space to explore your inner landscape. Through writing, you create a powerful opportunity to process complex emotions, identify behavioral patterns, gain deeper insights into your relationship anxieties, and develop greater self-understanding. It is a therapeutic tool that allows you to unpack your emotional experiences with honesty and compassion.

Different journaling approaches can support your emotional healing journey. A gratitude journal helps shift your mindset from negativity to appreciation, especially when struggling with anxiety attachment. By documenting the positive aspects of your life, you can counterbalance anxious thoughts and cultivate a more balanced emotional state.

An emotional journal is a judgment-free zone where you can freely express your anxieties, fears, and frustrations. This approach allows you to vent and explore your emotions, providing relief and ultimately alleviating stress and gaining emotional clarity. A reflective journal combines gratitude and emotional exploration to comprehensively view your daily experiences and inner responses.

Free writing emerges as a powerful technique to connect with your subconscious mind. Writing without worrying about grammar, spelling, or structure allows for a stream-of-consciousness approach that can unearth hidden thoughts and feelings. This method offers profound insights into your emotional landscape, revealing patterns and perspectives you might not discover through more structured writing.

Structured journaling prompts can guide your self-reflection, especially when dealing with anxiety attachment. Thoughtful questions can help you explore your emotional experiences more deeply. Consider exploring prompts that encourage you to examine the origins of your anxieties, recognize moments of security in your relationships, and understand your growth journey.

Implementing a Daily Self-Reflection Practice

Creating a consistent routine is essential for meaningful self-reflection. Choose a dedicated time for journaling that feels natural and sustainable. Some find morning reflections before starting the day most beneficial, while others prefer evening journaling to process daily experiences. You might combine your reflection practice with other self-care activities like walking or enjoying herbal tea, making it a holistic part of your growth routine.

Modern technology offers additional support through reflection apps and digital tools. These resources can provide journaling prompts, send helpful reminders, and offer a structured space for recording your thoughts, making the practice more accessible and consistent.

Reflection as a Decision-Making Tool

Self-reflection transcends understanding your past—it becomes a strategic approach to making intentional future choices. Before making significant decisions in your relationships, examine your core values, assess your long-term goals, and consider potential outcomes. This practice helps you align your choices with your emotional well-being, creating a more mindful approach to personal and relational challenges and instilling confidence in your decisions.

The Transformative Impact of Self-Reflection

Committing to regular self-reflection and journaling offers a path to profound personal transformation. You'll develop improved emotional intelligence, understand the roots of your anxiety attachment, and cultivate healthier relationship patterns. More importantly, you'll learn to approach yourself with greater self-compassion, making more conscious and aligned decisions.

Remember, self-reflection is a journey of continuous growth. Be patient and kind to yourself as you develop this powerful personal and emotional healing practice. Each word you write and each reflection moment brings you closer to understanding yourself more deeply and creating the relationships you desire.

RESOURCES FOR CONTINUOUS LEARNING IN ATTACHMENT RECOVERY

Learning continuously is a powerful catalyst for personal growth and emotional healing. By actively engaging your mind and cultivating curiosity, you create a dynamic pathway to understanding yourself and your relationships more deeply. Learning becomes more than an academic pursuit—it's a transformative journey of self-discovery and personal development.

Ongoing education is your gateway to becoming more adaptable, innovative, and resilient. As you expose yourself to new knowledge and perspectives, you develop the capacity to view challenges through a more nuanced lens. This approach is particularly crucial for individuals recovering from anxiety attachment. It offers tools and insights that can fundamentally reshape your approach to relationships and emotional well-being, bringing a sense of relief and hope.

Recommended Books for Attachment and Personal Growth

Amir Levine and Rachel Heller's *Attached* represents a cornerstone text for anyone navigating attachment challenges. This comprehensive book offers profound insights into how different attachment styles impact relationships, providing practical strategies for building more secure and fulfilling connections. Readers will find compassionate guidance that helps them understand their relational patterns and work toward healthier interactions.

Daniel Goleman's *Emotional Intelligence* explores how emotional awareness can transform personal and professional relationships. The book offers critical tools for understanding and managing emotions, which is especially valuable for individuals working through attachment anxiety.

Eckhart Tolle's *The Power of Now* complements these insights by emphasizing the importance of mindful presence. His teachings offer a powerful approach to reducing anxiety by anchoring oneself in the present moment. For those struggling with attachment-related stress, Tolle's work can provide a transformative perspective on managing emotional turbulence.

Online Learning: Flexible Paths to Personal Growth

Modern technology has revolutionized personal development through accessible online learning platforms. Websites like Coursera, Udemy, and Skillshare offer comprehensive courses on critical topics such as mindfulness, emotional regulation, and relationship skills. You can seamlessly integrate these courses into your daily life to provide flexible learning options.

Interactive online workshops led by personal development experts offer precious experiences. Unlike traditional learning methods, these sessions provide hands-on, practical approaches to understanding and implementing personal growth strategies. They create opportunities for direct engagement, allowing you to learn from experienced professionals while connecting with a community of people on similar journeys, fostering a sense of connection and understanding.

Embracing a Lifelong Learning Mindset

Personal growth is not a destination but a continuous journey. By consistently exposing yourself to new ideas, perspectives, and learning opportunities, you create a dynamic approach to personal development. This mindset of curiosity and openness becomes a powerful tool in your attachment recovery process.

Remember that learning takes many forms. While books and online courses are valuable, they complement other growth strategies like therapy, support groups, and personal reflection. Each resource offers a unique perspective that can contribute to your understanding and healing.

Practical Tips for Continued Learning

Consider creating a personal learning plan that includes the following:

- Regular reading time
- Scheduled online course participation
- As discussed in the previous section, journaling to reflect on new insights
- Discussing learned concepts with a therapist or support group

Your Ongoing Journey of Discovery

The approaches and resources discussed in this chapter are not mere suggestions but invitations to a deeper understanding of yourself and your relationships. Each book you read, each course you take, and each moment of reflection brings you closer to creating the secure, fulfilling connections you deserve.

Approach your learning journey with patience, compassion, and an open heart. Your commitment to personal growth is a powerful act of self-love and healing.

THE ROLE OF THERAPY AND PROFESSIONAL HELP

As we have seen, anxious attachment can significantly impact how we experience relationships. They often lead to a cycle of insecurity, a persistent need for reassurance from our partners, and a fear of abandonment. Therapy can be a transformative step for those working to overcome these challenges.

Consider seeing a therapist who specializes in inner child work. A professional can offer valuable insights and advice. Look for someone trained in trauma-informed care who makes you feel safe and supported. The right therapeutic relationship can make a significant difference, but finding a therapist who resonates with you is vital.

I worked with a therapist with over twenty years of experience in trauma-informed care. She emphasized the importance of patience and self-compassion in the healing process. Our sessions taught me that healing the inner child is like tending to a wounded part of yourself. It requires consistent care and understanding. I was given helpful exercises such as writing a dialogue between my adult self and inner child to foster communication and trust.

Here is how therapy and professional help are critical in healing and recovery.

1. **Understanding Attachment Styles**: Therapy provides a safe space for us to explore our attachment styles. A trained counselor can help us identify the roots of our anxious attachment, often tracing back to early relationships and experiences. This understanding can bring relief, allowing us to gain insight and heal, knowing that past experiences shape current behaviors and feelings.

2. **Developing Healthier Relationship Patterns**: Through therapy, we can recognize unhealthy relationship patterns,

such as clinging, excessive need for validation, or fear-driven behaviors. Therapists can guide us in developing healthier communication styles and coping strategies that promote secure attachment. This growth can lead to more stable and fulfilling relationships over time.

3. **Building Self-Esteem and Self-Worth**: Anxious attachment often stems from low self-esteem and inadequacy. Therapy can help us work on self-acceptance and self-worth, empowering them to approach relationships from a place of strength rather than neediness. As we cultivate a stronger sense of self, they become more capable of forming healthy, balanced partnerships and instilling confidence.

4. **Practicing Emotional Regulation**: Therapy offers tools and techniques for managing anxiety and emotional responses. By learning mindfulness, grounding techniques, and emotional regulation strategies, we can better handle our fears and insecurities in relationships. This practice leads to decreased anxiety and a more remarkable ability to engage in constructive interactions with partners.

5. **Creating Secure Attachments**: A therapist, with their professional training and experience, can assist us in identifying and fostering secure attachments. This may involve exploring current relationships and understanding what qualities in partners foster security versus insecurity. The therapist can guide us to seek and nurture relationships based on mutual respect and understanding, reinforcing healthier attachment styles.

6. **Establishing Boundaries**: One common struggle for those of us with anxious attachment is an inability to develop or maintain personal boundaries. Therapy encourages us to recognize and communicate our needs effectively to our partners. Establishing boundaries helps to foster respect and support within relationships, creating a more balanced dynamic.

7. **Foster Connection through Group Therapy**: Group therapy can also benefit those with anxious attachment styles. Connecting with others with similar experiences can provide validation, reduce feelings of isolation, and offer insights into different coping strategies. This communal support can reinforce healing and provide additional perspectives on forming healthy relationships, creating a sense of belonging and support.

Therapy and professional help can be invaluable resources for many of us seeking to recover from anxious attachment. Through increasing self-awareness, developing healthier relationship patterns, and learning effective coping strategies, we can break free from cycles of anxiety and insecurity. With time and commitment, therapy can pave the way for secure, loving relationships that foster personal growth and emotional fulfillment. Remember, the journey to healing and growth is unique for everyone. However, with proper support and commitment, overcoming anxious attachments and building healthier, more fulfilling relationships are possible.

LIFESTYLE CHANGES FOR LONG-TERM ANXIETY MANAGEMENT

As we have seen throughout this book, managing anxiety, particularly in the context of attachment recovery, requires thoughtful lifestyle changes that can promote emotional well-being and resilience. Here are several essential practices to consider:

1. **Develop Coping Strategies**: Learn and practice the coping mechanisms we discussed throughout the book. Having a repertoire of strategies can empower you to handle anxiety when it arises.

2. **Establish Healthy Routines**: Creating a structured daily routine can provide a sense of predictability and security. It can also be constructive for those recovering from attachment-related anxiety. For instance, wake up at the same time each day, have regular meals, and incorporate healthy activities we discussed earlier.

3. **Limit Exposure to Stressors**: Identify and minimize exposure to people, environments, or media that exacerbate anxiety. Setting boundaries in relationships and taking breaks from social media can significantly reduce overwhelming feelings.

4. **Nurture a Balanced Diet**: What we eat daily is vital to our mental health. Aim to have a balanced diet of rich, whole foods. Eat a mix of vegetables, lean protein, fruits, and whole grains. Staying adequately hydrated and reducing caffeine and sugar consumption can also contribute to lower anxiety levels.

5. **Cultivate Supportive Relationships**: Building and cultivating healthy relationships can help combat feelings of loneliness and insecurity. Foster connections with friends, family, or support groups that understand your experiences and can provide encouragement and empathy during challenging times.

6. **Seek Professional Guidance**: Consulting with a counselor or therapist specializing in attachment can provide invaluable tools and perspectives. Treatment can offer a safe space to explore underlying patterns and develop strategies for long-term recovery.

7. **Set Realistic Goals**: Establishing small and achievable goals can be a source of encouragement that can help build confidence and a sense of accomplishment. Celebrate progress, no matter how small, and be patient with yourself as you navigate the recovery process.

Making these lifestyle changes can significantly improve how you recover from anxiety related to attachment. Our recovery journeys are unique, so finding what resonates best with you and being kind to yourself throughout the process is essential.

DEVELOPING A PERSONAL GROWTH PLAN

Personal growth is a journey of change, self-discovery, and evolution—not a destination. For individuals recovering from anxious attachment, creating a structured personal growth plan becomes a beacon of hope, a crucial strategy for healing and building emotional resilience.

The Foundations of a Personal Growth Plan

A comprehensive personal growth plan goes beyond simple goal setting. It requires deep self-reflection, an honest assessment of your current emotional landscape, and a compassionate approach to personal development. The plan serves as a roadmap, helping you navigate the complex terrain of emotional healing and relationship growth.

Begin by conducting a thorough self-assessment. Examine your current emotional patterns, relationship dynamics, and most vulnerable areas. This process isn't about criticism but creating a compassionate understanding of your inner world. Consider your past relationship experiences, attachment triggers, and the emotional challenges that have consistently surfaced in your life.

Critical Components of an Effective Growth Plan

Your personal growth plan should address multiple emotional and relational well-being dimensions. Start by identifying specific areas for development. These might include:

- Emotional regulation skills
- Communication capabilities
- Self-confidence and self-trust
- Understanding and managing attachment triggers
- Developing healthier relationship patterns

Create measurable, achievable goals for each of these areas. Instead of vague intentions, craft specific objectives that you can track and celebrate. For instance, rather than saying, "I want to be less anxious," develop a goal like "I will practice three grounding techniques daily for the next three months" or "I will communicate my needs clearly in my relationship without apologizing for having them."

Implementing Your Growth Strategy

Consistency is the cornerstone of meaningful personal development. Design a daily and weekly framework that supports your growth objectives. This framework might involve the following:

- Morning meditation or journaling
- Weekly therapy or coaching sessions
- Regular self-reflection exercises
- Specific communication practice with your partner
- Dedicated time for personal learning and skill development

Technology and various resources can support your growth plan. Consider using the following:

- Habit-tracking apps
- Journaling platforms
- Online courses on emotional intelligence
- Meditation and mindfulness applications
- Support group connections

Overcoming Obstacles and Maintaining Motivation

Personal growth is not a linear path. You will encounter challenges, setbacks, and moments of doubt. Develop a resilience strategy that acknowledges these potential obstacles. Create a support system that includes professional guidance, trusted friends or family, and potentially a support group for individuals working through attachment challenges.

Embrace self-compassion throughout your journey. Understand that healing is a process, and every small step is significant. Celebrate your progress, no matter how incremental it might seem, knowing that you are caring for yourself in the best possible way.

Periodic Review and Adaptation

Your personal growth plan is a living document. Schedule regular review periods—perhaps quarterly—to assess your progress, adjust your strategies, and set new intentions. This plan might involve the following:

- Reviewing your initial goals
- Acknowledging your achievements
- Identifying new areas for development
- Adjusting your approach based on your learnings

The Holistic Nature of Personal Growth

Remember that personal growth extends beyond specific relationship skills. It encompasses your entire being—mental, emotional, physical, and spiritual. Integrate practices that nurture all these aspects, such as:

- Regular physical exercise
- Nutrition that supports mental health
- Creative expression
- Spiritual or mindfulness practices
- Continuous learning

A Journey of Transformation

Your personal growth plan is more than a series of objectives. It's a profound commitment to yourself—a declaration that you are worthy of healthy, secure relationships and inner peace. Approach this journey with patience, curiosity, and unwavering compassion for yourself.

As you move forward, trust in your capacity for change. Each step you take is toward healing, understanding, and, ultimately, the loving, secure relationships you deserve.

AFTERWORD

We have concluded our journey through the complexities of anxious attachment. You now understand the roots of this attachment style and practical strategies for overcoming it. I hope I have shown you the best path toward healthier, more secure relationships in this book.

SUMMARY OF KEY INSIGHTS

Let's reflect on what you have learned. We began by exploring the origins of anxious attachment. You learned about its evolutionary roots and the impact of early caregiving behaviors. You discovered how childhood experiences and societal influences shape your attachment style. This foundational knowledge laid the groundwork for understanding the emotional and psychological landscape you navigate daily.

We then explored the neuroscience behind attachment, examining brain structures and neurochemical processes that influence your behaviors. You gained insights into how your brain responds to stress and attachment cues and the potential for neuroplasticity to change these patterns. This knowledge has equipped you to approach your attachment style with compassion and curiosity.

It is essential to be able to identify anxious attachment in yourself. I offered tools and information you can use to achieve that, including self-assessment tools, reflective exercises, and case studies. You became more aware of your behaviors and their origins. Recognizing these patterns is the first step toward change, and your increased self-awareness paves the way for stronger, healthier relationships.

I provided practical strategies for managing anxiety, jealousy, and overthinking, including tools for immediate relief and long-term change. Self-soothing techniques, grounding exercises, cognitive-behavioral strategies, and visualization practices are now part of your toolkit. These methods empower you to regulate your emotions and reduce the intensity of your anxiety.

Enhancing self-awareness and emotional regulation through mindfulness, guided meditations, and self-compassion exercises further solidified your growth. These techniques help you stay present, manage emotions, and cultivate inner peace.

We also focused extensively on rebuilding trust and emotional security in relationships. You learned effective communication techniques, conflict resolution strategies, and ways to create a secure foundation with your partner. These are fundamental skills for fostering trust and deepening emotional intimacy.

Inner child healing was explored to address unresolved traumas and unmet needs from your past. You began a profound healing and self-compassion journey by reconnecting with your inner child. Remember the importance of this work in transforming your attachment style and building a more secure sense of self.

Another critical area was strengthening relationship skills, such as effective communication, setting boundaries, active listening, and empathetic responses. These skills are the building blocks of healthy, fulfilling relationships.

Finally, we discussed the importance of ongoing personal growth and development. You learned to continuously self-reflect, seek support from communities and resources, and create a personal growth plan. This commitment to lifelong learning ensures that your journey toward secure attachment and lasting love continues.

PRACTICE WHAT YOU LEARN AND CELEBRATE PROGRESS

As you reach the end of this book, take a moment to reflect on how far you have come. You have already taken courageous steps toward healing and growth by exploring your attachment patterns, confronting old wounds, and practicing new strategies. Your progress will be evident and should be celebrated. Remember, progress is not about perfection but about showing up for yourself each day, even when challenging. Celebrate the small victories: the moments of emotional clarity, healthier conversations, and growing trust in yourself and others. Keep practicing the tools you have learned here, knowing that every effort you make builds the foundation for a more secure and fulfilling future. You deserve love, connection, and peace—not just from your relationships but from within. Embrace this journey, stay committed to your growth, and trust that with time and persistence, you are creating a life filled with the lasting love and emotional security you have always deserved.

You now have all the fundamental knowledge and tools needed to change your attachment style and foster healthier relationships. But remember, this journey is ongoing. Actively apply the strategies and exercises this book provides to your daily life. I recommend revisiting chapters as needed and continually using the tools I provide to improve further. On a personal note, please accept my thanks for embarking on this journey with me. Your willingness to explore, reflect, and grow is inspirational. I hope I have provided valuable insights and practical tools for your journey toward healing and growth.

Remember, lasting love and secure, healthy relationships are possible. By applying the teachings of this book, you can create the fulfilling connections you deserve. Keep believing in your ability to change and grow. Your journey toward a more secure, loving future has just begun.

APPENDIX

SUPPORTING PARTNERS WITH ANXIOUS ATTACHMENT

THIS SECTION IS AIMED AT PARTNERS OF PEOPLE WITH ANXIOUS attachments. It is a short primer to give loved ones who may not understand anxious attachment and recovery and to promote open dialogue and avenues of communication and support. It also provides a different perspective for those in anxious attachment recovery of what their partners may see in the relationship.

Recognizing Anxious Attachment in Others

Recognizing anxious attachment behaviors in others is a crucial step in providing support. It requires understanding the intricate dynamics of attachment styles and recognizing the emotional needs that arise both in ourselves and those we care for. While self-awareness of our attachment patterns can often illuminate our challenges, it may be significantly different when we observe these patterns in others.

When identifying anxious attachment behaviors in someone else, we may recognize the confusion, emotional highs and lows, and the constant need for reassurance that can characterize their interactions. This awareness invites empathy as we strive to create a safe space for them to express their fears and anxieties. However, it also calls for us to remain mindful of our responses and boundaries as we navigate their emotional landscape's complexities without becoming overwhelmed.

By exploring how to support a partner or loved one through recovery, we become better equipped to foster healthier relationships while managing our emotional well-being. This journey of mutual understanding and support can lead to deeper connections, improved communication, and, ultimately, the healing of attachment wounds for both individuals involved.

Behaviors to Look Out For

Specific behavioral indicators can let you recognize signs of anxious attachment in other people. Inconsistency in how the person communicates tends to be one of the most common signs. Someone with an anxious attachment may sometimes overwhelm you with messages because they are looking for closeness and affirmation. However, another day, that person may be completely silent because they fear seeming too needy. This kind of inconsistency can be highly confusing and emotionally drains everyone involved. For example, they might often send you texts asking for reassurance that everything is okay between you, even when there has not been any evidence of issues. Their deep-seated fear of abandonment creates the person's frequent need for reassurance.

Other common signs of anxious attachment are jealousy and possessiveness. If someone has an anxious attachment, they may exhibit intense jealousy over apparently trivial interactions. They may have trouble dealing with the fact that you have relationships with other people, even if those relationships are entirely platonic. Some common manifestations of this possessiveness include constantly asking about a partner's whereabouts, who they spend time with, and what they do. They may interpret neutral behaviors as signs of disinterest or infidelity. These behaviors can create a cycle of conflict and mistrust, making fostering a healthy, balanced relationship complicated.

People with anxious attachment styles may also experience frequent emotional highs and lows, with drastic and sudden mood and behavior changes. That is why people in relationships with them sometimes feel like they are on an emotional rollercoaster. People with an anxious attachment may be affectionate and ecstatic one minute and upset and distant the next. These mood swings often result from internal conflict between their craving for closeness and fear of rejection. Partners of people with anxious attachment can find it challenging to navigate the emotional dynamics of the relationship.

How Anxious Attachment Impacts a Relationship

It is crucial to understand how much anxious attachment styles can impact the dynamics of a relationship. The frequent need for reassurance often means that there are communication problems. This can create a cycle in which the partner with anxious attachment constantly seeks validation. At the same time, a feeling of overwhelm causes the other to withdraw. This cyclical characteristic of reassurance-seeking and withdrawal can lead to less trust and a problematic pattern of conflict to get past. Both partners may have difficulty finding a stable footing because they feel constantly engaged in emotional negotiations.

These problematic relational patterns may become a fixed part of the relationship, which can cause frequent conflict. When someone with anxious attachment has intense reactions to misunderstandings and actions or words they perceive as rejection, this can cause significant conflict. With these conflict cycles, both people may end up feeling like they are walking on eggshells. Both partners will probably be hyper-aware of what the other person is feeling, wanting to avoid causing anxiety or arguments. These kinds of patterns can cause breakdowns in trust and communication, as well as feelings of being emotionally drained.

How to Support Your Partner

Empathy is vital when supporting a partner with an anxious attachment. It is essential to practice understanding and compassion in your approach to conversations about attachment. Make sure you use listening techniques, as they can be transformational when it comes to communication. If your partner wants to tell you about their anxieties and fears, listen patiently and do not interrupt. Maintain eye contact and nod, showing that you are present and attentive. Make statements like, "I know how anxious you get when I do not respond immediately." Giving them this validation of their emotions can help your partner feel heard and understood.

Make your partner feel safe in your open dialogue. This safe space will make your partner feel better about sharing their feelings without fearing being dismissed or judged. Let them know that their emotions are valid and ensure that they know you are there for them, offering support. You could ask your partner if they would like to set aside a regular time to express their feelings about the relationship and any concerns that might arise. You can significantly reduce some of your partner's anxiety by creating an environment of trust and openness.

Consistent communication and reassurance are critical strategies for supporting your partner with an anxious attachment. Check with your partner regularly and reassure them of your love and commitment. You can make your partner with anxious attachment feel much better just by sending thoughtful texts that ease their fears. Of course, you will need to set healthy boundaries while showing compassion. Communicate your limits and personal needs clearly but in a manner that is also kind and understanding. Help your partner understand that your boundaries are not a rejection and are simply necessary for you to maintain a balanced and healthy relationship.

Professional help and therapy can also benefit someone with an anxious attachment. Sometimes, a person needs more support than their partner can give. If you feel it is helpful, consider suggesting therapy as an option. Do this in a supportive way, communicating that treatment could help them develop valuable tools and coping mechanisms for anxiety management to feel secure in the relationship. Remind them that treatment can provide a safe space.

Remember, people with anxious attachments need recognition and support. If you have a partner with an anxious attachment style, you need to understand the roots of their behaviors and show empathy. This will help you build a stronger, more loving relationship.

FURTHER READING

John Bowlby's Attachment Theory, Saul McLeod, https://www.simplypsychology.org/bowlby.html

Contributions of Attachment Theory and Research: A Framework for Future Research, Translation, and Policy, Jude Cassidy et al., https://www.ncbi.nlm.nih.gov/pmc/articles/PMC4085672/

Neural basis underlying the trait of attachment anxiety and avoidance revealed by the amplitude of low-frequency fluctuations and resting-state functional connectivity, Min Deng et al., https://bmcneurosci.biomedcentral.com/articles/10.1186/s12868-021-00617-4/

Culture and Child Attachment Patterns: a Behavioral Systems Synthesis, Paul S Strand et at., https://www.ncbi.nlm.nih.gov/pmc/articles/PMC6901642/

8 Attachment Style Questionnaires & Tests to Assess Clients, Alicia Nortje, https://positivepsychology.com/attachment-style-tests/

The Power of Journaling for Well-being: A Path to Self-Discovery and Healing, https://dhwblog.dukehealth.org/the-power-of-journaling-for-well-being-a-path-to-self-discovery-and-healing/

How to Identify and Manage Your Emotional Triggers, https://www.healthline.com/health/mental-health/emotional-triggers/

Trauma of the Past: The Impact of Adverse Childhood Experiences on Adult Attachment, Money Beliefs and Behaviors, and Financial Transparency, Dr. Bruce Ross et al., https://newprairiepress.org/cgi/viewcontent.cgi?article=1280&context=jft/

Self-Soothing Techniques to Cope with Anxiety, Wendy Rose Gould, https://www.verywellmind.com/how-to-self-soothe-when-coping-with-anxiety-5199606/

30 Grounding Techniques to Quiet Distressing Thoughts, https://www.healthline.com/health/grounding-techniques/

An Overview of Attachment Anxiety, Arlin Cuncic, https://www.verywellmind.com/attachment-anxiety-4692761/

Eight Visualization Techniques for Stress Reduction, https://www.betterhelp.com/advice/stress/9-visualization-techniques-for-stress-reduction/

Effective Engagement Requires Trust and Being Trustworthy, Consuelo H Wilkins, https://www.ncbi.nlm.nih.gov/pmc/articles/PMC6143205/

5 Effective Communication Techniques for Couples, https://www.counsellinginmelbourne.com.au/communication-techniques-for-couples/

Contributions of Attachment Theory and Research: A Framework for Future Research, Translation, and Policy, Jude Cassidy et al., https://www.ncbi.nlm.nih.gov/pmc/articles/PMC4085672/

Why You May Have Trust Issues and How to Overcome Them, Kendra Cherry, https://www.verywellmind.com/why-you-may-have-trust-issues-and-how-to-overcome-them-5215390/

Inner Child Healing: 35 Practical Tools for Growing Beyond Your Past, Jeremy Sutton, https://positivepsychology.com/inner-child-healing/

John Bradshaw and The Power of Inner Child Work, Joan E Childs, https://joanechilds.com/john-bradshaw-and-the-power-of-inner-child-work/

EMDR Therapy for Childhood Trauma, Shelley Flannery, https://childmind.org/article/emdr-therapy-for-childhood-trauma/

Emotion Regulation in Close Relationships: The Role of Individual Differences and Situational Context, Wan-Lan Chen et al., https://www.ncbi.nlm.nih.gov/pmc/articles/PMC8355482/

Cognitive Reappraisal, https://www.psychologytoday.com/us/basics/cognitive-reappraisal/

8 Powerful Self-Compassion Exercises & Worksheets, https://positivepsychology.com/self-compassion-exercises-worksheets/

How to Improve Your Relationships With Healthy Communication, Elizabeth Scott, https://www.verywellmind.com/managing-conflict-in-relationships-communication-tips-3144967/

Setting Healthy Boundaries in Relationships, Sheldon Reid, https://www.helpguide.org/relationships/social-connection/setting-healthy-boundaries-in-relationships/

Active Listening: A Key to Deeper Intimacy and Understanding in Your Relationship, Mara Hirschfeld, https://holdinghopemft.com/active-listening-a-key-to-deeper-intimacy-and-understanding-in-your-relationship/

What Does Secure Attachment Look and Feel Like? Plus How to Develop It, Sanjana Gupta, https://www.verywellmind.com/secure-attachment-signs-benefits-and-how-to-cultivate-it-8628802/

The Importance of Self-Reflection: How Looking Inward Can Improve Your Mental

Health, Sanjana Gupta, https://www.verywellmind.com/self-reflection-importance-benefits-and-strategies-7500858/

21 Best Emotional Intelligence Books to Improve EQ, https://positivepsychology.com/best-emotional-intelligence-books/

Support groups: Make connections, get help, https://www.mayoclinic.org/healthy-lifestyle/stress-management/in-depth/support-groups/art-20044655/

ELIZA BENNETT

FREEDOM
from
AVOIDANT
Attachment

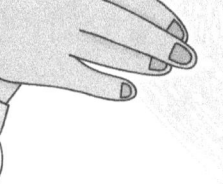
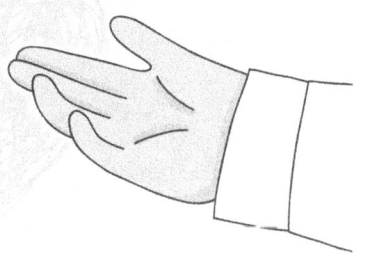

Transform Avoidance into Connection
by Understanding Dismissive Patterns,
Identifying Triggers, and Building a
Secure Relationship

INTRODUCTION

I once overheard a conversation in a bustling coffee shop that resonated deeply. A woman was candidly sharing her struggles with relationships. "I just can't seem to get close to people," she confessed with a tinge of frustration. Her words, I realized, echoed a shared experience. They mirrored the journey of many who grapple with avoidant attachment. This prevalent yet often misconstrued pattern can leave us feeling isolated, even when surrounded by those who care about us. In this shared struggle, you are not alone.

Avoidant attachment is a way of relating to others when getting too close feels overwhelming. It is like having a personal space bubble that is too big. This pattern often starts in childhood as a way to protect ourselves from getting hurt. But over the years, it can lead to feeling lonely and having relationships that do not feel quite right. Understanding this concept is the first step in turning these patterns into relationships that feel safe and loving.

My book will help you transform your life from avoidance to connection. I want to instill in you the belief that change is not just a distant dream but a tangible reality within your grasp. You can transition toward secure attachments that bring joy and fulfillment. We will explore ways to recognize dismissive patterns, identify triggers, and build secure relationships.

I am passionate about this work because I have seen the impact avoidant attachment can have. In my life, I have watched many people close to me struggle with this challenge. The distance and pain it caused were profound. These experiences fueled my desire to help others overcome similar struggles, showing me the power of transformation and the beauty of connection.

This book is structured to take you on a journey of discovery and transformation. The first chapters explore the origins and signs of avoidant attachment. We discuss how these patterns develop and how they affect our relationships. As we move forward, we delve into understanding their roots and identifying personal triggers. The latter chapters focus on practical strategies to foster secure attachments. We look at ways to build trust and intimacy and nurture healthy connections.

While the road to change can be daunting, I want to reassure you that you are not alone. I am your companion, offering practical tools and supportive guidance to help you navigate your journey. Each chapter is meticulously designed to provide insights and exercises that will support your growth and healing. As you progress, you will find that the effort you invest leads to meaningful rewards.

Self-awareness is a key element of this transformation. By engaging with the material, you will embark on a path of self-discovery. This journey encourages you to look within to understand your patterns and embrace opportunities for growth. It is about becoming more open to love, trust, and vulnerability.

I invite you to embrace this journey with an open heart and mind. The path to secure, loving relationships is within reach. Together, we can work through the challenges and celebrate the victories. Let us begin this transformative journey toward deeper connections and a more fulfilling life. The possibility of change awaits.

CHAPTER 1
UNDERSTANDING AVOIDANT ATTACHMENT

A COLLEAGUE ONCE SHARED A STORY THAT MIGHT RESONATE WITH you. After years of shallow relationships, he met someone who seemed perfect. Yet, whenever things became too intimate, he felt an overwhelming urge to pull away. It was as if an invisible force prevented him from embracing connection. This is a common experience for those with avoidant attachment—an attachment style that can deeply impact how we form and sustain meaningful relationships. However, understanding its roots is not just crucial —it is transformative. It is a beacon of hope that allows you to see the patterns that have shaped your life and the pathways to change. This chapter focuses on uncovering the origins of avoidant attachment, offering insight into why you might feel the way you do, and helping you to recognize how these patterns influence your current relationships. Let us explore this together, diving into the core theories and ideas that shed light on the development of avoidant attachment.

THE ROOTS OF AVOIDANT ATTACHMENT: CHILDHOOD WOUNDS AND EARLY EXPERIENCES

Understanding avoidant attachment begins with the pioneering work of John Bowlby and Mary Ainsworth. Bowlby, a British psychoanalyst, believed that children are biologically programmed to develop attachments as a means of survival. He proposed that these attachments form during a critical period in early childhood, typically up to five years of age. Bowlby suggested that the nature of these initial attachments creates an internal working model, a mental blueprint that guides future relationships. His theory emphasized the importance of a primary attachment figure, often a parent, whose behaviors shape the child's perception of relationships. Mary Ainsworth expanded on Bowlby's ideas through her groundbreaking "Strange Situation" experiment, which observed children's reactions to separations and reunions with their caregivers. This research identified several attachment styles, including the "avoidant style," where children showed little distress upon separation and avoided contact during reunion. These behaviors often reflect early experiences with caregivers who may have been emotionally distant or inconsistent. Ainsworth's work underscored the significance of caregiver sensitivity, suggesting that a lack of emotional responsiveness from caregivers can lead to an avoidant attachment style.

Early childhood experiences play a pivotal role in shaping avoidant attachment. Children who experience neglect or emotional unavailability from caregivers often learn to suppress their need for closeness as a self-protective measure. When a child's bids for attention are frequently ignored or met with indifference, they may begin to associate vulnerability with rejection. This can lead to the development of self-reliance, where the child learns to depend on themselves rather than risk disappointment. Inconsistent caregiving, where attention and affection are unpredictable, can further reinforce these patterns. Children in such environments often become adept at masking their emotions, shielding themselves from the pain of unmet needs. As these children grow, they may carry these patterns into adulthood, struggling with intimacy and connection in their personal relationships. The role of these early experiences in shaping avoidant attachment is profound and cannot be overstated.

The neurological underpinnings of avoidant attachment offer additional insight into how these patterns develop. Research indicates that the amygdala, a part of the brain that processes emotions and detects threats, plays a crucial role. For individuals with avoidant attachment, the amygdala may become sensitized to emotional closeness, interpreting it as a threat. This can trigger a physiological response that encourages distancing behaviors. Moreover, the brain's neuroplasticity, its ability to form new connections and pathways, suggests that attachment styles are not fixed. While early experiences set the stage, the brain retains the capacity to change and adapt throughout life, offering hope for those seeking to shift from avoidance to secure attachment.

The patterns established in childhood often manifest in adult relationships as avoidance of emotional intimacy and a strong inclination toward independence. You may find that you prioritize self-reliance, viewing emotional closeness as a potential risk. This can result in a reluctance to open up or share vulnerabilities with others—a protective mechanism learned early on. While this self-sufficiency can serve you well in certain aspects of life, it may also lead to challenges in forming deep, meaningful connections. However, recognizing these patterns is an important step toward change. By understanding the roots of avoidant attachment, you begin to see how early experiences have shaped your relationship dynamics. This awareness is the foundation for building more secure and fulfilling connections, offering hope for a more connected and inspiring future.

IDENTIFYING DISMISSIVE PATTERNS

In relationships, dismissive behaviors often go unnoticed but can cause profound disconnection. These behaviors manifest as emotional distancing tactics, where one might keep conversations superficial, avoiding topics that require vulnerability. For instance, when asked about their day, imagine someone offering only the bare minimum of detail or a partner who consistently changes the subject when conversations become too personal. This subtle withdrawal can create a chasm between people, fostering feelings of loneliness for both.

Emotional distancing is not limited to silence or brevity. It often involves the use of humor as a shield. Picture a friend who, when faced with a serious question about their feelings, responds with a joke, redirecting the conversation. This tactic can diffuse tension momentarily but leaves deeper issues unresolved. Such patterns are more than habits; they stem from a psychological need to protect oneself.

Intellectualization is another defense mechanism. It occurs when individuals focus on facts or logic to avoid confronting emotions. In a heated discussion, for example, someone might cling to data or historical references, steering clear of the emotional core of the matter. This behavior is rooted in a fear of vulnerability and dependence. By staying in the realm of the intellectual, individuals maintain control over the situation, safeguarding their emotional autonomy.

The motivations behind these dismissive patterns are often complex. Fear of vulnerability looms large, as opening up emotionally might feel like relinquishing control. For those with avoidant attachment, dependence on others can feel threatening. The desire to maintain autonomy becomes paramount, leading to behaviors that might push others away. This need for control can be traced back to early experiences, where relying on others may have led to disappointment or rejection.

Recognizing these patterns is the first step toward change. Reflective journaling could be a powerful tool in this process for some people. It allows you to explore your interactions and identify moments where you may have deflected genuine connection. Consider setting aside time each week to jot down instances where you felt the urge to distance yourself emotionally. Reflect on what triggered this reaction and how it made you feel. This self-reflection empowers you to take control of your attachment style and make positive changes. It is not just a tool but a powerful weapon in your arsenal that empowers you to take control of your attachment style and make positive changes.

Another method is seeking feedback from those around you. Feedback sessions can provide valuable insights. Ask trusted friends or close family members to share their perspectives on your communication style. How do they perceive your responses during emotionally charged conversations? This external viewpoint can illuminate blind spots you might not see on your own, providing support and understanding as you navigate your attachment style.

As you become more attuned to these dismissive tendencies, you can begin to address them. The goal is not to criticize but to understand. By acknowledging these patterns, you open the door to healthier ways of relating. Embracing vulnerability, although daunting, can lead to deeper connections and a richer emotional life. This shift requires patience and compassion for yourself and those you interact with. Remember, change is a gradual process, and each step you take brings you closer to more fulfilling relationships.

THE IMPACT ON PERSONAL RELATIONSHIPS

Avoidant attachment can cast a shadow over romantic relationships, often manifesting as emotional unavailability. When partners seek closeness, those with avoidant tendencies may retreat, creating a barrier that is difficult to overcome. This emotional distance can make expressing affection challenging. It is not uncommon to hear someone say, "I love you," only to be met with silence or a change of subject. For the partner, this can feel like rejection, fostering insecurity and doubt. Over time, these moments of withdrawal can accumulate, leading to a cycle of frustration and misunderstanding. Avoidant individuals might not even realize the extent of their emotional unavailability. They may believe they are being open, yet their actions suggest otherwise. This disconnect between intention and behavior can strain relationships, leaving both partners feeling isolated.

Friendships and family dynamics are not immune to the effects of avoidant attachment. Superficial connections often characterize friendships, where interactions remain on the surface. While discussions about the latest movies or weekend plans are common, conversations rarely venture into deeper emotional territory. This can result in friendships that lack depth and intimacy. In family settings, avoidant individuals might withdraw during conflicts, preferring silence to confrontation. This withdrawal can prevent issues from being addressed, leading to unresolved tension. Family members may perceive this as indifference or a lack of concern, further complicating relationships. Avoidant attachment can create a pattern of emotional detachment, making it difficult to form and maintain meaningful connections with those closest to us.

The cycle of relationship dissatisfaction often begins with these patterns of emotional distancing and withdrawal. Avoidant individuals struggle with emotional depth, finding it difficult to engage in the kind of vulnerable exchanges that strengthen bonds. Their partners, family members, or friends, in turn, may perceive this as neglect or emotional coldness, leading to feelings of inadequacy and loneliness. Eventually, these perceptions can erode the foundation of a relationship, leading to break-ups or persistent dissatisfaction. This cycle can repeat itself across different relationships, with each person in a relationship with the avoidant person facing the same challenges. It can feel as though no matter how hard people try, the outcome remains unchanged, leaving everyone feeling stuck and powerless.

Breaking free from these patterns requires deliberate effort and a willingness to change. Developing emotional literacy is a crucial first step if you have avoidant tendencies. This involves becoming attuned to your emotions and learning to express them more openly. It might feel uncomfortable at first, but with practice, it becomes easier. Engaging in honest and open dialogue with loved ones can also help bridge the emotional gap. This means sharing your thoughts and feelings, even when they are difficult to articulate. It is about creating a space where both parties feel heard and understood. Again, seeking feedback from trusted partners, family, or friends can provide valuable insights into how your behaviors are perceived. This external perspective can help illuminate blind spots, offering a clearer picture of how your actions impact your relationships.

Reflection Section: Strengthening Emotional Connections

Consider setting aside time weekly to reflect on your interactions. Ask yourself: *When did I feel the urge to withdraw? What emotions was I trying to avoid?* How did my actions affect my partner, family member, or friend? Jot down your thoughts in a journal, and revisit them regularly to track your progress. After several months, this practice can help you identify patterns and triggers, paving the way for change. Engaging in this reflective process allows for personal insight and growth, empowering you to take control of your relational dynamics.

AVOIDANT ATTACHMENT IN PROFESSIONAL SETTINGS

Avoidant attachment does not limit its influence to personal relationships; it often extends into professional environments, subtly shaping how we navigate the workplace. Picture a team meeting where ideas are exchanged freely. For an individual with avoidant tendencies, the thought of voicing an opinion might feel daunting. This reluctance to collaborate stems from a deep-seated preference for working independently. In a setting that thrives on teamwork, such behavior can create barriers to effective collaboration. The preference for independent tasks offers a sense of control and safety, shielding us from the uncertainties of group dynamics. This inclination can lead to missed opportunities for growth and learning that only arise through shared experiences and diverse perspectives. Opting out of collaborative projects may limit their exposure to new ideas and innovations that could enhance their skills and broaden their horizons.

The impact of avoidant attachment in the workplace does not stop at mere collaboration. It extends further into career advancement, where networking and mentorship play pivotal roles. Networking, often seen as the lifeblood of professional growth, requires engagement and openness. However, the same tendencies that lead to emotional distancing in personal relationships can surface here, resulting in a reluctance to engage in networking events or seek mentorship opportunities. This can hinder career progression, as building relationships with colleagues and industry peers is crucial for professional development. Avoidant individuals might shy away from leadership roles, finding the prospect of delegating tasks or managing others uncomfortable. This avoidance can stifle career advancement, as leadership often demands the very interpersonal skills that avoidant individuals find challenging to exercise.

Emotional intelligence is a crucial factor in overcoming these avoidant tendencies at work. It is being able to recognize, understand, and manage our emotions while also empathizing with the feelings of others. In a professional context, emotional intelligence can transform interactions, enabling individuals to navigate interpersonal relationships with empathy and insight. By honing emotional intelligence, we can begin to recognize patterns of avoidance and work toward regulating these responses. This involves becoming more attuned to personal emotions and understanding how they influence behavior in the workplace. Developing this skill can pave the way for more meaningful connections with colleagues and foster an environment where open communication thrives. Empathy, a core component of emotional intelligence, helps us see situations from others' perspectives, facilitating smoother collaborations and reducing the friction that avoidant behaviors might create.

To cultivate a more inclusive and connected work environment, practical strategies can be employed. Participating in team-building exercises offers a structured way to engage with colleagues, breaking down barriers that avoidance might erect. These activities encourage interaction in a non-threatening context, allowing us to build rapport and trust gradually. Professional coaching and mentorship can also play a transformative role. Engaging with a coach provides a safe space to review personal challenges and develop strategies to overcome them. Conversely, mentorship offers guidance and insight from someone who has traversed similar paths, providing a model for effective interpersonal engagement. These resources can empower us to get out of our comfort zones and embrace moments for growth. They ultimately lead us to a more fulfilling and successful professional life.

SELF-REFLECTION: RECOGNIZING YOUR ATTACHMENT STYLE

Understanding your attachment style is a significant step toward fostering healthier relationships. It begins with self-reflection and a willingness to look inward. One practical starting point is to engage with online attachment-style quizzes. These tools offer a structured way to assess your tendencies and provide insights into how these patterns manifest in your interactions with others. While these quizzes are not definitive, they are a useful starting point for deeper exploration. Consider them a mirror reflecting aspects of your relational self that you may not have fully acknowledged. They can illuminate patterns that have long influenced how you connect with others.

Beyond quizzes, reflective writing exercises about past relationships can be powerful tools for self-discovery. Set aside time to write about your experiences with partners, family, and friends. Think about moments where you felt particularly connected or distant. What emotions did these interactions evoke? Were there common themes or triggers that seemed to recur? By examining these narratives, you can begin to identify behaviors that align with avoidant tendencies. This process is not about judgment but understanding. It is about recognizing patterns that have shaped your relational world.

Linking these behaviors to avoidant tendencies is crucial in the path to change. Reflect on your past and present relationships. Do you notice a tendency to pull away when emotions become too intense? Are there specific situations that trigger a desire to retreat? Understanding these patterns lets you anticipate and manage them better. It also empowers you to respond differently in future interactions. By recognizing your emotional triggers and responses, you can start to shift how you engage with others, paving the way for more meaningful connections.

Personalized Attachment Style Assessment and Interpretation

The journey toward understanding your attachment style begins with more comprehensive self-assessment tools. These tools are designed to provide insight into how you relate to others, offering a window into your relational patterns. Among these tools are detailed questionnaires with scoring guides, which allow you to reflect on your behaviors and responses within relationships. These questionnaires are structured to help you identify tendencies you may not have consciously recognized before. They offer a framework for introspection, encouraging you to think about how you approach intimacy, independence, and emotional expression.

Interactive online assessments also play a pivotal role in this exploration. They provide personalized feedback that can illuminate aspects of your attachment style, offering tailored insights that resonate with your experiences. Such assessments often include scenarios that mimic real-life interactions, prompting you to consider your emotional responses in a safe, reflective space. The feedback from these assessments can serve as a catalyst for deeper self-reflection, helping you connect the dots between your current behaviors and past experiences. As you work through these tools, remember that they are not definitive. They offer guidance, but your self-awareness and personal context provide the richest understanding.

Interpreting the results of these assessments is a crucial step in your self-awareness journey. Attachment styles are typically categorized as secure, anxious, or avoidant, each with distinct characteristics and implications. A secure attachment style reflects comfort with intimacy and autonomy, while an anxious style may involve a preoccupation with relationships. On the other hand, as we have pointed out, avoidant attachment often manifests as emotional distance and a preference for self-reliance. Understanding where you fall within these categories can offer clarity on how you navigate relationships. It allows you to recognize patterns that may contribute to relational challenges and provides a starting point for change.

The insights gained from these assessments should encourage ongoing self-reflection. Consider keeping a behavioral diary to track your interactions and emotional responses every week. This practice can reveal patterns that may not be immediately apparent, offering valuable insights into how your attachment style influences your daily life. Regularly setting reminders for self-assessments can also be beneficial. These periodic check-ins provide an opportunity to observe changes and growth, helping you to stay attuned to your emotional landscape.

For those eager to delve deeper into the realm of attachment, numerous resources are available to support your exploration. Recommended books and articles on attachment theory can provide a more nuanced understanding of the dynamics at play. Engaging with these resources can enrich your knowledge and offer diverse perspectives on attachment-related experiences. Online forums and communities serve as platforms for peer support, where you can share insights and learn from others on similar paths. These communities foster a sense of belonging and offer encouragement as you navigate the complexities of attachment.

Resource List: Attachment Exploration

- **Recommend Book and Articles**: Delve into *Attached* by Amir Levine and Rachel Heller for insights into adult attachment theory, or explore scholarly articles that offer deeper academic perspectives (see our Further Reading section at the end of the book).
- **Online Communities**: Consider joining forums such as Reddit's "Attachment Theory" community, where you can engage in discussions and gain support from others on a similar path.

Engage with these resources to broaden your understanding and connect with others who share your journey.

As you embark on this path of self-reflection, it is vital to approach yourself with kindness and patience. Practicing self-compassion involves recognizing that everyone has flaws and areas for growth. Self-forgiveness is a fundamental part of this process. It allows you to acknowledge past mistakes without being defined by them. Embrace affirmations and positive self-talk as tools to foster a more compassionate inner dialogue. Remind yourself that growth is a continuous process that requires time and patience. Treat yourself with the same kindness you would offer a friend. That way, you create a nurturing space for transformation.

Setting personal growth goals is an integral part of transforming your attachment style. Begin by identifying specific areas you wish to improve. Perhaps you want to be more open in expressing your emotions or become more comfortable with vulnerability. Whatever your goals, make sure they are clear and actionable. Create a personal development plan with specific milestones to track your progress. This plan acts as a roadmap, guiding you as you work toward your goals. Celebrate small victories as you go along. Each step forward takes you that much closer to your desired relational life.

As this chapter closes, remember that self-reflection is a powerful catalyst for change. By understanding your attachment style and embracing self-compassion, you put down the groundwork for healthier and more fulfilling relationships. These insights enhance your interactions with others and deepen your connection to yourself. As you continue this process, hold onto the belief that transformation is within reach. With patience and perseverance, you can cultivate the secure and loving connections you seek.

CHAPTER 2
DEEPER UNDERSTANDING AND AWARENESS OF AVOIDANT ATTACHMENT

PICTURE YOURSELF IN A BUSTLING SOCIAL SETTING, OBSERVING someone effortlessly connecting with others while you are on the fringes of conversations. This hesitation could indicate the avoidant attachment style, which values distance over a connection. Understanding your attachment style is akin to having a map that guides you through the complex terrain of your relationships. This chapter is your guide to comprehending and being aware of your avoidant attachment, providing opportunities to delve into even more strategies regarding your attachment style.

UNDERSTANDING YOUR CORE WOUNDS

At the core of avoidant attachment lies a range of core wounds—emotional scars from early experiences that shape our self-relationships and relationships with others. These wounds often stem from pivotal moments in childhood that lead to a sense of disconnection, neglect, or emotional unavailability. Delving into these core wounds is not just crucial but profoundly empowering. They form the foundation of our attachment styles and significantly influence our adult relationships. However, understanding them gives us the power to change our responses, putting us in the driver's seat of our emotional journey.

Core wounds often manifest in feelings of inadequacy, fear of intimacy, and a pervasive sense of unworthiness. For individuals with avoidant attachment, these feelings can lead to the development of protective mechanisms designed to shield them from emotional pain. These protective mechanisms could include distancing behaviors such as avoiding deep conversations, withdrawing emotionally during conflicts, finding excuses to avoid social gatherings, or even overworking to avoid emotional situations. Recognizing these wounds is the first important step toward healing and transformation.

Understanding your core wounds involves a journey of self-reflection and awareness. It may require revisiting past experiences to identify how they have influenced your beliefs about relationships and intimacy. Ask yourself: *What were the critical moments in my childhood that shaped my views on love and connection? How have these experiences manifested in my current relationships?*

As we touched on in the previous chapter, a common theme among many individuals with avoidant attachment is a history of unreliable or emotionally distant caregivers. This often leads to internal narratives that promote self-sufficiency at the cost of intimacy. Recognizing and acknowledging these narratives is essential for breaking the cycle of avoidance. By doing so, you can begin to challenge and reframe the negative beliefs that have held you back.

Additionally, exploring your core wounds helps illuminate your triggers—those situations or interactions that provoke a defensive response. Understanding what triggers your avoidant behaviors can empower you to respond more consciously rather than reactively. For example, feelings of being overwhelmed or vulnerable may prompt you to withdraw. By acknowledging these triggers, you can work toward developing healthier coping mechanisms and fostering a deeper sense of connection with others.

Ultimately, the process of understanding your core wounds is not about assigning blame but rather about fostering compassion for yourself. As you learn to acknowledge and process these wounds, you create space for healing and the possibility of establishing secure connections. By transforming avoidance into awareness, you open the door to genuine intimacy and emotional resilience, allowing for nurturing relationships that celebrate your authentic self.

IDENTIFYING EMOTIONAL TRIGGERS

Emotional triggers are like hidden landmines in the landscape of our relationships, waiting to be activated by specific situations or interactions. When triggered, they often lead to intense emotional responses, disrupting harmony and understanding. These triggers usually stem from past experiences, are deeply ingrained in our psyche, and affect how we perceive and react in the present. However, understanding these triggers can bring a profound sense of relief, as it lets us recognize when our reactions are more about old wounds than the current situation, easing the tension in our relationships and providing a sense of calm and control.

Identifying your emotional triggers requires thoughtful introspection and a willingness to engage in self-inquiry. Start by reflecting on recent interactions that elicited strong emotional reactions. Ask yourself, *What about that moment made me feel uncomfortable or defensive?* Again, consider keeping a journal where you document these instances. Write down the situation, your feelings, and any physical sensations you experienced. As weeks pass, patterns may emerge, revealing specific themes or scenarios that consistently trigger your avoidant behaviors. Once again, this reflective practice can be complemented by getting feedback from trusted friends or family members. Sometimes, others can see patterns in our behavior that we might miss. Open a dialogue with someone you trust and ask for their observations on how you react in certain situations. These talks can provide valuable insights into your emotional landscape.

The origins of these emotional triggers often lie in our past, shaped by childhood experiences or previous relationships. If, as a child, you learned that expressing needs led to disappointment or rejection, you might have developed a trigger around vulnerability. Similarly, a history of relationships where trust was broken can lead to triggers related to intimacy or dependence. By linking these past experiences to your current emotional responses, you have a deeper understanding of why certain situations provoke strong reactions. This awareness can empower you to separate the past from the present and approach situations with greater clarity and calm.

Developing strategies to manage these triggers is an essential step in mitigating their impact. But it is not just about mitigation. It is about control. One effective approach is to cultivate coping mechanisms that help you remain grounded when faced with a trigger. Mindfulness methods like guided meditation, deep breathing, or a short walk can be particularly beneficial. These practices encourage you to stay present and observe your emotions without judgment, allowing you to respond thoughtfully rather than react impulsively. Engaging in mindfulness regularly can enhance your emotional regulation skills, making it easier to navigate challenging interactions. Other coping mechanisms could include journaling, talking to a trusted friend, or engaging in a physical activity. This sense of control can build your confidence, making it easier to implement these strategies when triggers arise.

BUILDING EMOTIONAL SELF-AWARENESS

Emotional self-awareness is recognizing and understanding your feelings and how they affect your thinking and behaviors. It is a cornerstone of personal growth and healthy relationships. When emotionally self-aware, you can navigate social interactions with greater ease and empathy. This awareness allows you to identify and articulate your feelings, reducing misunderstandings and enhancing communication. It also connects closely with emotional intelligence, which involves recognizing your emotions and those of others. By honing emotional self-awareness, you are better equipped to respond to emotional challenges with resilience and clarity, improving your mental health and relational interactions. The benefits extend beyond personal insight; they foster a deeper connection with those around you, leading to more meaningful and supportive relationships and a profound sense of emotional preparedness.

Engaging in practical exercises can be very beneficial in cultivating this self-awareness. One method is mood tracking, which can be done using apps or a simple journal. By noting your emotions at different times of the day, you begin to see patterns in your emotional responses. This practice helps identify triggers and understand the context in which certain emotions arise. For instance, you might notice a surge of anxiety every Monday morning, prompting you to explore what about that time triggers such a response. Another exercise is a daily reflection on emotional experiences. Set aside a few minutes each day to think about the emotions you felt and what prompted them. Write down these reflections, focusing on how these emotions influenced your actions and decisions. Over a while, these practices can illuminate your emotional landscape, offering insights into how your feelings shape your interactions.

Mindfulness plays a vital role in improving emotional self-awareness. It involves paying attention to the present moment without judgment, allowing you to observe your emotions as they arise. Through mindfulness practices, such as breathing exercises, you can stay grounded when emotions intensify. These exercises help you remain present, reducing the tendency to react impulsively. For example, when you feel anger building, taking slow, deep breaths can help you pause and consider your response. Guided meditations focusing on emotional exploration further deepen this practice. They prompt you to explore emotions with curiosity, encouraging a non-reactive stance. Such meditations guide you through acknowledging emotions, understanding their origin, and letting them pass without clinging to them. Regular mindfulness cultivates awareness that permeates your daily life, fostering a calmer, more measured approach to emotional challenges.

The journey of emotional self-awareness is ongoing and requires a commitment to continuous exploration. Creating a personalized emotional development plan can guide this process. Start by setting specific goals for your emotional growth, such as developing greater patience or reducing anxiety in social settings. Write down steps to achieve these goals, incorporating practices like journaling or mindfulness into your routine. Regularly review and adjust your plan as you gain insights and progress. Additionally, dedicate time for introspection, whether it is through meditation, quiet reflection, or engaging with nature. This time allows you to connect with your inner self, assess your emotional state, and recalibrate your approach to challenges. By prioritizing emotional self-awareness, you empower yourself to navigate the complexities of relationships and life with greater understanding and empathy.

UNDERSTANDING AVOIDANT BEHAVIORS IN CONFLICT

Imagine you are in a disagreement with a partner. The conversation escalates, and suddenly, there is a wall. You find yourself emotionally checked out, hearing words but not processing them. This is a classic avoidant conflict behavior—stonewalling or withdrawing entirely when things get heated. It is a protective mechanism, a way to avoid the discomfort that comes with confrontation. For many with avoidant attachment, facing conflict feels like standing on shaky ground. The thought of exposing vulnerabilities or emotions can be overwhelming, leading to a retreat into silence. This withdrawal might seem like a safe haven, but it often leaves issues unresolved, allowing resentment to fester. Over the years, these unaddressed conflicts can pile up, creating a rift in the relationship. Trust erodes, and emotional intimacy fades as partners feel shut out and unimportant.

The motivations behind the avoidance of conflicts are deeply rooted. At its core is a fear of vulnerability. Opening up in the heat of an argument might feel like an invitation to be hurt. There is a desire to maintain control and manage emotions and situations. This control protects against the chaos of emotional exposure. But it can also mean that significant issues remain unspoken, festering beneath the surface. You might find that conflicts are avoided not because they are unimportant but because the emotional stakes feel too high. This avoidance creates a cycle where conflicts are not resolved but delayed, leading to more significant issues down the line.

The impact of these avoidant behaviors on relationships can be profound. When partners, family members, or friends consistently face a wall of silence or emotional absence, they may begin to question the strength and validity of the relationship. Trust, the foundation of every healthy relationship, can start to crumble. Without open communication, misunderstandings thrive, and others may feel increasingly isolated. The lack of resolution leaves wounds open, which can deepen as time passes, eroding the connection that once existed. Emotional intimacy, the closeness from sharing and understanding each other's inner worlds, becomes more challenging. As each conflict ends without resolution, the space between you and your significant others grows, filled with unspoken words and unmet needs.

To approach conflict in a healthier, more constructive manner, it is crucial to embrace new strategies. Assertive communication is a powerful tool in this transformation. It involves expressing your thoughts and needs clearly and respectfully, without aggression or passivity. Start by using "I" statements, focusing on your feelings rather than placing blame. For example, instead of saying, "You never listen to me," try, "I feel unheard when we don't discuss things." This shift in language can open dialogue and reduce defensiveness. Active listening complements assertive communication by ensuring both people feel heard. It requires you to engage fully, reflecting back what you hear to confirm understanding. This practice fosters empathy, allowing you to see the situation from the other person's perspective. By acknowledging their feelings, you build a bridge of understanding, making it easier to find common ground.

Empathy plays a crucial role during disagreements. It helps you step outside your experience and consider how others might feel. Practicing empathy involves asking questions and genuinely listening to the answers, even when they might be difficult to hear. It is about creating a safe space for both people to discuss their thoughts and feelings without fear of judgment. When empathy is present, conflicts transform from battles to collaborative problem-solving opportunities. Both people can work together to find solutions that honor each other's needs and perspectives. This approach resolves the immediate issue and strengthens the relationship, building trust and deepening emotional intimacy. By incorporating these strategies, you pave the way for healthier interactions, creating a foundation for a more connected and resilient relationship. We will explore strategies for conflict resolution in more depth in Chapter 8.

OVERCOMING FEAR OF INTIMACY

Intimacy is a multifaceted concept, pivotal for meaningful relationships. It goes beyond physical closeness, encompassing emotional intimacy, which involves sharing our innermost thoughts and feelings. This level of openness deepens connections, fostering a bond that withstands life's challenges. Emotional intimacy allows you to be seen and understood, creating a foundation of trust and vulnerability. It is the glue that holds relationships together, providing a space where people feel safe to express their true selves. Without it, relationships can feel superficial, lacking the depth that brings fulfillment and joy. Yet, many find themselves hesitating at the threshold of intimacy, unsure of how to step forward without fear.

Avoidant individuals often grapple with a fear of intimacy, a barrier rooted in past experiences. Memories of betrayal or rejection can linger, casting a shadow over present relationships. These experiences can instill a belief that vulnerability equates to risk, leading to a protective instinct to keep others at a distance. Internal beliefs about self-worth also play a role, as those who doubt their value may fear that true intimacy will expose their perceived inadequacies. This fear can manifest as reluctance to engage emotionally, keeping relationships at arm's length to avoid potential pain. The result is often a cycle of loneliness and isolation, where the desire for connection is overshadowed by the fear of being hurt or rejected.

To embrace intimacy, starting small can make the journey less daunting. Begin with small acts of vulnerability, like sharing a personal story or admitting a fear. These moments of openness, though seemingly minor, can pave the way for a deeper connection. They build a bridge of trust, demonstrating to you and your partner, family member, or friend that vulnerability does not always lead to harm. Consistent, open communication also plays a vital role. Regularly discussing thoughts and feelings with others fosters an environment where intimacy can thrive. It encourages honesty and transparency and fosters a safe space for both people to express themselves without fear of judgment. After a few months, these practices can begin dismantling the walls that fear has built, allowing intimacy to flourish.

Building trust with oneself is equally vital in overcoming the fear of intimacy. Trusting yourself involves believing in your resilience and ability to handle emotional exposure. Exercises in self-trust and self-compassion can support this process. Practice affirmations that reinforce your worth and remind you that you are capable and deserve love. Engaging in activities that nurture your self-esteem, such as pursuing hobbies or setting personal goals, can also strengthen this trust. As you cultivate self-trust, your capacity to trust others naturally expands, creating a foundation for deeper connections.

Strengthening trust in relationships is crucial for fostering intimacy. Shared experiences, like traveling together or embarking on a new project, can build a sense of teamwork and mutual support. These experiences create memories and bonds that deepen over the years. They also provide opportunities to practice vulnerability in a supportive environment. By navigating challenges together, you learn to rely on each other, reinforcing the trust that intimacy requires. This process takes time and patience, but each step brings you closer to the fulfilling relationships you desire. We will explore ways to deepen trust and intimacy even further in Chapters 5 and 6.

UNDERSTANDING SHAME AND SELF-WORTH

The relationship between shame and avoidant attachment runs deep, often beginning in our earliest experiences of disconnection and perceived unworthiness. When young children experience consistent emotional unavailability or criticism from caregivers, they associate their needs and feelings with a sense of being fundamentally flawed. This creates what we call the shame-withdrawal cycle, where the experience of shame triggers emotional withdrawal, which then reinforces feelings of isolation and unworthiness.

Consider Tammy's story of growing up, with her academic achievements celebrated while her emotional needs were often dismissed with phrases like "Don't be so sensitive" or "You're too needy." As an adult, Tammy found herself unable to ask for support at work or in relationships, experiencing intense shame whenever she felt vulnerable. Her pattern of withdrawal, while protective in childhood, now prevented her from forming the deep connections she desired.

Understanding shame requires distinguishing between healthy shame—which serves as a moral compass and helps us maintain social bonds—and toxic shame, which convinces us we are inherently defective. For those with avoidant attachment, toxic shame often manifests as perfectionism, emotional distance, and an intense fear of being "seen." This shame becomes a lens through which all relationships are viewed, creating a self-fulfilling prophecy of disconnection.

Building Self-Worth Beyond Achievement

Building authentic self-worth begins with recognizing how deeply our sense of value has been tied to external validation and achievement. Many individuals with avoidant attachment develop what psychologists call a "false self"—a carefully constructed persona based on accomplishments, competence, and self-sufficiency. While this strategy may bring professional success, it often leaves a profound inner emptiness.

Take Wendell's experience as a successful entrepreneur. He appeared to have everything —wealth, status, and peer admiration. Yet in therapy, Wendell revealed that he felt like an impostor, constantly afraid that others would discover he was not truly worthy of connection. His worth was so entangled with his achievements that any failure felt catastrophic, leading him to avoid close relationships where he might be judged imperfect.

The process of developing internal validation requires a fundamental shift in self-relationship. This involves learning to recognize and honor our inherent worth separate from our accomplishments. Through consistent self-reflection and compassionate self-dialogue, we challenge the deeply held belief that we must earn love through performance or self-sufficiency.

Breaking the Shame Cycle

Disrupting entrenched shame patterns requires both awareness and active intervention. The first step is learning to recognize shame reactions in their earliest stages. These often begin with subtle physical sensations—a tightening in the chest, a desire to disappear, or a sudden sense of exposure. By developing this awareness, we can respond differently to shame triggers rather than automatically withdrawing.

Ellen's journey illustrates this transformation. As a teacher, she initially responded to any classroom challenges by becoming rigid and withdrawn, her shame about potential imperfection preventing her from connecting with students or seeking colleague support. Through therapy, Ellen learned to recognize her shame response as it emerged. She developed a practice of taking three deep breaths when feeling triggered and reminding herself that vulnerability is not weakness but rather a pathway to authentic connection.

The development of shame resilience involves creating new neural pathways through repeated experiences of safe vulnerability. This might begin in therapy, where the consistent presence of an attuned therapist helps reconstruct our expectations of a relationship. As we experience acceptance in moments of vulnerability, our nervous system gradually learns that connection, rather than withdrawal, can be a source of safety.

SOMATIC AWARENESS AND HEALING

Our bodies hold the imprint of our attachment histories, often expressing through tension patterns what we cannot yet verbalize. Understanding the somatic dimension of avoidant attachment opens new healing pathways beyond cognitive insight. When properly attended to, the body's wisdom can guide us toward greater security and connection.

The case of James exemplifies the importance of body-based awareness. Despite years of talk therapy, James struggled to understand why he consistently withdrew from potential romantic partners. Through somatic work, he discovered that he habitually held his breath and tensed his shoulders when others expressed care for him. This physical pattern, developed in childhood to protect against disappointment, actively maintained his avoidance in adult relationships.

Somatic Exercises for Regulation

Through intentional somatic practices, the body's wisdom in healing attachment wounds becomes accessible. These exercises bridge our conscious awareness with the deeper, often unconscious, patterns that maintain avoidant attachment. Through regular practice, we can begin to reshape our nervous system's default responses to connection and intimacy.

Dr. Rachel Chen, a trauma-informed therapist, shares her client, Michael's transformation. Initially, Michael could only identify his attachment activation through hindsight after withdrawing from connections. Through guided somatic work, he learned to recognize the subtle tightening in his throat that preceded emotional shutdown. This awareness became his early warning system, allowing him to pause and implement regulation strategies before withdrawal.

Breathwork is a fundamental tool in attachment healing, as our breathing patterns directly influence our nervous system. "box breathing"—inhaling for four counts, holding for four, exhaling for four, and holding for four—helps activate the parasympathetic nervous system, creating a physiological state more conducive to connection. When practiced regularly, these breathing patterns can become automatic responses to attachment stress, replacing old withdrawal patterns.

As we conclude this chapter, consider how these insights into intimacy, trust, and self-worth can transform relationships. You can build more profound, more meaningful connections by embracing vulnerability, nurturing self-trust, fostering open communication, and breaking the shame cycle. These steps set the stage for creating secure attachments, the focus of our next exploration.

CHAPTER 3
CULTURAL AND GLOBAL CONTEXTS OF ATTACHMENT

IMAGINE STANDING IN A VIBRANT MARKET, ALIVE WITH COLORS, sounds, and scents worldwide. Each stall represents a different culture, offering unique flavors and traditions. Just as these stalls add richness to the marketplace, cultural norms and values are pivotal in shaping our understanding of relationships and attachment. These norms significantly influence how we express our emotions and perceive independence, impacting our attachment styles.

Understanding attachment patterns must be viewed through cultural diversity and modern social contexts. What might be interpreted as avoidant behavior in one culture could represent healthy boundaries in another. This complexity becomes particularly evident in our increasingly interconnected world, where relationships often span cultural boundaries.

Consider the experience of Mei, a first-generation Chinese American therapist working with predominantly Western clients. She observed how her cultural background, which valued emotional restraint and indirect communication, initially led to her being labeled as avoidant by Western colleagues. Through a deeper exploration of cultural attachment variations, she began to understand how cultural values shape the expression of attachment needs and the pathways to security.

Religious and spiritual traditions also significantly influence attachment patterns and healing approaches. For instance, in some Buddhist communities, the practice of non-attachment is highly valued, potentially creating confusion around Western attachment theory's emphasis on secure dependency. Understanding these cultural and spiritual nuances helps create more inclusive and practical approaches to attachment healing. This chapter will explore how these cultural influences shape avoidant attachment and affect our relationships across different societies.

UNDERSTANDING CULTURAL ATTACHMENT VARIATIONS

Cultural norms significantly influence attachment styles, with a clear distinction between collectivist and individualist societies. For instance, in collectivist cultures like those found in many Asian and African countries, the norm of prioritizing community, family, and interdependence can lead to avoidant attachment when individuals suppress personal needs to maintain harmony. In contrast, individualist cultures, prevalent in Western countries, value independence, self-reliance, and personal achievement. This focus can lead to avoidant attachments as individuals learn to prioritize autonomy over emotional connection. The societal expectation of self-sufficiency can create a barrier to forming close relationships, as emotional expression may be viewed as a sign of weakness or dependency.

Cultural upbringing is crucial in shaping attachment behaviors, with parenting styles varying across cultures. Authoritarian parenting, defined by strict demands and limited responsiveness, is prevalent in many cultures and can contribute to avoidant attachment. In these settings, children may learn to suppress their emotions and need to meet parental expectations, leading to a detachment from their emotional experiences. The ongoing influence of cultural expectations is evident in how these children navigate their relationships in adulthood. Conversely, cultures emphasizing emotional expression and nurturing caregiving often foster secure attachments. The role of extended family in attachment formation also varies culturally. In many collectivist cultures, extended family members play an integral role in a child's upbringing, providing additional sources of attachment. This can reinforce secure attachments through consistent caregiving or contribute to an avoidant attachment if family dynamics are complex or unpredictable.

Perceptions of avoidant behaviors differ across cultures, reflecting varying attitudes toward emotional expression and vulnerability. In some cultures, emotional stoicism is perceived as a strength, embodying resilience and self-control. This perspective can lead individuals to view avoidant behaviors positively as a way to maintain composure and avoid emotional entanglements. In contrast, other cultures may value vulnerability and interdependence, viewing emotional openness as a path to deeper connections. These cultural attitudes influence how individuals perceive and express their attachment styles, shaping their relational dynamics and emotional experiences.

Avoidant behaviors manifest uniquely in different cultural contexts, influenced by societal norms and expectations. In high-context cultures, where communication relies heavily on implicit understanding and nonverbal cues, individuals may avoid conflict to preserve harmony and relationships. This means that in these cultures, people often communicate in ways that are more indirect and rely on shared cultural knowledge. This avoidance can lead to unspoken tensions and unresolved issues, as confrontation is usually discouraged. Conversely, in low-context cultures, where communication is explicit and direct, individuals may prioritize privacy and personal space, leading to avoidant behaviors emphasizing autonomy over connection. People tend to communicate more directly in these cultures and rely less on shared cultural knowledge. These cultural preferences shape how individuals navigate their relationships, influencing the development and expression of avoidant attachment.

Interactive Element: Reflection Exercise on Cultural Influences

Take a moment to reflect on your cultural background and how it might have shaped your attachment style. Consider the following questions:

- How do cultural norms in your upbringing influence your view on emotional expression and independence?
- In what ways do you see cultural expectations affecting your attachment behaviors today?

- How might understanding these cultural influences empower you to navigate your relationships consciously?

Use these reflections to explore the cultural context of your attachment style, deepening your understanding of how cultural norms shape your relational experiences. This awareness can offer new insights into your behaviors, helping you bridge cultural divides and foster more meaningful connections.

EMBRACING DIVERSITY IN ATTACHMENT STYLES

Attachment styles do not exist in a vacuum in the rich tapestry of human relationships. They weave through the cultural and social fabric surrounding them, each representing a unique blend of influences. Recognizing the diversity within attachment styles is crucial, as it highlights how cultural contexts shape our emotional connections. In culturally diverse societies, attachment styles are not homogeneous. Secure, anxious, and avoidant styles adapt and manifest differently, colored by the cultural nuances that define them. This recognition of diversity within attachment styles opens our minds to the unique and intricate nature of human relationships, allowing us to see beyond a one-size-fits-all approach and appreciate the richness of different perspectives.

Exploring the benefits of diverse attachment perspectives enriches our understanding and broadens our relational horizons. For example, collectivist cultures often emphasize the importance of community and support, teaching us valuable lessons about the strength and resilience found in interdependence. These cultures show how collective support systems can create a safety net that fosters secure attachment. They provide individuals with the confidence to explore and express their emotions. On the other hand, individualistic cultures highlight the value of independence and self-reliance, reminding us of the importance of personal autonomy within relationships. This perspective, which encourages the development of personal boundaries and self-awareness, is essential for healthy attachment. By learning from these diverse approaches, we gain a deeper appreciation for how attachment can be expressed and nurtured, recognizing that each perspective offers unique insights into the human experience. This broadened understanding can enrich our relationships and interactions with others.

Embracing openness to multiple attachment narratives invites us to value the diversity of experiences and stories that shape our emotional worlds. Sharing multicultural stories and personal experiences allows us to see the world through different lenses, offering new perspectives on attachment. These narratives reveal the varied pathways to emotional connection, highlighting how people navigate and understand their relationships. Whether it is the story of a family that values interdependence or an individual who finds strength in solitude, each narrative contributes to a richer understanding of attachment. By valuing these diverse pathways, we celebrate the individuality and creativity of forming connections, acknowledging that there is no one right way to love and relate to others.

From a clinical view, therapists and counselors should adopt practical strategies that honor cultural differences to ensure that attachment work is inclusive and respects diversity. Culturally sensitive communication techniques are vital, as they help therapists and clients navigate conversations with empathy and respect. This involves being mindful of cultural norms and values and adjusting our communication style to accommodate different perspectives. Encouraging culturally informed therapeutic practices can further enhance inclusivity in attachment work. Therapists and counselors should incorporate cultural insights into their practice, acknowledging the unique cultural influences that shape their clients' attachment styles. This approach fosters a supportive environment where people feel seen and understood, empowering them to explore and transform their attachment patterns authentically. Cultivating these inclusive practices creates spaces where all individuals can meaningfully engage with attachment work, regardless of their cultural background.

Case Study: Cultural Adaptation in Therapy

Consider the story of Mei, a young woman from a collectivist culture who sought therapy in a Western context. Her therapist recognized the importance of family in Mei's life, incorporating family-oriented strategies into the sessions. By integrating Mei's cultural values into the therapeutic process, the therapist created a space where Mei felt comfortable exploring her attachment style. This culturally informed approach respected Mei's background and empowered her to navigate her relationships authentically and confidently. Mei's story illustrates the power of embracing diversity in attachment work, highlighting the transformative potential of culturally sensitive practices. (We will explore the importance of therapeutic fit in more depth in Chapter 9.)

CROSS-CULTURAL RELATIONSHIP DYNAMICS

Imagine two people from different corners of the world, each carrying their traditions and customs, coming together to build a life. Cultural backgrounds intricately shape relationship dynamics, influencing how partners interact, communicate, and set expectations. In some cultures, relationship roles and responsibilities are clearly defined, often influenced by traditions passed down through generations. For instance, in many societies, there may be an expectation for one partner to take on specific household duties or financial responsibilities. These roles can be deeply ingrained, reflecting cultural values and norms that dictate how partners should contribute to the relationship.

Additionally, cultural traditions such as courtship, marriage, and family planning can significantly impact relationship milestones. What might be considered a romantic gesture in one culture could be seen as inappropriate in another, highlighting the importance of understanding and respecting these differences. When individuals from diverse backgrounds come together, navigating these variations requires openness and adaptability, as each partner brings their cultural expectations to the relationship.

Cross-cultural relationships often face unique challenges that require careful navigation. Differing family expectations can pose significant hurdles, as families may hold traditional views that clash. For example, one partner's family might expect a formal engagement and marriage ceremony, while the other might prioritize personal choice over tradition. Balancing these expectations can be daunting, requiring clear communication and compromise to honor both cultures. Language and communication barriers also present challenges, as linguistic differences can lead to misinterpretations and misunderstandings. Even when partners share a common language, cultural nuances can affect how messages are conveyed and received. Miscommunication can strain relationships, making developing effective strategies to bridge these gaps crucial. Partners must learn to communicate with patience and empathy, recognizing that cultural differences can influence how each person expresses emotions and intentions.

Despite these challenges, cross-cultural relationships offer unique strengths and opportunities for growth. The blending of diverse perspectives can lead to innovative solutions and enriched experiences. Each partner brings their own worldview, which is shaped by their cultural background, which can broaden their understanding and appreciation of different ways of life. This diversity fosters creativity and adaptability as partners learn to navigate and embrace their differences. Additionally, navigating cultural differences builds resilience. It strengthens the relationship as partners work together to overcome obstacles. These experiences can deepen the emotional bond, fostering a sense of unity and collaboration. Cross-cultural relationships encourage personal growth as individuals gain insight into their cultural identities and develop a greater appreciation for the richness of diversity.

Practical tools can be employed to enhance understanding and harmony in cross-cultural relationships. Engaging in cultural exchange activities and experiences can provide valuable insights into each other's backgrounds and traditions. Participating in cultural events, cooking traditional meals together, or learning each other's languages can foster appreciation and respect for each culture's uniqueness. These activities create opportunities for shared discovery, allowing partners or friends to connect more deeply. Creating a shared cultural space within the relationship can also strengthen the bond. This involves integrating elements from both cultures into daily life, such as celebrating holidays from each partner's background or establishing new traditions that honor both heritages. By blending cultural influences, partners create a unique cultural identity that reflects their shared journey. These practices promote inclusion and understanding, building a strong foundation for a successful relationship.

RESPECTING CULTURAL VARIATIONS IN ATTACHMENT

Respecting cultural differences in attachment is pivotal in fostering understanding and empathy. We must look beyond our cultural lenses and appreciate how attachment manifests globally. Avoiding ethnocentric judgments is crucial. It is important not to view our cultural practices as the standard by which others are measured. Instead, embracing cultural humility allows us to explore attachment with an open heart and mind. Cultural humility involves recognizing that our understanding is limited and that there is always more to learn from others' experiences and perspectives. This mindset fosters respect for how people connect and form attachments, acknowledging that no single way is superior.

Cultural awareness has a significant role in building stronger, more empathetic relationships. By understanding the cultural context in which our partners operate, we can better appreciate their perspectives and responses. This awareness allows us to navigate interactions with sensitivity and awareness, recognizing how cultural values and norms influence behaviors and expectations. Incorporating cultural knowledge into relationship decisions enables us to make choices that honor both peoples' backgrounds, fostering harmony and mutual respect. For instance, considering each partner's cultural traditions and values can strengthen the relationship when planning significant life events or discussing future goals. This approach enhances communication and deepens the emotional connection, as both people feel seen and valued.

Culturally respectful communication is key to ensuring that interactions are inclusive and considerate of cultural differences. Adapting communication styles to align with cultural norms helps facilitate understanding and reduce potential conflicts. For example, straightforward and clear communication can prevent misunderstandings in cultures where direct communication is valued; conversely, in coordinating indirect communication, being sensitive to nonverbal cues and using subtle language may be more effective. Practicing active cultural listening—attuning oneself to the cultural nuances in conversations—and empathy enhances our ability to engage in meaningful dialogue. It involves being present, asking open-ended questions, and showing genuine interest in understanding the other person's perspective. This practice can bridge cultural divides, fostering a sense of connection and trust.

Learning from diverse cultural practices enriches our relationships and broadens our perspectives. Celebrating multicultural traditions and customs allows us to embrace the richness of different cultures and incorporate their wisdom into our lives. Participating in cultural festivals, ceremonies, or family gatherings gives us insight into the values and beliefs that shape different communities. Incorporating multicultural rituals into our relationship life can also deepen our connection to our partners and their backgrounds. Whether adopting a traditional practice or creating new rituals that honor both cultures, these experiences foster a sense of belonging and unity. They remind us of the beauty of diversity and the myriad ways we can express love and connection.

Imagine a couple integrating each other's cultural customs into their daily routine. They might start their mornings with a traditional breakfast from one partner's culture and end their evenings with a bedtime ritual from the other. This blending of traditions creates a unique cultural tapestry that reflects their shared journey. It also is a constant reminder of their commitment to understanding and valuing each other's heritage. By embracing these diverse practices, they enrich their relationship and strengthen their appreciation for the cultural influences that have shaped them.

Respecting cultural variations in attachment opens the possibility of more profound, meaningful connections. Valuing the diverse ways people form attachments cultivates empathy and understanding, creating a world where all forms of connection are honored and celebrated. This approach enriches our relationships and contributes to a more inclusive and harmonious global community.

INCLUSIVE STRATEGIES FOR A GLOBAL COMMUNITY

As we consider the needs of a global village, it is vital to acknowledge the diverse backgrounds, experiences, and perspectives we all bring to the table. People from different parts of the world may approach attachment with various cultural lenses, which shape their understanding and interactions. Acknowledging these differences enriches our discussions about attachment, allowing us to tailor strategies that truly resonate. By considering global perspectives, we create an inclusive dialogue that embraces the unique experiences of individuals from all walks of life. This approach ensures that the strategies presented are culturally relevant and respectful of the diversity that defines our global community.

Offering inclusive strategies for attachment improvement requires flexibility and adaptability. I am all about providing tools that can be molded to fit different cultural contexts, recognizing that one size does not fit all. Flexible attachment exercises are key, as they allow individuals to engage with the material in a way that aligns with their cultural values and norms. Encouraging readers to adapt techniques to their cultural context empowers them to take ownership of their attachment journey, fostering a sense of agency and confidence. This adaptability ensures the strategies are practical and meaningful, resonating with the individual's unique cultural identity and experiences.

Technology also plays a crucial role in bridging cultural gaps and supporting attachment work on a global scale. It offers a platform where individuals from different backgrounds can come together, share insights, and learn from each other. Online communities provide a space for cross-cultural attachment support, where people can connect with others who share similar experiences and challenges. These communities foster a sense of belonging and offer a supportive network that transcends geographical boundaries. Additionally, virtual resources for culturally informed attachment education provide access to diverse perspectives and knowledge. These resources empower individuals to explore attachment in a way that respects and honors their cultural heritage, enhancing their understanding and growth. However, we must be mindful of setting healthy expectations and boundaries around digital communication (more about this in the Appendix).

Promoting global empathy and connection is central to fostering a world where attachment work is inclusive and impactful. Engaging in international conversations about attachment encourages exchanging ideas and experiences, broadening our understanding of how attachment manifests across cultures. This dialogue fosters empathy as we learn to appreciate the unique challenges and triumphs individuals from different backgrounds face. Building international networks of attachment support and learning further strengthens this connection, creating a web of support that spans the globe. These networks offer collaboration, learning, and growth opportunities, enriching our collective understanding of attachment and its role in our lives.

In the grand tapestry of human connection, each thread represents a unique cultural perspective, weaving together a rich and diverse narrative. By embracing these perspectives, we create a world where attachment work is inclusive and transformative, empowering individuals to build meaningful, authentic, and resilient connections. As we move forward, we explore the intricate interplay of culture and attachment, recognizing the beauty and complexity that define our shared humanity. This journey is one of discovery and growth, fueled by a commitment to understanding and honoring the varied ways we connect and relate to one another.

CHAPTER 4
BRIDGING AWARENESS AND CHANGE

THE JOURNEY FROM AWARENESS TO ACTIVE CHANGE REPRESENTS A crucial transition in addressing avoidant attachment patterns. This bridge period requires careful attention to both internal readiness for change and external support systems that will facilitate transformation.

Consider the experience of Dr. Emily Chen, who documented her transition from understanding to action in her work with attachment patterns. She describes this period as "standing in the doorway between knowing and becoming," emphasizing the importance of honoring the past protective function of avoidant patterns and the possibility of more secure attachment. She created a roadmap for others navigating this crucial transition through journals and recorded self-reflections.

Preparing for change involves creating what attachment theorists call a "secure base for exploration." This means establishing reliable support systems and self-care practices that can sustain us through the vulnerability of transformation. These foundations include therapeutic relationships, supportive friendships, somatic practices, and clear protocols for managing attachment activation during the change process.

IMPLEMENTING SUSTAINABLE CHANGE

The transition from theoretical understanding to practical change requires a carefully structured approach that honors our desire for growth and our nervous system's need for safety. This implementation phase often represents the most challenging aspect of attachment work, as it requires us to act in ways that initially feel counterintuitive or threaten our emotional safety.

The experience of Dr. Nathan Rivera, a clinical psychologist who documented his attachment journey, provides valuable insights into this implementation process. Despite his professional understanding of attachment theory, Nathan struggled to maintain connection during periods of stress. He developed the "micro-steps approach," focusing on implementing tiny, manageable changes in his daily interactions. For instance, he began by simply noticing his impulse to withdraw without changing his behavior. Over time, he progressed to pausing for five seconds before withdrawing, then gradually extending this pause while developing alternative responses.

Creating sustainable change requires understanding the difference between behavioral modification and genuine transformation. A software engineer, Amy, initially approached her attachment work as though debugging code, looking for problematic behaviors to eliminate. Through work with her therapist, she understood that sustainable change required a more profound reorganization of her emotional operating system. This meant changing specific behaviors and developing new ways of experiencing and responding to emotional connections.

MANAGING RESISTANCE AND SETBACKS

Resistance to change often emerges subtly, particularly for those with avoidant attachment patterns who have developed sophisticated strategies for maintaining emotional distance. Understanding resistance as a protective response rather than a failure allows us to work with it productively rather than against it.

Professor Marcus Chen's longitudinal study of attachment change provides valuable insights into the nature of setbacks in this work. His research followed fifty individuals through their attachment transformation journey, documenting what he termed "recursive growth patterns"—where apparent setbacks served as opportunities for deeper integration of new patterns. One participant, Linda, described how a period of intense withdrawal following a vulnerable emotional exchange initially felt like a failure but ultimately led to a deeper understanding of her attachment needs and triggers.

The development of resilience during setbacks involves creating what attachment theorist Mary Main called "earned security." This process requires building internal resources that allow us to maintain a connection to our growth process, even during periods of activation or withdrawal. These resources include self-compassion practices, clear protocols for re-engagement after withdrawal, and reliable support systems that understand the non-linear nature of attachment healing.

CREATING LASTING TRANSFORMATION

Establishing lasting transformation in attachment patterns requires attention to internal and external maintenance strategies. This involves creating what attachment researchers call "islands of security"—reliable practices and relationships that support ongoing growth even during challenging periods.

The long-term success story of Mitchell and Susan, partners who identified with avoidant attachment, demonstrates the importance of creating sustainable change practices. After initial progress in therapy, they developed what they called their "secure connection protocol"—a set of daily and weekly practices designed to maintain their growth trajectory. This included daily check-ins about emotional states, weekly vulnerability practices, and monthly reviews of their attachment progress. Importantly, they built flexibility into their system, recognizing that different periods of life require different levels of active attention to attachment work.

Training the nervous system for lasting change requires what neuroscientists call "repetition in novelty," which means practicing new connection patterns in varying contexts and situations. Dr. Rachel Goldman's research on attachment transformation highlights the importance of gradually expanding the contexts in which we practice secure attachment behaviors. This might begin with practicing new patterns in therapy, then with close friends, and eventually in more challenging relationships or situations.

INTEGRATION AND ONGOING GROWTH

The final phase of attachment work involves integrating new patterns so profoundly that they become our default way of relating. This integration process requires an understanding that attachment security is not a destination but a dynamic state that requires ongoing attention and care.

Professor Dr. Elizabeth Chen's forty-year study of attachment transformation reveals that individuals who achieve lasting change share specific characteristics in their approach to integration. They maintain what she calls "conscious attachment practice"—regular reflection on their patterns, ongoing engagement with growth opportunities, and active cultivation of secure relationships. Rather than seeing their attachment work as complete, they view it as an ongoing process of refinement and deepening.

The creation of a personal attachment legacy represents a powerful aspect of integration. This involves transforming our patterns and becoming secure attachment sources for others. William, a teacher who documented his attachment journey over fifteen years, discovered that his healing process enabled him to create more secure classroom environments for his students. His story demonstrates how personal attachment work can ripple outward, contributing to broader social transformation.

The journey of attachment transformation ultimately leads us toward what attachment theorist John Bowlby called "felt security" —a deep, embodied sense of safety in connection that allows for intimacy and autonomy. This state is not characterized by the absence of attachment activation but by our increased capacity to maintain connection through various emotional states and challenges. It represents not the end of our attachment journey but the beginning of a new way of being in a relationship with ourselves and others. With that in mind, let us now explore how we can make those first steps of change from avoidant to secure attachment.

CHAPTER 5

TRANSFORMING AVOIDANT PATTERNS THROUGH TRUST AND EMOTIONAL INTIMACY

Transforming avoidant patterns is key to deepening connections in relationships. This chapter focuses on building mutual trust through honest communication and accountability, allowing people in various relationships to engage fully. We also explore the role of emotional intimacy in sharing thoughts and feelings, which helps dismantle barriers to connection. By practicing intentional exercises and fostering open dialogue, we can begin to build a safe space for vulnerability in our relationships.

FOUNDATION OF TRUST AFTER AVOIDANCE

Mutual trust, the cornerstone of any healthy relationship, is not a one-way street but a bridge that spans a vast chasm, connecting two worlds. This trust bridge, built on shared experiences and mutual understanding, allows both parties to be vulnerable without fear of betrayal, fostering deeper connections and greater intimacy. When trust is broken, it can feel as if the bridge has collapsed, leaving both parties stranded on opposite sides, struggling to find a way back to each other. Picture a couple sitting at their kitchen table, casually discussing their weekend plans. The ease of their conversation reflects a foundation of trust built over time through consistent honesty and shared understanding. These simple interactions highlight how trust is not built solely during significant events but in daily exchanges where partners feel safe to express themselves without fear of judgment. Trust often reveals itself in the small, everyday moments.

To cultivate trust, begin with consistent honesty and transparency. This means aligning your words with your actions, creating a reliable pattern on which others can depend. Transparency involves openly sharing your thoughts and feelings, even when they are difficult to express. By doing so, you eliminate secrecy and foster an environment where trust can flourish. Gradually opening up can be especially effective for those recovering from avoidant patterns. Vulnerability does not have to happen all at once—it can start with sharing a meaningful experience or expressing a minor worry. These small moments of openness invite your partner to do the same, slowly deepening the emotional connection.

Building the trust back up after breaking it requires patience and conscious effort. You can begin with sincere apologies and accountability. Acknowledge the harm caused and take responsibility for your actions without making excuses. Let the person know you understand your behavior's impact and are committed to making amends. Being transparent about your intentions and motivations can also prevent misunderstandings from escalating. When you explain why you made a particular decision or how you feel about a situation, you offer clarity that strengthens trust. Open conversations about misunderstandings help both partners feel seen and understood, reinforcing the relationship's stability. Along the same lines, mutual understanding, the ability to comprehend and respect each other's perspectives, is vital in trust-building. It helps resolve conflicts and make decisions that benefit both parties.

Establishing and respecting personal boundaries is another crucial aspect of trust-building. Clearly communicating your limits—such as needing alone time or identifying sensitive topics—helps your partner understand and respect your needs. Likewise, honoring your partner's boundaries shows you value their autonomy. This mutual respect fosters a safe space where trust can naturally grow. Another vital step is following through on promises and commitments. When you say you will do something, ensure that you follow through. This consistency builds reliability, reinforcing the belief that you are dependable. As time passes, these small acts of honesty and reliability form the bedrock of trust, creating a strong and lasting foundation for your relationships.

Implementing trust-building rituals or activities can also help restore the connection. These might include regular check-ins, where you discuss your feelings and progress, or shared activities that strengthen your bond, like going for a walk or cooking a meal together. For instance, you could set aside a specific weekly time for a "trust-building talk" where you openly share your feelings and concerns. Or you could plan a "trust-building day" where you engage in activities that require teamwork and cooperation, such as a cooking challenge or a DIY project. These rituals provide a structured way to rebuild trust, offering tangible steps toward healing and reconciliation. Remember, rebuilding trust takes time, but restoring the bridge that once connected you is possible with effort and dedication.

Mutual trust is essential for the health and longevity of any relationship. Trust-building should never be a one-sided effort; it requires the active participation of both parties. Encourage open dialogue about trust issues, creating a space where both people feel safe to express their concerns and needs. This dialogue fosters mutual understanding and allows you to address the problems before they escalate. But how do you engage in these open discussions effectively? Start by setting aside a particular time to talk about trust, ensuring that both of you are in a calm and receptive state of mind. As we talked about in Chapter 2, use "I" statements like "I feel...," "I need...," or "I am concerned about..." to express your feelings and concerns, and actively listen to the other person's perspective without interrupting. Collaborating on trust-building exercises can further enhance this process. Consider engaging in activities requiring teamwork and cooperation, strengthening the relationship. These exercises can take many forms, from problem-solving tasks like planning a trip to shared hobbies like cooking a meal together, each offering an opportunity to work together toward a common goal. By nurturing mutual trust, you create a resilient bond capable of withstanding the challenges that inevitably arise in relationships.

Reflection Section: Trust-Building Checklist

This section provides questions to help you evaluate and enhance trust in your relationships. By reflecting on these questions often, you can ensure your trust-building efforts remain steady and effective.

- **Openness Audit**: Do you share your thoughts and feelings transparently?
- **Apology Acknowledgment**: Have you taken responsibility for past mistakes?
- **Consistency Check**: Are your actions aligned with your words?
- **Commitment Review**: Are you following through on promises?
- **Mutual Dialogue**: Are you engaging in open discussions about trust?

Use this checklist to evaluate and enhance trust in your relationships. Regular reflection can help you remain on track and ensure your trust-building efforts remain steady and effective. Please take a few moments to consider these questions and reflect on how you can apply the insights to your relationships.

INITIAL STEPS IN EMOTIONAL CONNECTION

Imagine sitting with someone you care about deeply, feeling the warmth that comes from their presence and the profound connection you share. This is emotional intimacy at its core—a closeness transcending physical presence and tapping into what it truly means to know and understand another person. Emotional intimacy—a deep bond beyond physical interactions—is essential for relationship satisfaction. It enables individuals to express their deepest thoughts, feelings, and dreams. It is the kind of bond where you feel seen and understood, creating a profound sense of safety and acceptance.

This level of intimacy plays a crucial role in relationship satisfaction, as it helps build trust and empathy, fostering more substantial, more resilient relationships. When emotional intimacy is present, it is a glue that holds relationships together, providing the emotional support needed to weather life's ups and downs. It allows people, especially partners, to navigate challenges with a united front, enhancing individual and collective well-being. The benefits of emotional intimacy are manifold, leading to deeper connections that enrich your relational experiences and contribute to a fulfilling life. Emotional intimacy is built through shared emotional experiences—laughter, tears, or even comfortable silence—that weave a fabric of trust and understanding. These shared moments create a safe space where both individuals feel valued, accepted, and deeply connected.

Enhancing emotional closeness can be achieved through intentional exercises encouraging openness and empathy. One simple yet powerful practice is sharing daily highs and lows with your partner, family member, or friend. Set aside time each day to discuss the moments that brought joy and those that were challenging. This exercise fosters communication and offers a window into each other's emotional worlds, deepening understanding and connection. Another effective exercise is practicing active empathy through shared experiences. This involves engaging in activities requiring collaboration and support, such as cooking a meal, taking a class, or volunteering together. These shared experiences create a bond because they require you to work together, understand each other's needs, and support each other, strengthening your emotional connection and fostering emotional intimacy. Another powerful method to deepen emotional intimacy is sharing personal narratives and life stories. Take turns recounting experiences that have shaped who you are, from childhood memories to significant life events. This practice allows partners, family members, or friends to explore more profound layers of each other's personalities, fostering empathy and a stronger emotional bond.

Despite its benefits, emotional intimacy often encounters barriers that can hinder its development. Fear of judgment or rejection is a common obstacle, preventing individuals from opening up fully. To overcome this, it is vital to create an environment where both people feel safe to express themselves without fear of criticism. Start by acknowledging these fears and discussing them openly with the other person. This dialogue can help dispel misconceptions and build a foundation of trust. It is also essential to actively listen and validate the other person's feelings without judgment. Affirming and validating the other person's emotions is equally important in creating emotional safety. Acknowledge their feelings as real and significant, even if they differ from your perspective. This validation nurtures a secure environment where both people feel comfortable expressing themselves openly, deepening the foundation of trust in the relationship.

To foster a safe space for emotional expression, you could establish "emotional safety rules" such as no interrupting, judgment, or dismissive responses. Gradually opening up emotionally can also be achieved through incremental sharing, where you begin with small disclosures and progressively increase the depth as comfort grows. This method lets you test the waters and build confidence in sharing and vulnerability. Over months, these steps can begin to help dismantle the barriers to emotional intimacy, paving the way for a richer, more connected relationship.

Maintaining emotional intimacy is not a one-time task. It is an ongoing effort. It requires a commitment to nurturing the connection. Regular check-ins with other people, especially partners, are essential to sustaining this intimacy. Schedule time to discuss your feelings, needs, and goals, ensuring you remain aligned and connected. These check-ins provide an opportunity to address any concerns and celebrate successes, reinforcing the bond between you and providing a sense of reassurance and connection. Taking part in activities that promote emotional bonding is another effective way to maintain intimacy. Consider embarking on new adventures together, whether exploring a hobby, traveling to a new destination, or volunteering for a cause you both care about. These shared experiences create lasting memories and deepen your connection, continually strengthening the emotional intimacy that forms the heart of your relationship.

DEVELOPING HEALTHY COMMUNICATION SKILLS

Imagine trying to tune a radio to a clear station amid static. This is what communication can feel like when avoidant patterns are at play. Effective communication is the tool that cuts through the noise, allowing clarity and understanding to emerge. It is pivotal in transforming these patterns into secure attachments where both people feel heard and valued. Through communication, conflicts can be resolved not by who speaks the loudest but by who listens the best. It enhances understanding by allowing you to see the world through the other person's eyes, fostering empathy and connection. When communication flows freely, it becomes the bridge between trust and intimacy travel.

Practical communication techniques can transform how you connect with others. As mentioned, one such method involves using "I" statements to express feelings without casting blame. Instead of saying, "You never listen to me," try, "I feel unheard when we don't discuss things." This shifts the focus from blame to personal experience, reducing defensiveness and opening the door to dialogue. Active listening is equally crucial. It means fully concentrating on what the other person is saying and reflecting their words back to them to confirm understanding. This might sound like, "So, you're saying you felt left out when I went out with friends?" Reflective responses demonstrate your engagement and empathy, building deeper connections through sincere exchanges.

Communication pitfalls often trip us up, leading to misunderstandings and conflicts. Avoiding assumptions and mind-reading is vital. It is easy to assume you know what the other person is thinking, but this often leads to miscommunication. Instead, ask clarifying questions to ensure you are on the same page. Managing defensiveness is another common hurdle. When criticized, the natural reaction is often to defend ourselves. However, by taking a moment to breathe and consider the feedback, you can respond thoughtfully rather than reactively. This approach fosters a more constructive and open dialogue, allowing for growth and understanding. Criticism can be hard to hear, but it often holds the key to unlocking deeper understanding when approached with an open mind.

Practice is key to building these communication skills. Role-playing difficult conversations can provide a safe space to explore and refine your communication techniques. Think of a challenging topic and take turns playing each other's roles. This exercise helps you understand The other person's perspective and offers insight into your communication style. Exercises in expressing needs and boundaries can further enhance your skills. Practice articulating what you need from the other person, whether it is more quality time or space to pursue personal interests. Clearly stating your boundaries and needs invites mutual understanding and respect, laying a foundation for a healthier relationship dynamic.

Interactive Element: Communication Role-Play Exercise

- **Scenario Setup**: Choose a familiar conflict, like differing plans for the weekend.
- **Role-Swap**: Partner A expresses their needs using "I" statements while Partner B actively listens and reflects.
- **Switch Roles**: Partner B shares their perspective, and Partner A practices active listening.
- **Debrief**: Discuss what felt challenging and what was learned.

Use this exercise to explore communication dynamics and discover new ways to connect. Practicing these techniques in a controlled setting helps build confidence, making applying them in real-life situations easier. Remember, effective communication is a skill. It grows with practice and patience, leading to more secure and satisfying relationships.

MANAGING EMOTIONAL DETACHMENT

Emotional detachment is often a protective shield, guarding against the discomfort of vulnerability. It is a defense mechanism to cope with past wounds or present uncertainties. For some, this detachment feels like a safe harbor where emotions cannot overwhelm or hurt. However, this can create an invisible barrier in relationships, leaving partners, family members, or friends feeling isolated and unsupported. The warmth of connection fades when one partner feels emotionally absent, and the relationship can suffer. Significant others may feel they are reaching out to someone who is no longer there, leading to feelings of neglect and loneliness. This emotional distance can chip away at the foundation of support and understanding vital for a thriving relationship.

Re-engaging emotionally requires a conscious effort to reconnect with your feelings. As mentioned, mindfulness practices can be particularly effective, helping you become more present in your emotional experiences. Mindfulness lets you observe your emotions without judgment by focusing on the here and now, encouraging you to feel rather than suppress. Consider putting aside a few minutes daily to engage in mindfulness meditation, focusing on your breathing and body sensations. This practice can help you connect better with your emotions, fostering a sense of presence that counteracts detachment. Journaling is another valuable tool in this process. By writing down your feelings and thoughts, you can explore and articulate emotions that might otherwise remain unexamined. Journaling provides a safe space to process experiences and reflect on how they affect your emotional landscape, offering insights into patterns and triggers.

Emotional regulation plays an essential role in managing detachment. It involves recognizing and naming emotions as they arise, a skill that can help prevent feelings from becoming overwhelming. Start by identifying what you are feeling in the moment and giving it a name—whether it is anger, sadness, or joy. This simple labeling can create distance between you and your emotions, allowing you to respond rather than react. Breathing exercises can also support emotional regulation. Breathe slow and deep to calm your nervous system when emotions intensify. This practice can help reduce the urge to detach, making staying engaged with your feelings and those around you easier.

Getting support from loved ones is another crucial step in re-engaging emotionally. Sharing your experiences with others you trust can provide validation and perspective, helping you feel less alone. Seek out a person you trust, whether a friend or family member. Talk to them about what you are going through and ask for their support as you work on reconnecting with your emotions. Their feedback can offer insights into how detachment affects relationships, clarifying what needs to change. Involving others in your process can create a sense of accountability, encouraging you to stay committed to your emotional growth. Trusted individuals can offer encouragement and celebrate your progress, reinforcing your efforts to re-engage emotionally.

Interactive Element: Emotional Awareness Exercise

- **Daily Emotion Check-In**: Spend five minutes each day identifying and naming your emotions.
- **Journaling Prompt**: Reflect on a recent experience that triggered emotional detachment. What emotions were present? How did you respond?
- **Mindfulness Practice**: Set a timer for three minutes and focus on your breath, noticing any emotions that arise without judgment.

These exercises can help you become more attuned to your emotional state, promoting engagement and connection in your relationships. Regular practice can transform emotional detachment from a protective mechanism into an opportunity for growth and deeper understanding. Embracing your emotions and seeking support opens the door to more prosperous, fulfilling relationships.

EMBRACING VULNERABILITY IN RELATIONSHIPS

Vulnerability in relationships often gets a bad rap, yet it is one of the most profound elements that lead to genuine connections. To be vulnerable means to open yourself up to reveal parts of yourself that are tender and true. It is not about exposing weaknesses but about sharing your authentic self, warts, and all. This openness creates a pathway to genuine connection, allowing you to experience deeper intimacy with the other person. When you allow someone to see you as you truly are, you invite them to do the same, fostering a mutual understanding that forms the bedrock of secure attachment. There is a paradox here. By embracing vulnerability, you actually become stronger. This strength comes not from putting up defenses but knowing that you can be open and still be okay. It is about resilience, about understanding that even if you stumble, you can get back up, and your relationship can weather the storm.

However, the notion of being vulnerable can evoke fear. The thought of laying bare your innermost thoughts and feelings can be daunting because the risk of judgment and rejection comes with it. Many fear that showing their vulnerabilities will be seen as weak or inadequate. This misconception often stems from societal norms that equate strength with stoicism and emotional self-reliance. Yet, true strength lies in the ability to stand firm in your truth and embrace and own your imperfections. It involves stepping into uncertainty with the courage to face whatever comes, knowing that vulnerability is not a liability but a powerful tool for connection.

To cultivate vulnerability, share personal stories and experiences with the other person. These narratives do not have to be epic tales; they can be simple anecdotes that reveal your desires, fears, or dreams. By sharing these pieces of yourself, you invite the other person into your world, allowing them to understand you on a deeper level. Practicing openness in everyday interactions can further encourage vulnerability. Instead of defaulting to surface-level conversations, challenge yourself to go deeper. When asked how your day was, instead of saying "fine," share the parts that mattered—the small victories, the frustrations, the moments that made you pause. By consistently practicing openness, you create a habit of vulnerability, making it a natural part of your interactions.

The rewards of embracing vulnerability are significant. For one, it deepens trust. When you show your true self, you tell the other person you fully trust them. This fosters a reciprocal trust, encouraging them to be open with you in return. As each layer of vulnerability is revealed, mutual understanding blossoms. You begin to see each other as allies on a shared path, navigating life's challenges together. Vulnerability also enhances emotional resilience. By facing your fears and opening up, you build a support network that bolsters you in times of need. This network provides a cushion, softening the blows of life's inevitable hardships. Knowing you have someone who sees and supports you in your most vulnerable moments gives you the strength to face whatever comes.

As this chapter closes, consider how vulnerability can transform your relationships. By embracing it, you pave the way for deeper connections built on a foundation of trust and mutual understanding. This sets the stage for creating secure attachments where love and resilience flourish together. Looking ahead, we will explore how these principles can apply broadly, fostering growth and fulfillment in all areas of life.

CHAPTER 6
BUILDING SECURE ATTACHMENTS

IMAGINE YOURSELF IN A BUSTLING AIRPORT, WITNESSING THE heartwarming reunions of travelers with their loved ones. The sheer joy and relief in their eyes tell a story of trust and connection that transcends words. This scene beautifully captures the essence of secure attachment—a bond characterized by trust, empathy, and effective communication. Secure attachment is the foundation of healthy relationships, offering safety and support for individuals to thrive. It fosters an environment where people feel appreciated and heard, promoting open and sincere communication. In contrast, insecure attachment styles, such as anxious or avoidant, can lead to miscommunication and emotional distance, often resulting in relationships fraught with tension and misunderstanding. You can build resilient, fulfilling, and enduring relationships by understanding and nurturing secure attachments.

FOUNDATIONS OF SECURE ATTACHMENT

As we discussed at the beginning of the book, secure attachment is rooted in psychological and emotional well-being. It begins with positive self-esteem and self-worth, enabling you to engage authentically and confidently with others. When you believe in your value, you approach relationships with openness and trust rather than fear and defensiveness. This self-assurance is the cornerstone of secure attachment, allowing you to express your needs without hesitation. Emotional regulation, a vital skill, plays a significant role in managing your emotions effectively. By recognizing and responding to your feelings in a balanced way, you can navigate conflicts and challenges with composure and empathy, feeling empowered and in control. This ability to regulate emotions is a hallmark of secure attachment, fostering stability and understanding in relationships. It is not just about managing conflicts but about feeling empowered to navigate them in a way that strengthens the relationship. These psychological and emotional elements create a framework for secure attachment, empowering you to connect with others in meaningful and lasting ways.

The development of secure attachment often begins in childhood and is influenced by early experiences with caregivers. Consistent and reliable caregiving provides security as children learn to trust their needs will be fulfilled. This trust forms the basis of secure attachment, allowing children to explore the world confidently. Positive reinforcement and emotional support from caregivers strengthen this bond, as children feel valued and loved. These nurturing experiences lay the groundwork for secure attachment, shaping how individuals perceive and engage in relationships. When caregivers respond sensitively and consistently, they instill a sense of safety and predictability, which fosters secure attachment. This early foundation helps individuals develop healthy relational patterns characterized by trust, empathy, and effective communication. Understanding the role of these early experiences can help us gain insight into our current attachment patterns and how we can work toward secure attachments, enlightening us and fostering self-awareness.

In adult relationships, secure attachment offers numerous benefits that enhance emotional resilience and satisfaction. Those with secure attachments are better equipped to handle stress and adversity, as they possess a stable foundation of self-worth and emotional regulation. This resilience allows them to navigate challenges gracefully and have a positive outlook even in difficult times. Secure attachment also contributes to greater satisfaction and longevity in relationships, as it fosters open communication and mutual support. People feel safe expressing their needs and emotions, knowing they will receive understanding and compassion. This creates a cycle of trust and intimacy, where both people feel valued and respected. The emotional resilience and satisfaction accompanying secure attachment lay the foundation for enduring relationships characterized by love, trust, and shared growth. These benefits are not out of reach but a potential that can be realized through understanding and nurturing secure attachments.

Reflection Section: Building Secure Attachments

- **Self-Assessment**: If you have not done so already, reflect on your current attachment style. Do you feel secure in your relationships, or do you often experience anxiety or avoidance? Consider how your early experiences may have influenced your attachment patterns.
- **Caregiver Influence**: Consider your caregivers and how their behavior shaped your understanding of relationships. How have these early experiences influenced your approach to attachment as an adult?
- **Emotional Regulation**: Practice mindful breathing or journaling techniques to enhance emotional regulation. How do these practices help you manage emotions in your relationships?
- **Building Trust**: Identify ways to build trust and empathy in your relationships. What steps can you take to foster open communication and mutual support?

Engaging with these reflections can help you understand your attachment style and work toward building secure attachments. As discussed in previous chapters, cultivating trust, empathy, and effective communication can create resilient and fulfilling relationships. We will continue to build on these principles by exploring these ideas more fully.

CULTIVATING A SECURE ATTACHMENT MINDSET

Imagine looking at relationships as a refuge, a place where support and security intertwine seamlessly. This perspective forms the core of a secure attachment mindset. Here, relationships are not burdens or obligations but sources of mutual strength and reassurance. Embracing this mindset means understanding that interdependence is not a sign of weakness but a healthy balance between autonomy and connection. It is about recognizing that you do not have to face life's challenges alone. You can rely on others while still standing firm in your identity. This balance fosters a sense of belonging, where both people contribute to each other's well-being. Seeing relationships in this light transforms them into partnerships where support flows both ways, creating a nurturing environment that encourages personal growth and shared happiness.

Cultivating this secure mindset begins with challenging negative beliefs about relationships. Many of us carry assumptions shaped by past experiences or societal pressures, such as the notion that needing help is a sign of dependency. Start by identifying these beliefs and questioning their validity. Are they based on reality, or are they remnants of past wounds? Replace these limiting notions with positive affirmations that reflect a healthier perspective. Tell yourself that seeking support is a strength, not a flaw. Practicing positive self-talk can reinforce these new beliefs. When doubt creeps in, remind yourself of your worth and the value you bring to your relationships. These affirmations can serve as anchors, keeping you grounded in a mindset that embraces interdependence and mutual support.

Self-awareness is vital in developing a secure attachment mindset. It involves reflecting on your relationship patterns and understanding how they were formed. Take time to identify insecurities that may hinder your ability to connect with others.

These insecurities might stem from past relationships or childhood experiences. By acknowledging them, you can begin the process of healing. Self-awareness allows you to see how these patterns influence your interactions, empowering you to make conscious choices that align with your desire for secure attachment. It provides clarity and insight, helping you navigate relationships with intention and authenticity. As you become more attuned to your internal landscape, you can address insecurities compassionately, paving the way for healthier connections.

A growth-oriented perspective encourages you to view relationships as dynamic entities that can evolve and adapt as years pass. Embrace change as a natural part of any partnership. Relationships are not static; they require flexibility and openness to thrive. Instead of fearing change, see it as an opportunity for growth and enrichment. Celebrate progress and small victories along the way. Acknowledge the milestones you reach together, whether they are emotional breakthroughs or shared achievements. These celebrations reinforce the bond between you and others, highlighting your journey together. This perspective fosters resilience, enabling you to navigate life's ups and downs with grace and unity. By cultivating a mindset that values growth, you create a solid base for lasting and fulfilling relationships.

As you work toward a secure attachment mindset, remember it is a continuous process. It is about embracing the complexities of relationships with an open heart and a willingness to learn. Each step forward, no matter how small, contributes to a deeper understanding of yourself and your connections with others.

ADVANCING TRUST IN SECURE RELATIONSHIPS

Imagine a couple sitting at their kitchen table, discussing their weekend plans effortlessly. Their conversation reflects a deep trust that has been nurtured over time. Advancing trust in a secure relationship involves more than just establishing it; it requires continual growth through consistent, honest communication and intentional actions.

Consistent and transparent communication remains the backbone of trust. Sharing significant thoughts and feelings openly while respecting personal boundaries reinforces the bond between partners. This does not require disclosing every minute detail of daily life but involves being forthcoming about meaningful matters. This level of openness signals that transparency is valued, creating an environment where trust deepens over time.

Reliability is equally essential in advancing trust. Continuously following through on promises—whether handling everyday tasks like picking up groceries or offering unwavering support during difficult times—strengthens the belief that one partner can depend on the other. This steady dependability reassures both partners, fostering a secure and trustworthy relationship foundation.

Deepening trust also involves a growing willingness to share personal thoughts and emotions. Gradual vulnerability invites deeper connection. Sharing experiences that evoke emotion or discussing personal challenges allows both partners to feel seen and understood. Couples cultivate a deeper emotional bond by encouraging this mutual vulnerability, solidifying their trust.

Transparency is not only about sharing thoughts but also about clarifying intentions and motivations. Explaining the reasons behind decisions or actions reduces misunderstandings and strengthens trust. Addressing any confusion or misinterpretation promptly shows a proactive commitment to the relationship. Open dialogue about misunderstandings reflects a dedication to maintaining clarity and mutual respect.

Respecting and adapting to each other's evolving boundaries further advances trust. As relationships grow, personal needs and comfort zones may shift. Regular discussions about individual boundaries—such as the need for personal space or sensitive topics—demonstrate care and respect for each other's autonomy. Honoring these boundaries reassures both partners that their emotional safety is a shared priority.

Advancing trust in secure relationships is a continuous process of intentional communication, reliability, vulnerability, transparency, and boundary respect. By nurturing these elements, couples can deepen their connection, reinforcing a resilient and lasting trust that evolves with the relationship.

MASTERING DEEP EMOTIONAL CONNECTION

Imagine sitting with someone you care about deeply, feeling the warmth that comes from their presence and the profound connection you share. This is emotional intimacy at its most transformative level—a closeness transcending physical presence and tapping into what it means to know and be known by another person. Deep emotional intimacy forms the bedrock of profound connection, creating a sacred space where both individuals can reveal their innermost thoughts, fears, and aspirations without judgment. It is cultivated through shared emotional experiences, those precious moments where shared laughter, witnessed tears, or comfortable silence weaves an unbreakable bond. These experiences create a tapestry of trust and understanding, fostering a deep sense of safety and validation.

When emotional intimacy reaches this master level, it becomes more than just the heartbeat of a relationship—it transforms into its very soul, nurturing a profound sense of belonging and mutual growth. This depth of connection requires dedicated practice and intention. Consider implementing advanced emotional connection exercises into your daily life. One powerful approach is establishing sacred emotional check-in rituals with significant others. These are not merely casual conversations but intentional spaces for deep exploration of feelings, dreams, and vulnerabilities. They might take the form of weekly reflection walks or dedicated evening connection sessions where phones are turned off and presence is prioritized.

The art of sharing personal narratives evolves at this level into what we might call "sacred storytelling"—taking turns not just recounting life experiences but exploring their more profound meaning and impact on your current patterns and beliefs. This practice reveals the multilayered nature of your personality and invites others into the complex tapestry of your inner world, fostering profound emotional bonds. These advanced exercises cultivate what psychologists call "radical vulnerability"—a state where both individuals feel safe enough to share surface-level emotions and their deepest fears, hopes, and authentic selves.

Creating an environment for this depth of emotional intimacy requires mastering several key elements. Active listening transforms into what we might call "soul listening"—where you're not just hearing words but sensing the underlying emotions, unspoken needs, and subtle nuances in communication. This deep, empathetic presence lets you connect with others almost intuitively, creating a space where they feel heard and truly understood.

The practice of validation evolves beyond simple acknowledgment into what we might call "emotional resonance," where one can recognize and deeply attune to another's emotional experience. This creates a profound sense of being emotionally held and understood, fostering the deepest levels of intimacy possible in human connection.

Managing barriers at this level involves recognizing that fear of vulnerability is not just about potential rejection but often connects to our deepest existential concerns about being indeed known. Working through these fears requires courage and a fundamental shift in how we view vulnerability—seeing it not as a risk to be managed but as the gateway to the most meaningful connections possible in our lives.

Mastering these elements makes emotional intimacy not just a component of our relationships but their very essence, creating profoundly healing and transforming growth-promoting connections. This mastery allows us to develop relationships characterized by extraordinary depth, authenticity, and mutual understanding.

LONG-TERM STRATEGIES FOR SECURE RELATIONSHIPS

Imagine watching a movie where two characters evolve over a period of time, their relationship deepening through countless shared experiences and challenges. This evolution mirrors the principles necessary for maintaining secure relationships. At its core lies a commitment to ongoing communication and connection. This does not mean endless conversations but regular, meaningful exchanges that keep both people in tune. It is about creating a rhythm of interaction where checking in becomes second nature. Whether it is a quick chat over breakfast or a more profound discussion at the end of the day, these interactions build a tapestry of understanding that strengthens the relationship. Prioritizing mutual respect and understanding is equally vital. It involves recognizing each other's perspectives and valuing them, even when they differ from yours. This respect fosters a climate of cooperation, where both people feel valued and heard, ensuring the relationship remains harmonious and resilient.

Securing relationship longevity requires practical strategies that adapt to the ebb and flow of life. Regularly revisiting and renegotiating relationship goals and boundaries is one such strategy. Life changes, and so do people. What worked in the past may no longer serve in the present. By periodically assessing your goals and boundaries, you ensure they remain relevant and supportive. This process involves open discussions where both people express their needs and aspirations, adjusting the relationship's trajectory as necessary. Engaging in shared activities that promote bonding is another way to sustain the relationship.

These activities might include hobbies, travel, or exploring new interests together. These shared experiences create memories and connections that enrich the relationship, reinforcing your bond.

Flexibility is the thread that weaves through these strategies, allowing relationships to adapt and flourish. Being open to change and new experiences together keeps the relationship dynamic and alive. It means embracing opportunities that arise, whether they are planned or spontaneous. This openness to change fosters a sense of adventure and growth, inviting both parties to explore and learn together. Adjusting to life transitions as a team further reinforces this flexibility. Life is full of unexpected turns, from career shifts to family changes. You strengthen the relationship's resilience by approaching these transitions as a united front. Supporting each other through these changes ensures that both people feel secure and valued, reinforcing the relationship's foundation of trust and cooperation.

Fostering a supportive partnership involves encouraging individual growth within the relationship. Each partner should feel free to pursue their interests and goals, knowing they have the support of their partner. This encouragement strengthens the individual's sense of self and enriches the relationship, as both bring new experiences and perspectives. Providing emotional and practical support during challenges is another key aspect of a supportive partnership. Whether offering a listening ear during a tough day or helping with practical tasks, this support reinforces the bond between partners. It shows a commitment to each other's well-being, creating a partnership where both individuals feel nurtured and secure.

As we close this chapter, remember that secure relationships require consistent effort and adaptability. Committing to ongoing communication, embracing flexibility, and fostering a supportive partnership lays the groundwork for a resilient and deeply fulfilling relationship. Building and maintaining secure attachments is a continuing process with opportunities for growth and connection. The following chapter will explore how these principles can create even deeper emotional bonds and a more profound sense of intimacy in our many different relationships.

CHAPTER 7
NAVIGATING DIFFERENT RELATIONSHIP CONTEXTS

NAVIGATING RELATIONSHIPS CAN BE PARTICULARLY CHALLENGING FOR individuals with avoidant attachment styles. This chapter explores the complex dynamics at play, beginning with the unique hurdles faced during the dating process. We delve into the intricacies of developing romantic intimacy, highlighting the gradual approach necessary for those who fear vulnerability while also craving connection. Furthermore, we examine the profound impact of rejection sensitivity, illustrating how past experiences can shape present interactions and relationships. Family systems often mirror these attachment patterns, presenting both the origins of avoidant behavior and opportunities for healing. Finally, we discuss creating new family dynamics that foster emotional availability and connection. Each section offers examples, insights, and strategies for understanding and overcoming the challenges of avoidant attachment, ultimately paving the way for healthier relationships.

DATING WITH AVOIDANT ATTACHMENT

The dating landscape can be particularly daunting for individuals with avoidant attachment patterns. The early stages of a romantic connection often trigger intense attachment system activation, leading to a push-pull dynamic that can perplex both parties.

"Attachment system activation" refers to the psychological process by which individuals seek comfort and connection from significant others, particularly during stress or distress. This concept is rooted in the attachment theory we discussed in Chapter 1. When individuals experience feelings of threat or insecurity, their attachment system is activated, prompting them to reach out for support from those they feel bonded with, such as partners, family members, or close friends. The activation of this system can influence behavior, emotions, and decisions, driving individuals to seek proximity and comfort from loved ones to cope with anxiety or uncertainty. It plays a vital role in relationships and overall emotional well-being.

We can look at one woman's dating journey, which illustrates some common patterns. After several promising relationships ended due to Lisa's unconscious withdrawal at signs of deepening intimacy, she began working with an attachment-informed dating coach. Together, they developed strategies for maintaining connection during activation, including transparent communication about her need for space and structured check-ins with potential partners.

Establishing dating boundaries is a delicate art that requires a balance between protection and connection. This might involve setting clear expectations about communication frequency, planning dates with built-in alone time, and developing scripts for discussing attachment needs early in relationships. The aim is not to eliminate attachment activation but to make it manageable and conducive to personal growth.

MANAGING REJECTION SENSITIVITY

The fear of rejection often lies at the heart of avoidant attachment patterns, creating a complex web of protective behaviors that paradoxically increase the likelihood of experiencing rejection. Understanding rejection sensitivity requires examining how early experiences of emotional unavailability or inconsistent caregiving create heightened vigilance to potential abandonment.

The transformation of Karen, a marketing executive, illustrates how rejection sensitivity can be effectively managed. Early in her career, Karen interpreted any constructive feedback as a personal rejection, leading her to maintain an emotional distance from colleagues and miss mentorship opportunities. Through dedicated work with her therapist, she developed what she called her "rejection resilience toolkit." This included techniques for distinguishing between genuine rejection and perceived threats and strategies for maintaining connection during periods of heightened sensitivity.

Building rejection resilience involves a crucial understanding that not all disconnections signify rejection. When Thomas, a graduate student, began examining his rejection sensitivity, he discovered that his automatic interpretation of unanswered text messages as rejection stemmed from childhood experiences of emotional neglect. Through mindful awareness practice, he learned to pause before acting on these interpretations, creating space for alternative explanations and more measured responses.

BUILDING ROMANTIC INTIMACY

Developing romantic intimacy with an avoidant attachment style requires a gradual, intentional approach that honors the need for connection and the fear of vulnerability. This process involves creating what attachment theorist John Bowlby called a "secure base" to explore deeper intimacy levels.

The successful journey of partners David and Jason demonstrates this approach. Both identifying with avoidant attachment patterns, they initially struggled with emotional intimacy. Through couples therapy, they developed a practice they called "scheduled vulnerability"—setting aside specific times for deeper emotional sharing while maintaining clear boundaries around alone time. This structure provided the safety needed to increase their capacity for intimacy gradually.

Physical intimacy and attachment intertwine in complex ways for individuals with avoidant patterns. The body's response to physical closeness can trigger attachment activation, leading to withdrawal after intimate encounters. Understanding this connection allows for developing strategies to maintain an emotional presence during physical intimacy.

FAMILY RELATIONSHIPS AND ATTACHMENT HEALING

The family system often serves as both the source of avoidant attachment patterns and a crucial arena for healing. Working with family relationships requires understanding that current tensions usually reflect multi-generational patterns of emotional distance and unmet attachment needs.

Maria's work with her family demonstrates the complexity of this healing process. Growing up in a family that prided itself on emotional stoicism, Maria struggled to connect with her teenage daughter, who openly expressed emotional needs. Through family therapy, Maria discovered that her avoidant patterns reflected her grandmother's survival strategy during times of war—emotional distance had once served as protection but now hindered family connection. This understanding allowed Maria to begin bridging the generational gap, creating new patterns of emotional availability for her daughter.

Setting boundaries within family systems requires particular finesse when working with avoidant attachment. These boundaries must serve dual purposes: protecting against overwhelming emotional demands while remaining permeable enough for genuine connection. The process involves communicating needs while remaining open to family members' emotional responses.

CREATING NEW FAMILY DYNAMICS

Transforming family patterns requires sustained effort and patience from all involved members. Each small change in communication or behavior can create ripple effects throughout the family system, sometimes meeting resistance before leading to positive change.

The Johnson family's experience exemplifies this transformative process. When the eldest son, Robert, began addressing his avoidant attachment patterns in therapy, he initially faced resistance from family members accustomed to their emotionally distant dynamic. The family's breakthrough came during a holiday gathering when Robert shared his journey using the metaphor of a bridge built slowly over troubled waters. This image helped his family understand the challenge and the possibility of creating new connection patterns.

Fostering healthy connections within the family system involves creating what attachment theorists call "earned secure attachment." This process requires consistent, small steps toward greater emotional availability, with each family member moving at their own pace while remaining committed to a deeper connection.

PROFESSIONAL RELATIONSHIPS AND ATTACHMENT

The workplace often uniquely triggers attachment patterns, particularly for individuals with avoidant attachment styles who may have developed high achievement as a compensation strategy. Understanding how attachment manifests in professional settings allows for more effective navigation of workplace relationships while maintaining appropriate boundaries.

Dr. Sarah Martinez's research with corporate leaders revealed how avoidant attachment patterns often manifest as workaholism or difficulty delegating tasks. By studying successful executives who had addressed their attachment patterns, she identified key strategies for maintaining professional effectiveness while developing more secure relationship patterns. These strategies emphasized the importance of mentorship, clear communication about work boundaries, and regular check-ins with team members.

Leadership roles present particular challenges for individuals with avoidant attachment, as they require maintaining professional authority and fostering secure connections within teams. The experience of James, a tech startup founder, demonstrates how awareness of attachment patterns can enhance leadership effectiveness. James developed protocols for staying engaged during challenging conversations by understanding his tendency to withdraw during team conflicts, ultimately creating a more psychologically safe environment for his entire organization.

CHAPTER 8
CONFLICT RESOLUTION AND RELATIONSHIP GROWTH

REMEMBER WHEN A DISAGREEMENT WITH A PARTNER, FAMILY MEMBER, or friend seemed impossible to overcome? The tension, frustration, and the feeling of being misunderstood may still be vivid. But what if I told you that these conflicts are not just hurdles but potential stepping stones to deeper connections and personal growth? This chapter presents a structured approach to conflict resolution that respects both parties' needs and fosters mutual understanding. By approaching conflicts with intention, you can turn them into opportunities for building stronger, healthier relationships.

UNDERSTANDING THE ROOT CAUSES OF CONFLICT

Resolving conflicts effectively begins with identifying the root cause. Often, disagreements on the surface mask deeper issues related to unmet needs or unexpressed emotions. For example, an argument about household chores might stem from feelings of imbalance or underappreciation. The sense of relief and empowerment gained through understanding these underlying issues can be enlightening. To pinpoint the root cause, open a dialogue with the other person where you both express underlying concerns. Ask questions beyond the immediate conflict, such as, "What do you need from me in this situation?" or "How does this make you feel?" By exploring these deeper issues, you can address the real problem rather than just the symptoms.

Once you understand the underlying issues, it is crucial to establish common goals for resolution. A shared objective might be to ensure that both people feel heard and respected or to find a compromise that meets everyone's needs. For instance, in a disagreement about household chores, a common goal could be establishing a fair division of labor that both parties agree on. Framing the conflict resolution process as a collaborative effort encourages cooperation and reduces defensiveness. When both parties work toward a common goal, the focus shifts from winning the argument to finding a solution that benefits the relationship. This mindset fosters a sense of partnership and shared responsibility, paving the way for more constructive discussions and a more profound understanding of connection.

Maintaining a calm and open mindset is essential when navigating conflicts. Emotional reactions often escalate tensions, making it challenging to communicate effectively. Instead, practice techniques that manage these reactions, such as taking deep breaths or pausing to collect your thoughts before responding. This reassures you that you are in control of the situation. Creating a safe space for open discussion also helps. Choose a time and place where both parties can talk without distractions or interruptions. Set ground rules that encourage respectful dialogue, such as allowing each person to speak without interruption and agreeing to listen with an open mind. These practices create an environment where both people feel safe to express themselves honestly.

Compromise and collaboration are essential to resolving conflicts in a way that strengthens relationships. Rather than adopting a win-lose mentality, strive for mutually beneficial solutions. This might involve finding middle ground or creating new options that neither party initially considered. Encourage collaborative problem-solving by brainstorming solutions together. Ask questions like, "How can we address both of our needs?" or "What are some alternatives we haven't explored?" This approach resolves the immediate conflict and builds trust and cooperation.

Conflict Resolution Checklist

- **Preparation**: Reflect on your feelings and identify the root cause of the conflict.
- **Setting**: Select a peaceful and private environment for the discussion.
- **Mindset**: Approach the conversation with an open mind and a willingness to listen.
- **Dialogue**: Express your needs using "I" statements and listen to the other person's perspective without interrupting.
- **Common Goals**: Identify shared objectives for resolution.

- **Compromise**: Brainstorm solutions that address both parties' needs.
- **Agreement**: Agree on actionable steps to move forward.

This checklist is a practical guide to navigating conflicts with intention and care. Following these steps, you can transform disagreements into opportunities for growth and deeper connection. With practice, this process becomes second nature, enhancing the health and longevity of your relationships.

THE CRUCIAL ROLE OF ACTIVE LISTENING AND EMPATHY EXERCISES IN CONFLICT RESOLUTION

Imagine a conversation where you feel truly heard. Your words are acknowledged and understood as if the other person has stepped into your shoes. This is the power of active listening—a crucial skill in resolving conflicts and fostering more profound connections. Active listening reduces misunderstandings and miscommunications, which often arise when we listen to respond rather than to understand. When you practice active listening, you validate the other person's perspective, showing them that their thoughts and feelings matter. This validation can dissolve tension, opening the door to meaningful dialogue and resolution.

To enhance your active listening skills, consider engaging in exercises that focus on reflective listening. This technique involves paraphrasing what the other person says and confirming your understanding before responding. For instance, if the other person shares a frustration, you might say, "So, you're feeling overwhelmed because of the work deadlines." This reflection shows that you are paying attention and allows you to correct any misinterpretations. Another effective practice is honing your nonverbal communication cues. Nonverbal signals like maintaining eye contact, nodding, or leaning slightly forward indicate engagement and interest. These cues reassure the other person that you are present and attentive, reinforcing your connection.

Empathy has a crucial role in building and maintaining connections. It involves putting yourself in another's shoes and seeing the world through their eyes. This perspective shift fosters understanding, allowing you to connect with their emotions and experiences deeply. Empathy bridges gaps that words cannot, creating a shared emotional experience that strengthens bonds. Techniques for cultivating empathy include empathy mapping exercises, where you explore another person's feelings, thoughts, and motivations. In an empathy mapping exercise, you consider what the other person might feel, think, and want. Consider writing down what you believe the other person is experiencing, then discuss it with them to gain a clearer understanding. This exercise encourages open communication and mutual understanding, laying the groundwork for a more empathetic relationship.

To keep empathy alive in your relationships, it is crucial to practice it regularly. Daily empathy reflections can be a simple yet powerful tool. Spend a few minutes each day reflecting on your interactions. Ask yourself how you demonstrated empathy and where you might improve. This reflection helps internalize empathetic behaviors, making them a natural part of your interactions. Partner empathy challenges can also strengthen these skills. Set aside time with your partner to discuss each other's perspectives on various topics, challenging yourselves to see through each other's eyes. This practice enhances empathy and deepens your connection. It helps cultivate a relationship built on mutual understanding and respect. You can also practice this with other significant relationships you may have.

THE IMPORTANCE OF SETTING REALISTIC RELATIONSHIP EXPECTATIONS

In relationships, expectations guide how we interact and what we anticipate from others. They shape our perceptions and influence our satisfaction. Realistic expectations are vital because they help us navigate relationships without unnecessary disappointment or frustration. When expectations align with reality, they foster a sense of balance and understanding. On the other hand, unrealistic expectations can lead to repeated feelings of letdown. For instance, expecting the other person always to know precisely what you need without expressing it sets both of you up for failure. This expectation ignores that everyone has different perspectives and that open communication is necessary. Setting realistic expectations creates a foundation for a healthy relationship where both people feel valued and understood.

Understanding what you expect from a relationship starts with self-reflection. Take time to think about what you truly need and want from the other person. Reflective journaling can be a helpful tool in this process. Write down your thoughts on a fulfilling relationship, considering communication, support, and shared activities. Once you have a clearer picture, discuss these expectations with the other person. This dialogue is crucial because it reveals whether your visions align and where adjustments may be needed. By articulating your needs and listening to and acknowledging the other person's needs, you can work together to create a relationship that meets both of your expectations.

Unrealistic expectations can strain a relationship. They often stem from idealized notions of how a relationship should be, influenced by media, past experiences, or societal pressures. Common unrealistic expectations include believing that conflicts should never occur, that people should always agree, or that love alone can solve all problems. These expectations overlook the complexity and effort required to maintain a healthy relationship. When expectations go unmet, disappointment and resentment can grow. You might start to see the other person as inadequate or feel unfulfilled, which can lead to conflict or even the dissolution of the relationship. Recognizing and addressing these unrealistic expectations is crucial for maintaining harmony and satisfaction.

Modifying your expectations can lead to a more satisfying relationship. Start by setting achievable relationship goals that consider both peoples' needs and limitations. These goals may include spending quality time together weekly or improving communication by having regular check-ins. Practicing acceptance and flexibility is also key. Understand that no relationship is perfect, and both people will have strengths and weaknesses. Accepting this reality allows you to appreciate the other person for who they are rather than who you want them to be. Flexibility in your expectations means being open to change and adapting as the relationship evolves. This adaptability can strengthen your bond and create a more resilient relationship.

OVERCOMING PERFECTIONISM IN RELATIONSHIPS

Perfectionism in relationships often manifests as the pressure to meet unattainable standards for yourself and the other person. This drive for flawlessness can lead to constant dissatisfaction, as pursuing perfection leaves little room for the natural imperfections that characterize human interactions. Minor issues can become magnified—for example, a partner might criticize an unwashed dish or an unsaid compliment, not because these things matter in themselves but because they symbolize a broader failure to meet an unattainable ideal. Over time, this relentless pursuit of perfection can trigger conflicts, erode intimacy, and create a disconnect as the focus shifts from appreciating each other's unique qualities to critiquing perceived flaws.

Examining the root causes of perfectionism can provide insight into its impact on relationships. Fear of rejection or failure often underlies perfectionist tendencies, driven by a deep-seated belief that being imperfect equates to being unworthy. These internalized beliefs about worthiness and success may come from past experiences—such as childhood environments where love or approval seemed conditional on achievement—or societal pressures that idolize flawlessness. Recognizing these sources is the first step in addressing perfectionism. By understanding where these beliefs originated, individuals can begin to challenge their validity and reframe their perspective on what it means to be in a healthy, fulfilling relationship.

Challenging perfectionist thoughts requires intentional effort, reflection, and self-compassion. Cognitive restructuring techniques can help reframe negative thoughts about imperfection. When perfectionist thoughts arise, such as *I must do this perfectly*, or *I've failed*, pause and ask whether this belief is realistic or helpful. Consider alternative perspectives, like *doing my best is enough* or *imperfections are part of being human*. Similarly, when dwelling on a perceived flaw in your partner or loved one, pause and ask whether this thought is based on reality or an unrealistic standard. Practicing self-compassion is also essential— treat yourself with the understanding and kindness you would give a friend. Celebrate small successes and progress, focusing on effort rather than outcome. This shift in thinking can create a more positive and supportive environment where people feel accepted and valued for who they are rather than what they think they should be.

Embracing imperfection as a growth opportunity can transform the dynamics of a relationship. Instead of viewing mistakes as failures, see them as chances to learn and connect on a deeper level. When a misstep occurs, approach it with curiosity rather than criticism. Ask the other person how they perceived the situation and share your perspective. This open dialogue fosters empathy and understanding, strengthening your bond. Celebrate the progress you and your partner, family member, or friend make together, acknowledging the growth from facing challenges as a team. Focus on the journey of development rather than the destination of perfection, appreciating the unique qualities and strengths each of you brings to the relationship. By shifting focus from striving for perfection to valuing authenticity and effort, you create a space where love can flourish, unencumbered by unrealistic expectations.

CREATING A GROWTH-ORIENTED RELATIONSHIP PLAN

When you focus on growth within your relationships, you create dynamic ones that can evolve over the years. This approach not only enhances satisfaction but also increases longevity. You build resilience and adaptability by emphasizing growth, equipping both people to handle life's inevitable changes. A growth-oriented mindset encourages mutual support, allowing each person to develop individually while strengthening the relationship as a whole. You become allies in each other's journeys, fostering an environment where both can thrive. This mutual development creates a robust foundation to weather challenges and celebrate successes together.

To develop a personalized growth plan, set specific, measurable relationship goals. These might include improving communication, spending more quality time together, or supporting each other's aspirations. Determine what success is for each goal. Then, realistic timelines can be set to achieve them. When goals are clear and measurable, they become more attainable, providing motivation and direction. Next, identify areas for improvement and collaboration. Discuss openly where the relationship thrives and where it might need more attention. Perhaps you both agree that you want to enhance your emotional intimacy or work on better conflict resolution. Make these areas a focus in your growth plan, outlining actionable steps you can take together to address them.

Monitoring progress is crucial to any growth plan. Regular relationship check-ins allow you to reflect on your journey and adjust your goals as needed. Schedule time for these discussions, ensuring they are safe for honest communication. During these check-ins, celebrate milestones and progress. Recognizing successes, no matter how small, reinforces positive behavior and keeps momentum. Consider keeping a progress journal where you document these reflections and celebrations. This journal is a tangible reminder of your commitment to growth and can encourage you during challenging times. By tracking your progress, you gain insight into what works and needs adjustment, ensuring your growth plan remains relevant and practical.

Fostering a mindset of continuous improvement is vital to maintaining growth. Embrace change and view it as an opportunity for learning. Life has many unexpected events, and a growth-oriented approach prepares you to adapt gracefully. Encourage each other to seek new experiences and challenges individually and together. This shared pursuit of growth keeps the relationship fresh and exciting, especially for couples. Cultivating a supportive and encouraging environment is equally important. Celebrate each other's successes and offer support during setbacks. Create a relationship culture where growth is not only expected but eagerly anticipated. This positive atmosphere inspires both people to strive for their best selves, individually and together.

Integrating these strategies into your relationship lays the groundwork for a thriving relationship built on mutual growth and development. This approach enhances your connection and sets the stage for a more fulfilling future. By focusing on growth, you ensure that your relationship remains vibrant and resilient, equipped to handle whatever comes your way. In the next chapter, we will explore how building secure attachments is the natural progression from this growth-focused mindset, leading to deeper connections and lasting happiness.

CHAPTER 9
INTEGRATING SELF-DISCOVERY WITH THERAPEUTIC SUPPORT

PICTURE YOURSELF STANDING AT THE EDGE OF A VAST FOREST. EACH tree represents a different aspect of your emotional landscape; some are familiar, and others are mysterious. Venturing into this forest alone can be daunting and overwhelming. This is where therapy comes into play, offering a guiding hand and a reliable map to navigate the complexities of your emotional world. Therapy provides a supportive and structured space where you can safely explore and transform your attachment styles, helping you understand how early experiences shape your present interactions. It is a process that invites you to delve into your emotions and empowers you, uncovering patterns that may have gone unnoticed and discovering pathways to more secure connections.

WHEN AND WHY TO SEEK SUPPORT

Therapy is a platform for building trust, not only with the therapist but also with yourself. The therapeutic alliance, which forms the foundation for this trust-building process, is a crucial aspect of therapy. Within this alliance, you find a space where your thoughts and feelings are validated and encouraged to express your deepest emotions without fear of judgment. This safe environment fosters vulnerability, allowing you to explore deep-seated emotional patterns that might remain buried. Through this exploration, you gain insights into how these patterns impact your relationships, empowering you to make conscious changes that enhance your emotional well-being. The therapeutic relationship's sense of safety and understanding creates a powerful catalyst for transformation.

Various therapeutic modalities can aid in transforming attachment styles, each offering unique benefits. Cognitive Behavioral Therapy (CBT) is particularly effective in reframing negative beliefs that may underlie avoidant behaviors. CBT helps you develop healthier thought patterns and behaviors by challenging and reshaping these beliefs. On the other hand, emotionally Focused Therapy (EFT) focuses on enhancing emotional connection, guiding you to express and process emotions in ways that foster intimacy and understanding. Attachment-based therapy offers a more direct approach, addressing specific attachment issues and helping you develop secure relational patterns. These therapies, individually or in combination, provide tailored support to meet your unique needs, guiding you toward healthier and more fulfilling relationships.

Therapy has many benefits for people struggling with avoidant attachment styles. It enhances emotional awareness, enabling you to identify and express your feelings more effectively. Through therapy, you learn to navigate relational interactions with confidence and empathy, building skills that improve your ability to connect with others. The therapeutic process encourages you to confront and embrace your emotions, fostering a sense of emotional resilience. As you become more attuned to your feelings, you gain the tools needed to manage them constructively, reducing the tendency to retreat into emotional distance. This newfound awareness and skill set empower you to engage in healthier, more meaningful relationships, bringing you closer to the secure attachments you desire.

Consistency in therapeutic engagement is vital for achieving meaningful change. Setting a regular therapy schedule ensures you remain committed to the process, providing the stability needed for growth. Consistent sessions allow you to build momentum, progressively working through challenges and celebrating victories. Dedicating to ongoing therapeutic goals reinforces your commitment to personal development, helping you stay focused on the path to transformation. Regular engagement with therapy offers a structured framework for accountability, encouraging you to explore your emotional landscape with intention and purpose. Through this commitment, you cultivate a mindset of continuous growth, embracing the potential for lasting change in your emotional and relational life.

Reflection Section: Therapeutic Engagement Checklist

- **Regular Schedule**: Have you established a consistent therapy schedule?
- **Therapeutic Alliance**: Do you feel safe and understood within the therapeutic relationship?

- **Modality Exploration**: Which therapeutic approaches have you explored, and which resonate with you?
- **Emotional Awareness**: How has therapy helped you recognize and express your emotions?
- **Commitment to Goals**: Are you actively pursuing your therapeutic goals with dedication?

Use this checklist to assess and enhance your therapeutic engagement, ensuring you remain aligned with your personal and relational development objectives.

FINDING THE RIGHT THERAPEUTIC SUPPORT

Choosing a therapist who truly understands your needs is crucial in your path to emotional healing. You are the central figure in this journey, and finding someone specializing in attachment issues can make a significant difference. A therapist with expertise in attachment theory will deeply understand how early relationships affect your current interactions. They can guide you through the complexities of avoidant attachment with insight and empathy. Finding a therapist whose communication style aligns with yours is also vital. Some therapists are more directive, while others take a more collaborative approach. Consider what type of interaction makes you feel most comfortable and empowered. This compatibility can enhance your therapy experience, making it more effective and fulfilling.

The relationship between you and your therapist, often called "therapeutic fit," is crucial to successful therapy. Building rapport and trust with your therapist creates a safe space for exploration and growth. Feeling understood and validated makes you more likely to open up and engage with the process thoroughly. This connection allows you to delve into deeper emotional patterns and work through them with support. A good therapeutic fit fosters a partnership where you and the therapist work together toward your healing goals. This relationship often holds the power to transform your emotional landscape, helping you develop healthier relational patterns.

Evaluating potential therapists can feel overwhelming, but having a strategy can simplify the process. Start with a consultation. It is a good opportunity to ask questions that matter to you. Inquire about their experience with attachment issues and their therapeutic approach. Discuss what you hope to achieve through therapy and gauge their response. This meeting can provide valuable insights into whether the therapist's expertise aligns with your needs. Consider scheduling trial sessions to assess comfort and effectiveness further. These sessions allow you to experience their style firsthand and decide if it feels right. Trust your instincts during this process; feeling at ease is essential to a good match.

In addition to traditional therapy, alternative support options can complement your healing journey. Online therapy platforms offer accessibility and convenience, allowing you to connect with therapists from your home. This can be particularly beneficial if you have a busy schedule or live in an area with limited in-person options. Support groups provide another layer of assistance. They offer a space to share experiences with others who understand what you are going through. These groups can cultivate a sense of community and belonging, providing peer support that can be incredibly validating and empowering. Other alternative options include self-help books, podcasts, and workshops, which can provide additional insights and tools for your healing journey. Engaging with others with similar challenges can broaden your understanding and offer new perspectives on your attachment style.

INTEGRATING BOOK INSIGHTS WITH COUNSELING

Integrating self-help insights with therapy can significantly enhance healing, providing a more holistic approach to personal growth. When you combine the exercises and reflections from this book with your therapeutic sessions, you reinforce the concepts you are working on in therapy. This dual approach can deepen your understanding and help you apply what you learn in real-world settings. The exercises in this book encourage self-reflection, allowing you to internalize therapeutic concepts and explore them more deeply. These exercises can uncover insights that may not arise during therapy sessions alone. This self-guided exploration complements the structured support of therapy, creating a rich framework for personal development.

Discussing the insights and exercises from the book with your therapist can also be incredibly beneficial. It lets you bring personal reflections into your therapy sessions, providing a starting point for deeper discussions. Sharing these reflections helps your therapist understand your thoughts and emotional responses, offering a more comprehensive view of your experiences. Together, you can explore how these insights relate to the issues you are working on in therapy, using them as a springboard for addressing complex topics. Whether it is a specific exercise or a chapter that resonated with you, these elements can facilitate meaningful conversations, helping you to address and resolve underlying challenges. This collaborative approach encourages open dialogue, fostering a partnership between you and your therapist as you work toward shared goals.

To work collaboratively with your therapist using book insights, it can be helpful to set joint goals based on the material. This involves discussing specific objectives you want to achieve and drawing on the concepts and exercises from the book. Your therapist can then tailor their approach to support these goals, providing guidance and feedback that aligns with your personal development plan. Regularly reviewing your progress on book-inspired tasks can help you stay on track and adjust as needed. This ongoing evaluation allows you to measure your growth and celebrate milestones, reinforcing your commitment to the process. You create a dynamic and supportive environment for change by actively engaging with books and therapy resources.

Maintaining a journal to track insights and progress can further enhance your engagement with therapeutic tools. This practice allows you to document your thoughts and experiences, creating a record of your journey. Journaling provides a space for reflection, helping you to process emotions and identify patterns that may influence your behavior. Over weeks and months, these entries can reveal valuable insights, offering a window into your growth and transformation. Creating a personal toolkit from books and therapy resources can also be empowering. This toolkit might include exercises, reflections, and strategies that resonate with you, providing a resource for managing challenges and fostering resilience. By actively using these tools, you enhance your ability to navigate emotional complexities, equipping yourself with the skills to build healthier, more secure relationships.

DEVELOPING A THERAPEUTIC ACTION PLAN

Think about setting out on a road trip without a map or GPS. You know the destination, but each turn and decision requires guesswork, which might lead to unexpected detours. A therapeutic action plan is your roadmap, providing structure and direction as you work toward transforming your attachment patterns. This plan clarifies your therapeutic goals, offering a clear vision of what you wish to achieve. You can see your progress and celebrate each step forward by setting specific milestones. A well-crafted action plan outlines your personal development journey, helping you navigate the complexities of emotional growth with confidence and purpose.

Creating a personalized action plan involves several steps tailored to your unique needs and aspirations. Begin by identifying particular areas where you seek change and growth. Reflect on the patterns and behaviors you wish to alter, considering how they impact your relationships. Once you clearly understand these areas, set realistic timelines for achieving your objectives. Break down your goals into attainable steps, ensuring each milestone is manageable. This process provides a sense of accomplishment and keeps you motivated and focused. You create a cohesive framework to support your emotional and relational development by aligning your plan with your therapeutic goals.

Accountability is crucial to the success of a therapeutic action plan. It ensures you stay committed to your goals, providing the support needed to overcome challenges. Involve your therapist in monitoring your progress, using sessions to discuss achievements and areas for improvement. This collaborative partnership allows you to work together toward common objectives. Additionally, consider enlisting a support partner, someone you trust to hold you accountable. This person can offer encouragement, celebrate successes, and provide perspective when encountering obstacles. Their involvement adds extra support, reinforcing your commitment to personal growth.

To effectively track and evaluate your progress, consider using practical tools that offer clarity and insight. Progress charts and checklists can be valuable resources, allowing you to visualize your achievements and identify areas that require further attention. These tools provide a tangible way to measure your development, offering a sense of direction and purpose. Regular reflection sessions can also enhance your ability to assess progress. Set aside time to evaluate your achievements, reflecting on the steps you have taken and the lessons learned along the way. This practice encourages self-awareness and helps you stay aligned with your goals, ensuring that your action plan remains relevant and practical.

Interactive Element: Action Plan Template

- **Goal Setting**: Define your primary objectives for personal and therapeutic growth.

- **Milestones**: Identify specific milestones that mark progress toward your goals.
- **Timeline**: Create a realistic timeline for reaching each milestone.
- **Accountability**: List your therapist's role and support partner's involvement in monitoring progress.
- **Evaluation Tools**: Choose tools like progress charts and checklists to track development.

Use this template to structure your therapeutic action plan, tailoring it to your needs and aspirations. Review and change your plan regularly as you progress, ensuring it remains a dynamic and supportive resource for your journey toward transformation.

LEVERAGING THERAPY FOR LONG-TERM ATTACHMENT SECURITY

Imagine therapy as a sturdy anchor in the sometimes turbulent sea of life. This anchor does not just stabilize you during storms; it helps you navigate calmer waters as well. The long-term benefits of sustained therapeutic work are profound, reinforcing secure attachment behaviors continuously. Regularly engaging in therapy creates a routine that nurtures emotional growth. This ongoing support helps solidify the new patterns you have worked hard to establish, making them second nature as time passes. As life throws new challenges, therapy acts as a compass, guiding you with strategies and insights tailored to your evolving needs. Whether it is a new job, a relationship shift, or personal growth, therapy provides a framework to adapt and thrive.

The journey does not end when formal therapy sessions conclude. Maintenance strategies become crucial in preserving the progress you have made. Regular self-check-ins and reflections are invaluable tools for staying attuned to your emotional state. Set aside time to reflect on your feelings and behaviors, identifying old patterns that might resurface. Continued practice of therapeutic exercises keeps you grounded, reinforcing the skills you have developed. These exercises, whether mindfulness practices or journaling, remind you of the work you have accomplished and your growth. They act as touchstones, helping you stay connected to your cultivated secure attachment.

Approaching therapy as a lifelong tool rather than a one-time fix changes how you view personal development. Life is dynamic, with transitions and changes that can unsettle even the most secure individuals. Returning to therapy during major life shifts can provide stability and insight to navigate these periods confidently. Periodic therapeutic "tune-ups" offer an opportunity to recalibrate, ensuring that your emotional resilience remains strong. These check-ins with a therapist can prevent regression, letting you address emerging issues before they become overwhelming. This proactive approach to therapy fosters a sense of empowerment, enabling you to take charge of your emotional well-being.

Adopting a mindset focused on lifelong growth and development transforms how you engage with therapy and personal growth. Viewing therapy as part of a more extensive process of self-discovery encourages you to embrace change as an opportunity for continued development. Each therapeutic encounter becomes a stepping stone, contributing to a deeper understanding of yourself and your relationships. This mindset invites you to see challenges as chances to learn and grow, cultivating resilience and adaptability. By embracing this perspective, you open yourself to the richness of life, ready to evolve and thrive in whatever circumstances arise.

In this chapter, we have explored how therapy can serve as a foundation for long-term attachment security. Sustained therapeutic engagement reinforces secure behaviors, helping you adapt to life's ever-changing landscape. Regular self-reflection and proactive therapy ensure lasting growth, turning therapy into a lifelong ally.

CHAPTER 10

FOUNDATIONS OF EMPOWERMENT AND GROWTH IN ATTACHMENT HEALING

THINK OF A SCULPTOR GRADUALLY CHISELING AWAY AT A PROTECTIVE marble shell, each careful stroke revealing the capacity for connection beneath. Just as a sculptor reveals the hidden beauty within the marble, the journey of personal growth and empowerment shapes the inner landscape of who we are. For those of us with avoidant attachment patterns, this shell represents the defensive barriers we have built—our tendency to withdraw, our comfort with emotional distance, and our reflexive self-reliance. Yet beneath these protective layers lies our innate ability to connect. The journey of transforming avoidant attachment requires a delicate balance of self-compassion and courage, acknowledging that our defensive patterns once served a vital purpose while recognizing they may no longer serve our current needs for connection. It takes lots of courage to embark on this journey, face our fears, and step into the unknown, but this courage empowers us.

THE JOURNEY TO SECURE ATTACHMENT

As we have seen, the path from avoidant to secure attachment begins with the understanding that our tendency to withdraw from emotional connection stems from early adaptive responses. Research with avoidant attachment clients reveals that self-compassion often feels threatening precisely because it activates the attachment system we have worked so hard to suppress. One individual, Michael, described his initial resistance to self-compassion practices as follows: "Being kind to myself felt more threatening than criticism. Criticism was familiar; it kept me moving, achieving, staying safe in my independence."

Cultivating self-compassion involves embracing a nonjudgmental attitude toward personal flaws. We are all imperfect, yet it is through these imperfections that we learn and grow. Accepting this truth is liberating, offering the freedom to be human without the burden of unrealistic expectations. When you nurture compassion toward yourself, you create a foundation for genuine self-acceptance. This self-compassion is not a weakness but a source of strength and freedom, empowering you to be your true self and live a life free from the weight of self-criticism.

We can begin with small, manageable steps toward self-compassion to navigate this challenge. Traditional loving-kindness meditation might feel overwhelming for those with avoidant attachment. Instead, start with "micro-moments of compassion." Close your eyes for thirty seconds, focusing on phrases like "My need for space is valid" or "I can be both independent and connected." These brief exercises help bypass our defensive reactions while gradually building tolerance for self-directed warmth.

James, a software engineer with avoidant attachment, developed his "emotional check-in protocol." Each morning, he would spend two minutes acknowledging one emotion and one need without trying to fix or change them. "At first, it felt mechanical, almost like debugging code," he shared. "But over time, it became a way to maintain emotional awareness without feeling overwhelmed."

Integrating self-compassion into daily life is a deliberate practice that requires effort and commitment. Start your day with affirmations reinforcing your worth and capabilities to set a positive tone. Equally important is setting aside time for self-reflection and care. Whether it is a quiet walk in nature or a few minutes of mindful breathing, these practices ground you in the present and nurture your well-being, fostering a compassionate outlook on life.

Interactive Element: Self-Compassion Checklist

- **Morning Affirmations**: Begin each day by affirming your worth and setting a positive intention.
- **Loving-Kindness Meditation**: Practice visualizing compassion and kindness for yourself and others.
- **Mindful Breathing**: Set aside time for deep breaths, grounding yourself in the present moment.
- **Reflective Journaling**: Write about daily experiences, focusing on self-kindness and understanding.

These practices cultivate an enduring sense of self-compassion, bringing about profound personal growth. By embracing this approach, you empower yourself to face life's challenges with resilience and grace, creating a life imbued with authenticity and joy.

EMPOWERMENT THROUGH KNOWLEDGE AND AWARENESS

For those with avoidant attachment, intellectual understanding often feels safer than emotional connection. This preference for knowledge can be used as a bridge toward greater emotional awareness. Dr. Mark Thompson's research on attachment styles shows that avoidant individuals often begin their healing journey through intellectual engagement before developing emotional capacity. Consider creating what Dr. Thompson calls an "attachment insight journal." Each week, record the following:

1. One attachment pattern you noticed.
2. The situation that triggered it.
3. Your bodily sensations during activation.
4. The emotional need beneath the pattern.
5. One small way you might respond differently next time.

A research scientist, Louise, found that approaching her attachment patterns with scientific curiosity helped reduce shame and increase awareness. "I started treating my attachment responses like data points in a longitudinal study," she explained. "This created enough emotional distance to observe my patterns without immediately withdrawing from them."

Increasing self-awareness is a key to personal empowerment. It guides us through the complex emotional landscapes of our lives. Understanding attachment theory gives us valuable insights into how early experiences shape our behaviors. It empowers us to make informed choices about our relationships. It is like a lighthouse, illuminating the path and helping us navigate troubled emotional waters.

Again, mindfulness meditation practices offer another structured way to cultivate this awareness. Traditional meditation might feel overwhelming for those with avoidant attachment, so start with brief moments of conscious attention. Set aside just two minutes daily to direct your attention to your breath and notice your thoughts with nonjudgmental awareness. This creates a safe space for self-reflection and insight while respecting your need for emotional regulation.

STRATEGIES FOR SUSTAINABLE PERSONAL CHANGE

For those with avoidant attachment, sustainable change requires balancing our need for independence with our growing capacity for connection. This balance begins with recognizing that independence and connection can coexist—they are not mutually exclusive states. Maya, a freelance designer, developed what she called her "connection capacity building" practice:

1. **Morning**: Brief emotional check-in (two minutes)

- Name one emotion
- Identify one relationship need

- Set one small connection intention for the day

2. **Throughout the Day**: Micro-connections

- Send one authentic message to a friend
- Share a genuine observation with a colleague
- Practice thirty seconds of eye contact in conversations

3. **Evening**: Integration practice (five minutes)

- Review moments of connection and withdrawal
- Acknowledge both independence and connection needs
- Plan the next day's balance points

For maintaining long-term change, Dr. James Wilson's research identifies key sustainability factors for those with avoidant attachment:

1. **Structure and Flexibility**: Create consistent connection practices while allowing for adaptation during high-stress periods. Rather than seeing withdrawal as a failure, plan for it: *If I need to withdraw, I'll communicate it and set a specific time to reconnect.*
2. **Progressive Challenge**: Gradually increase emotional exposure while maintaining successful experiences. Start with written communication, progress to voice calls, and then face-to-face vulnerability.
3. **Independence Integration**: Integrate both needs rather than viewing independence as an opposing connection.

> Schedule both connection time and explicit alone time, honoring both as valuable.

Remember that sustainable change is like a steady drumbeat—consistent and enduring rather than a sprint followed by exhaustion. This is particularly important for those with avoidant attachment, who might be tempted to approach emotional growth with the same intensity they bring to achievement-oriented goals. Here are some common challenges and solutions:

1. **Achievement-Based Regression**:

- **Challenge**: Returning to achievement focus during stress
- **Solution**: Create "connection metrics" alongside traditional goals

2. **Withdrawal Impulse**:

- **Challenge**: Strong urges to disconnect during intimacy
- **Solution**: Develop "partial withdrawal" strategies that maintain some connection

3. **Emotional Overwhelm**:

- **Challenge**: Feeling flooded when practicing connection
- **Solution**: Create emotional "container times" with clear start and endpoints

Dr. Wilson notes, "Sustainable change for those with avoidant attachment isn't about eliminating the avoidant response but expanding our capacity to choose connection even when avoidance feels safer." Remember, transforming avoidant attachment patterns is not about becoming a different person—it is about expanding your capacity for connection while honoring your need for independence. Each small step toward secure attachment builds upon the last, creating lasting change through consistent, mindful practice. The journey requires patience, self-compassion, and the understanding that growth happens gradually, one conscious choice at a time.

CHAPTER 11
TOOLS FOR TRANSFORMATION

THIS CHAPTER WILL EXPLORE THE TOOLS YOU NEED FOR YOUR transformative journey of understanding and redefining your attachment styles. You are at the center of this journey, and your active participation is crucial. Journaling for self-reflection can uncover deep insights that foster personal growth. At the same time, reflective questions will guide you in examining your relationship patterns, allowing you to understand how your past influences your present. We will introduce practical attachment exercises that can be seamlessly integrated into everyday life, helping to reinforce healthier responses in your interactions. We will also outline how to create a personalized attachment change plan, equipping you with the tools to navigate your unique path toward healthier attachments. Finally, building a supportive community, whether it is through therapy, support groups, or trusted friends, will be crucial in this process, as sharing experiences offers perspective and encouragement. These elements will lay the foundation for meaningful change and personal development, with you as the central figure in this journey.

COMPREHENSIVE JOURNALING PRACTICE

Consider journaling as a robust tool for self-reflection and personal growth. Just as a painter uses strokes to bring their vision to life, you can use words to paint the landscape of your inner world. This practice is more than just putting pen to paper; it is a journey that explores your thoughts, emotions, and experiences in a safe space. Through consistent journaling, you can process emotions, confront fears, celebrate victories, and develop clarity about your attachment style. Writing helps structure your internal dialogue, transforming abstract feelings into tangible insights that enhance self-awareness and emotional regulation. By examining how past experiences influence present relationships through written expression, you gain profound perspectives that guide your growth journey.

To assist in this exploration, consider incorporating a variety of journaling prompts into your practice. These prompts are designed to guide you in examining different facets of your attachment style and relationships. Start by reflecting on past relationship experiences. What were the dynamics like? How did you feel during moments of closeness or conflict? Another prompt might invite you to explore your current emotional triggers and responses. When do you feel the urge to withdraw, and what emotions arise in those moments? Understanding these triggers can empower you to navigate your feelings more effectively.

Additionally, consider writing about a time you felt deeply connected to someone. What factors contributed to that connection, and how can you cultivate similar experiences now? These prompts encourage introspection, helping you uncover insights that might otherwise remain hidden.

Making journaling a regular part of your routine helps maximize its positive impact on your life. Incorporate this practice into your routine to foster ongoing self-exploration. You should journal daily, taking a few moments each morning or evening to jot down your thoughts. Alternatively, a weekly journaling session can provide a dedicated space for deeper reflection. Set up a comfortable and quiet area where you can write undisturbed. This dedicated space signals to your mind that it is time to focus inward, creating a ritual supporting your self-discovery journey. Eventually, this practice becomes a valuable tool for maintaining self-awareness and emotional balance.

Reviewing past journal entries is an enlightening exercise that allows you to track emotional and behavioral changes over weeks, months, and years. As you read through your entries, you may notice recurring themes or patterns, such as a tendency to avoid intimacy during stressful periods. Identifying these patterns can inform your relationship approach, highlighting areas where growth is needed. Additionally, revisiting your entries can provide a sense of progress, reminding you how far you have come on your journey toward secure attachment. This sense of progress can instill a feeling of accomplishment, motivating you to continue building on your strengths and address challenges confidently and clearly.

Interactive Element: Journaling Prompts for Self-Exploration

- Reflect on a past relationship where you felt emotionally distant. What factors contributed to this distance, and how did it affect the relationship?
- Explore a recent situation that triggered a strong emotional response. What were you feeling, and what thoughts accompanied those feelings?
- Write about a time when you felt deeply connected to someone. What elements fostered that connection, and how can you bring similar qualities into current relationships?
- Consider a pattern you have noticed in your relationships. How does this pattern relate to your attachment style, and what steps can you take to address it?

As you engage with these prompts, allow yourself the freedom to explore without judgment. Journaling can support your development and understanding and provide a window into your inner world.

Reflective Questions for Deeper Learning

Reflective questioning illuminates the path to deeper self-understanding by encouraging critical thinking and introspection. These questions serve as mirrors, reflecting aspects of yourself that may remain unexplored, facilitating both personal and relational insights. Through this process, you uncover the underlying beliefs and values guiding your behaviors while gaining clarity about complex emotions and thoughts. Start by examining your values and relationship goals through targeted questions about vulnerability, trust, and partnership dynamics. Consider how your past influences your present ability to connect and what principles matter most in your relationships. This focused exploration offers a richer understanding of the factors shaping your interactions.

While these questions provide a starting point, I encourage you to create a personalized set of questions. Your unique experiences and challenges are the keys to unlocking a more profound understanding. Reflect on areas of curiosity or uncertainty in your life. There may be a recurring issue in your relationships that you cannot quite figure out. Formulate questions that address these specific dynamics. For example, if you often struggle with expressing emotions, you might ask, "What fears hold me from sharing my true feelings?" Tailoring questions in this way allows you to address the nuances of your experiences, leading to more targeted and meaningful introspection. This personalized approach ensures that your reflection is profoundly relevant and impactful, guiding you toward greater clarity and growth.

Once again, discussion also plays a vital role in the process of reflection. Conversations with trusted friends or partners about your reflective questions can enhance understanding and provide new perspectives. Sharing your insights and hearing others' viewpoints can deepen your comprehension of complex issues. It fosters a collaborative environment where mutual learning and support thrive. Consider participating in group discussions or workshops focused on personal growth. These settings offer a safe space to explore complex topics, allowing you to learn from others' experiences and gain diverse insights. The collective wisdom of a group can illuminate blind spots and broaden your perspective, enriching your reflective practice. Whether in intimate conversations or larger gatherings, discussing your reflections with others can amplify their impact, leading to profound personal and relational transformation.

Reflection plays a pivotal role in sustaining change, acting as a mirror that allows you to see your growth and adjust your course as needed. In the context of personal development, regular reflection sessions offer an opportunity to assess your progress, celebrate successes, and identify areas for improvement. It helps you stay connected with your journey, fostering greater self-awareness and emotional intelligence. In relationships, reflection can provide valuable insights into your partner's needs and feelings, promoting empathy and understanding. Consider keeping a reflective journal to document your thoughts, feelings, and experiences. This journal becomes a living record of your transformation, providing a tangible way to measure your progress and maintain momentum.

Interactive Element: Reflective Journal Prompts

- What new behaviors have you successfully integrated into your daily life?
- How have these changes impacted your relationships?
- What challenges have you encountered, and how have you overcome them?
- In what ways have you noticed growth in your emotional awareness?

PERSONALIZED GROWTH PLANNING AND GOAL SETTING

A tailored change plan is your transformation guide, providing structure and clarity while reflecting your unique strengths and challenges. You create a realistic roadmap that transforms abstract desires into tangible goals by aligning strategies with your traits and setting clear, achievable objectives. These objectives should stretch you just enough to encourage growth without overwhelming you, becoming milestones that build confidence and momentum. Begin by identifying and breaking specific attachment-related goals into manageable steps with realistic timelines. For instance, if improving communication is your goal, practice active listening daily. This systematic approach ensures steady progress while maintaining focus and accountability.

Setting Personal Growth Goals

For those with avoidant attachment patterns, goal setting often gravitates toward achievement rather than connection. We might feel more comfortable setting career advancement or skill development goals than emotional vulnerability. While these achievement-oriented goals have value, healing avoidant attachment requires us to expand our focus to include relationship-oriented goals.

Consider Rachelle's experience as a successful attorney. She excelled at setting and achieving professional goals. However, she initially resisted when her therapist suggested setting goals around the emotional connection. "I could plan a complex litigation strategy, but planning to be more vulnerable felt foreign and frightening." This resistance reflects how our attachment patterns can influence our personal development approach. Together, they developed what they called "balanced growth goals," pairing each achievement goal with a connection goal:

- **Achievement Goal #1**: Complete advanced certification in legal mediation
- **Connection Goal #1**: Share one personal feeling during each weekly team meeting
- **Achievement Goal #2**: Improve time management efficiency
- **Connection Goal #2**: Spend ten minutes in unstructured conversation with her partner daily

When creating these types of goals, you can use the SMART (specific, measurable, achievable, relevant, time-bound) framework while acknowledging attachment activation:

1. **Specific**: Instead of "be more open," try "share one vulnerability with my closest friend each week."
2. **Measurable**: Track the action and your attachment response (e.g., Did you feel the urge to withdraw?).
3. **Achievable**: Start small to manage attachment anxiety.
4. **Relevant**: Connect goals to your desire for secure attachment.
5. **Time-bound**: Set realistic timeframes that account for attachment challenges.

Just as standing at the edge of a vast field can feel overwhelming without a clear path, setting personal growth goals provides direction and focus for your healing journey. These goals serve as guideposts, helping you channel your efforts toward meaningful change while respecting your attachment-based needs for safety and control.

Tracking and evaluating your progress is vital in achieving personal growth goals. Keeping a personal growth journal can be an invaluable tool in this process. Dedicate weekly time to reflect on your progress, noting successes and challenges. This practice allows you to celebrate achievements and identify areas for improvement. Regularly reviewing your goals ensures they remain aligned with your evolving priorities, enabling you to adjust them as needed. Perhaps you realize that a goal is irrelevant or that you have accomplished more than anticipated. By revisiting your goals, you can make informed decisions about how to proceed, ensuring your growth efforts remain focused and effective.

Celebrating milestones and achievements is essential to maintaining motivation and reinforcing progress. Create a rewards system to acknowledge your accomplishments, no matter how small. When you reach a milestone, treat yourself to a special meal or a relaxing day off. These rewards serve as positive reinforcements, encouraging continued effort and dedication. Reflecting on growth and lessons learned is equally essential. Consider what you have gained from the process regarding achievements and insights. This reflection helps solidify your progress, embedding the changes you have made into your life. It also provides an opportunity to learn from setbacks, equipping you with the knowledge to navigate future challenges. As you celebrate your growth, remember that each step takes you closer to realizing your full potential.

Flexibility is crucial in planning, as life rarely unfolds exactly as expected. Your plan should be a living document, open to adjustments based on feedback and progress. Embrace new insights as they arise, allowing them to inform your path forward. This adaptability prevents stagnation, ensuring that your plan remains relevant and practical. As you progress, you might discover areas that require more attention or find that specific steps need reevaluation. By remaining open to evolution, you cultivate resilience and foster continuous growth. This willingness to adapt enhances your plan and strengthens your capacity to navigate life's uncertainties gracefully and confidently.

Monitoring and evaluating your plan is an ongoing process that keeps you aligned with your goals. Progress journals or digital apps can be invaluable tools for tracking your journey. Regularly record your achievements, setbacks, and reflections to gain insights into your progress. These records help you identify patterns, celebrate successes, and swiftly address challenges. Set aside time periodically to assess and revise your strategy, ensuring it evolves with your growth. During these reviews, ask yourself what has worked well and needs adjustment. This reflective practice reinforces accountability and keeps your efforts focused and intentional. It also provides a sense of accomplishment, reminding you how far you have come.

USE HEALTHY ATTACHMENT EXERCISES DAILY

Incorporating practical exercises into your daily routine can significantly reinforce your work on attachment, making the abstract tangible and the theoretical-practical. Imagine the satisfaction of having simple tools at your disposal, ready to be used whenever emotional regulation or relational skills need a boost. Here, we will briefly review valuable attachment exercises to practice daily.

Among these tools we have stressed are mindfulness practices designed to help you manage emotions effectively. One such practice is mindful breathing, where you focus on the rhythm of your breath to find calmness amid chaos. This exercise can be done anywhere, offering a refuge from the stress and an opportunity to center yourself. Another valuable exercise is a body scan meditation, which requires checking different areas of your body to notice where you are. Holding stress and consciously releasing it are simple mindfulness practices that are incredibly effective in helping you stay grounded.

As explored earlier in the book, communication exercises are also pivotal in enhancing your relational skills. Consider the practice of active listening, which involves genuinely paying attention to what others are saying without planning your response. This exercise can transform conversations, allowing for deeper understanding and connection. Another exercise is using "I" statements, which help you express feelings without blaming others. For instance, instead of saying, "You never listen to me," you might say, "I feel unheard when my thoughts are not acknowledged." These exercises encourage openness and honesty, fostering meaningful dialogues and reducing misunderstandings.

Variety is the spice of life, and the same applies to the exercises you choose to integrate into your routine. For those looking to build trust and openness, consider exercises like sharing daily reflections with a partner, trusted family member, or friend. This technique requires dedicating a specific period daily to share one thing you appreciate about each other, reinforcing positivity and connection. To foster emotional intimacy, you might engage in an activity called "emotional check-ins," where you regularly discuss your emotional state with others, identifying feelings and exploring their origins. These exercises cater to different needs and help strengthen the bonds of trust and intimacy in your relationships.

Finding Consistency Through Structure and Adaptation

Imagine you are on a scenic hike, winding through a lush, ever-changing landscape. The path is unclear, but each step brings you closer to your destination. This hike is akin to the journey of sustaining attachment transformation. It is one thing to start this process, but maintaining it requires dedication and a strategy to integrate new patterns into your everyday life. Consistency becomes your steady companion, providing stability needed to reinforce new habits and avoid slipping back into old patterns. Consistency sets the stage for long-term success by anchoring your progress in reliable, repeatable actions. It forms the foundation upon which transformation can thrive, ensuring that each new behavior becomes a natural part of your daily existence.

Consistency is not merely about repetition; it is about creating a sense of stability and predictability in your life. As emphasized in behavior support strategies, consistency aids in setting clear expectations and enhances self-esteem by providing a dependable framework for growth. By reinforcing new habits regularly, you build a strong foundation that supports emotional regulation and resilience. This reliability helps prevent complacency, which can be a silent adversary on your path to change. It is easy to fall back into comfortable but unproductive habits without consistent reinforcement. Consider consistency as the gentle yet persistent waves shaping the shore, gradually transforming the landscape over a lifetime. It is through this steady application that true, lasting transformation occurs.

Consider creating a structure that naturally incorporates attachment exercises to embed transformation into your daily routine. This might involve starting your day with a brief mindfulness practice, such as a five-minute meditation, or ending it with reflective journaling, where you write down three things you are grateful for. These small, deliberate actions can solidify new patterns and make them second nature. Utilizing technology can also be advantageous; apps and reminders can serve as gentle nudges, keeping you on track. For instance, setting reminders to practice gratitude or checking in with your emotions can help integrate these practices into your daily rhythm. The key is to weave these activities seamlessly into your life so they become as habitual as brushing your teeth. These practices will reinforce your progress and enrich your overall well-being as days pass.

Consistency is crucial for lasting change, so weaving these exercises into your daily life is essential. Setting reminders can help ensure that these practices become part of your routine. Whether it is a gentle nudge on your phone reminding you to take a mindful breath or an alarm signaling a time for an emotional check-in, these reminders keep you accountable. Integrate these exercises into existing routines, like practicing mindful breathing during your morning coffee or using "I" statements in your evening conversations. These small, consistent actions add up as days pass, gradually transforming your relational landscape.

Adapting exercises to suit your unique context is also key to making them effective. You should tailor these practices to fit your individual or relationship needs. For example, consider doing mindfulness exercises during lunch breaks if you find morning routines challenging. Adjust the intensity or frequency based on your progress and comfort level. If daily emotional check-ins feel overwhelming, start once a week. You can start with meetings and increase the frequency as you gain confidence. Remember, these exercises are meant to support your growth, so feel free to modify them to serve you best.

BUILDING A SUPPORTIVE COMMUNITY

Visualize standing on the edge of a vast ocean, waves crashing against the shore. While this scene might evoke feelings of solitude, the vastness becomes less daunting when surrounded by a supportive community. This network provides essential emotional support, diverse perspectives, and shared experiences that enrich your understanding of yourself and your relationships. Within this community, you find people who empathize with your challenges and celebrate your triumphs, offering insights you might not have considered alone.

Begin building this network by identifying supportive individuals in your life and considering both in-person and virtual connections through support groups or online forums. These varied channels create a comprehensive support system that adapts to your comfort level and schedule while consistently encouraging your attachment work. Also, joining online forums or social media groups focused on attachment work can expand your network beyond geographical boundaries. These platforms connect you with a worldwide community of individuals on similar paths, offering diverse insights and experiences. The digital space allows for flexible participation, enabling you to engage according to your schedule and comfort level.

Diversity and inclusivity within your support network are crucial for enriched learning and growth. Welcoming members from different backgrounds and experiences broaden the range of perspectives and insights available to the group. Diverse voices contribute to a richer tapestry of understanding, offering unique viewpoints that challenge assumptions and expand horizons. Celebrating this diversity means valuing each person's contribution and recognizing the strength that comes from many experiences. It creates an inclusive environment where all members feel seen, heard, and respected. This inclusivity fosters an atmosphere of openness and trust, where people can express themselves authentically without fear of judgment. In such a community, learning becomes a shared journey where each member benefits from the collective wisdom and support of the group.

One of the essential benefits of a supportive community is the mutual accountability it fosters. Accountability partners within your network can help maintain progress and motivation by setting shared goals and regular check-ins. These partners serve as cheerleaders and challengers, supporting your achievements while encouraging you to push beyond your comfort zone. Collaborative problem-solving within the community can lead to innovative solutions and more profound understanding as different perspectives are shared and considered. Peer feedback offers fresh insights into your attachment work, highlighting areas for growth and celebration. This mutual support and accountability environment creates a dynamic where progress is celebrated, and setbacks are viewed as opportunities for learning and development.

Sustaining Growth Through Support Systems

Adequate support systems are essential for long-term success in transforming attachment patterns. These support structures include professional guidance when needed, community resources, and peer support networks. They provide the foundation necessary for maintaining positive changes over time:

1. **Monitoring Progress**: Regularly assessing attachment patterns and relationship dynamics helps maintain positive changes. This involves staying attuned to family interactions, addressing challenges, and celebrating progress. Families can strengthen attachment bonds through consistent monitoring and adjustment and create lasting positive change.

2. **Building Resilience**: The ultimate goal in transforming attachment patterns is building resilience that can weather life's challenges. This involves developing adaptive coping mechanisms, maintaining healthy boundaries, and fostering open communication channels. As families develop these skills, they create a legacy of secure attachment that can benefit future generations.

Support and guidance from others can be invaluable in maintaining your transformation. Engaging with therapists, mentors, or peer groups provides a network of accountability and encouragement. Therapists can offer professional insights and strategies tailored to your unique needs, mentors can provide guidance based on their own experiences, and peer groups can offer shared experiences and mutual support. Scheduled periodic check-ins with a therapist or coach can guide you through challenges and strengthen your commitment to change. These professionals provide insights and strategies tailored to your unique needs, enhancing your capacity for growth.

Additionally, joining support networks or groups can create a sense of community where shared experiences and mutual support foster resilience. Within these communities, you can share your challenges and triumphs, learn from others' experiences, and receive encouragement and advice. These connections can inspire and motivate you, offering fresh perspectives and collective wisdom. They remind you that you are not alone and can achieve remarkable transformation together. This sense of community can make you feel understood and supported, strengthening your resolve to continue your personal growth and relationship improvement journey.

As this chapter draws to a close, consider the power of having a personalized attachment change plan. By tailoring your approach, you harness your strengths, address your challenges, and set a course for meaningful transformation. These structured steps pave the way for secure, fulfilling relationships, building a future where connection and growth thrive. With this plan in hand, you are equipped to embark on a journey of self-discovery and relational enrichment. Embrace the possibilities, and be confident in creating lasting change and meaningful connections.

CHAPTER 12
LEGACY AND LONG-TERM GROWTH

THIS FINAL CHAPTER WILL EXPLORE HOW TO BUILD SECURE AND meaningful relationships by creating a clear vision for the future. By identifying our core values and setting specific goals, we can navigate our journeys together with intention and purpose. We will discuss the importance of aligning our daily actions with this vision, fostering mutual support, and maintaining a positive mindset. Embracing lifelong learning and collaboration will empower us to strengthen our bonds and overcome challenges, ultimately guiding us toward fulfilling and resilient relationships.

CREATING YOUR VISION FOR SECURE RELATIONSHIPS

Envisioning your future in relationships is like charting a course for an adventurous trip. It is about setting a clear direction that aligns with your deepest values and aspirations, giving you a sense of purpose and focus. Defining the core values that you hold dear is the first step in crafting this vision. These values may include honesty, loyalty, or empathy—principles that guide your interactions and decisions. Reflect on what is essential to you in a relationship, and let these values shape your vision. They act as a compass, steering you toward relationships that reflect these ideals. Alongside these values, setting long-term relational goals helps lay the groundwork for a fulfilling future. These goals involve building a family, traveling together, or cultivating a shared passion. They are the milestones that mark your journey, providing motivation and excitement as you move forward.

Everyday actions are the building blocks of your long-term vision. It is vital to align these actions with the future you aspire to create. Begin by regularly revisiting and refining your vision statement. This process ensures that your goals remain relevant and inspiring as you grow and change. It is an opportunity to reflect on what is working and what might need adjustment. Think of your vision statement as a living document that evolves with you. Aligning daily choices with this vision involves making intentional decisions that support your goals. Whether spending quality time with your partner, family members, or friends, prioritizing communication, or investing in shared experiences, each choice contributes to realizing your vision. Though seemingly small, these actions accumulate over months and years, bringing your long-term goals within reach. They keep you grounded and focused, ensuring your daily life reflects your aspirations. This alignment with your long-term vision gives your daily actions a sense of purpose and commitment, bringing your goals within reach.

Mutual support is the cornerstone of achieving any long-term vision. It requires collaboration and shared effort, where both people are invested in the journey. Creating a partnership agreement can be a powerful tool in this endeavor. This agreement outlines shared objectives and commitments, such as regular date nights, open communication, or mutual respect, ensuring that both parties are aligned in pursuing the vision. It reminds you of the goals you have set together, fostering accountability and mutual support. Regular vision-alignment discussions further reinforce this collaboration. These conversations provide open dialogue where partners can express their hopes, concerns, and ideas. They help maintain clarity and focus, ensuring that both individuals are on the same page. This mutual support creates a sense of unity, where challenges are faced, and successes are shared. It strengthens the bond, making the relationship more resilient and fulfilling.

Maintaining hope and optimism is crucial for staying motivated and inspired. It is cultivating a positive outlook, even in the face of challenges. Practicing gratitude and appreciation in your relationships is a powerful tool to develop this mindset. Consistently recognizing the positive qualities of your relationship and expressing gratitude for the other person's presence reinforces your bond. It shifts the focus from what is lacking to what is abundant, creating an atmosphere of positivity and appreciation. This focus on gratitude helps you maintain a positive and appreciative mindset, even in the face of challenges, keeping your vision alive and your commitment strong.

Future Growth and Relationship Empowerment

In the ever-evolving landscape of personal growth and relationships, the mindset of lifelong learning becomes crucial. Imagine your journey as a tapestry, with each new experience adding a vibrant thread. Viewing challenges not as barriers but as chances for expansion allows you to weave a rich and diverse pattern. Every experience, whether a success or a setback, contributes to personal and relational development. This mindset encourages seeking new learning opportunities, such as workshops or classes, which can introduce fresh perspectives and skills. These experiences equip you with tools to navigate the complexities of relationships, enhancing personal satisfaction and relational harmony. By viewing growth as a continuous process, you remain open to change and learning, which can lead to profound transformations in how you connect with yourself and others.

Empowering relationships involves nurturing both individual and collective growth. It means creating a relationship where both partners feel empowered to be their best selves and support each other's growth. One practical approach is joint goal setting with your partner or family members. This process involves agreeing on common personal development objectives, relationship milestones, or shared dreams. By aligning your goals, you create a sense of partnership and shared purpose that strengthens your bond. Collaborative decision-making further empowers your relationship, creating a space where both perspectives are acknowledged and valued. This approach builds trust and mutual respect as decisions reflect both people's collective wisdom and desires. Regularly practicing these skills develops a cooperative dynamic where challenges are met with united effort and successes are celebrated. This empowerment enriches your relationship, allowing it to flourish as people grow individually and together.

Adaptability stands as a cornerstone in navigating the inevitable changes that life presents. The ability to remain flexible in the face of shifting dynamics is invaluable. It enables you to embrace change gracefully, turning potential disruptions into opportunities for growth. This adaptability involves developing strategies to manage unexpected challenges, such as changes in circumstances or evolving needs within the relationship. By cultivating resilience, you equip yourself to respond to these changes confidently and creatively. This mindset supports maintaining balance and harmony, even when faced with uncertainty. Embracing flexibility in relationship dynamics also means being open to adjusting roles and responsibilities as needed, reflecting the fluid nature of healthy partnerships. This adaptability fosters a sense of security and stability, as both people trust in their ability to navigate life's twists and turns together. It reassures you that you can handle whatever life throws your way, strengthening your sense of security and stability in your relationships.

Creating a culture of growth within your relationship involves fostering an environment where mutual empowerment and development are priorities. Celebrating shared successes and progress reinforces the positive aspects of your relationship, creating a strong foundation for future growth. These celebrations, whether big or small, recognize the efforts and achievements of both people, building a sense of accomplishment and motivation.

Encouraging open dialogue about personal growth aspirations further strengthens your connection, allowing each person to express their dreams and goals. This openness fosters understanding and support, creating a safe space where both people feel valued and encouraged to pursue their aspirations. This culture of growth transforms your relationship into a supportive ecosystem where each partner's growth is celebrated and nurtured. The synergy created by this mutual support enhances the overall quality of the relationship, enriching both individual lives and the shared journey.

As you journey through this chapter, remember that creating a long-term vision for your relationships is dynamic. It is about dreaming boldly, planning strategically, and acting consistently. It demands bravery and dedication, yet the rewards are profound. A clear vision guides your actions and enriches your relationships, making them more meaningful and satisfying. As you look forward to the next chapter, know that this vision is a foundation for building stronger, more secure connections. Let it inspire you and lead you to the fulfilling relational life you seek.

BREAKING THE CYCLE OF ATTACHMENT DISSATISFACTION

Reflect on your relationships, both past and present. You may notice a familiar pattern, a cycle of dissatisfaction that seems to replay with each new partner. These recurring patterns often stem from attachment styles established early in life, repeating themselves in a loop that feels inescapable. Perhaps you find yourself constantly seeking reassurance yet never feeling genuinely secure. Or maybe you maintain emotional distance, fearing the vulnerability that closeness demands. The emotional toll of this cycle can be exhausting, leaving you feeling unfulfilled and disconnected. Recognizing these patterns not as a fault but as a starting point for change is essential. Understanding them allows you to see your relationships with fresh eyes, acknowledging how they have impacted your happiness and well-being.

The cycle of avoidant attachment often manifests as a predictable pattern. As relationships deepen, we feel an increasing urge to withdraw, creating an emotional distance that confirms our belief that the connection is threatening. Dr. Elena Martinez's research identifies key phases in this cycle:

1. **Initial Engagement**: We may appear open and connected while maintaining internal distance.
2. **Activation Point**: As emotional intimacy increases, our attachment system activates.
3. **Withdrawal Phase**: We create distance through work, hobbies, or emotional shutdown.
4. **Confirmation Phase**: The resulting relationship strain reinforces our avoidant patterns.

Consider Tim's experience breaking this cycle: "I used to pride myself on being 'low maintenance' in relationships, not needing much contact or emotional connection. When my partner expressed hurt about my emotional distance, I'd withdraw further, seeing their need for connection as proof that closeness was overwhelming." Through therapy, Tim learned to recognize his withdrawal as a protective response rather than a personality trait.

To disrupt these patterns, we can implement what Dr. Sarah Martinez calls "conscious connection practices":

1. **Withdrawal Recognition**:

- Track situations that trigger your urge to withdraw.
- Notice physical sensations that precede emotional disconnection.
- Identify thought patterns that justify distance.

2. **Active Engagement Strategies**:

- When noticing withdrawal urges, practice staying present for just five minutes longer.
- Share your withdrawal process with trusted others: "I'm feeling the urge to pull away right now."
- Create structured connection points that feel manageable.

Dr. Sarah Chen's work with avoidant clients emphasizes the importance of "titrated exposure" to emotional connection. "Think of it like building physical endurance," she explains. "You wouldn't run a marathon without training. Similarly, we build emotional connection capacity gradually."

Understanding and Breaking Intergenerational Patterns

In previous chapters, we delved deeply into understanding avoidant attachment and the effects of childhood wounds, personal triggers, and the development of emotional intimacy. As we move forward, we must explore how to break intergenerational patterns that perpetuate avoidant attachment styles, creating a ripple effect across relationships and families.

At the heart of attachment work lies the crucial task of understanding how family history shapes our present relationships. Families carry forward genetic traits and emotional patterns that influence how we connect with others. These patterns often stretch back multiple generations, creating intricate webs of behavioral and emotional responses that become deeply embedded in family dynamics. Examining these historical threads, we can understand why certain attachment styles persist and how they influence current relationships.

1. **Cultural and Environmental Factors**: Family attachment patterns do not exist independently but are profoundly shaped by cultural, social, and historical contexts. Significant events like wars, economic hardships, or migrations can dramatically shape how families relate to one another across generations. These external factors often imprint on family systems, affecting everything from parenting styles to emotional expression. Understanding these contextual elements helps explain why specific patterns emerged and persisted within family lines.

2. **Identifying Pattern Recognition**: Recognizing attachment patterns requires careful observation and reflection. Family members often unconsciously replicate relationship dynamics experienced in childhood, perpetuating cycles that may span generations. These

patterns manifest in daily interactions, emotional responses, and approaches to conflict resolution. By developing awareness of these recurring themes, individuals can identify which patterns serve them well and which ones may need transformation.

Breaking the Cycle of Trauma: Understanding Trauma's Ripple Effect

Generational trauma operates like invisible threads connecting past experiences to present behaviors. This form of inherited trauma can manifest in various ways, from explicit fears and anxieties to subtle patterns of emotional withdrawal or overprotection. The impact of unresolved trauma often appears in how family members relate to one another, make decisions, and handle stress. Recognizing these patterns is essential for beginning the healing process.

1. **The Path to Healing**: Healing from generational trauma requires both individual and collective work within family systems. This journey involves acknowledging past wounds while developing new coping mechanisms and relationship patterns. Professional support often plays an essential role in this process, offering tools and perspectives to help family members process their experiences and develop healthier ways of relating to one another.

2. **Creating New Patterns**: Transforming trauma patterns begins with conscious awareness and intentional action. This includes developing new communication styles,

establishing healthy boundaries, and learning to respond rather than react to emotional triggers. Through consistent practice and support, families can gradually replace harmful patterns with nurturing ones that promote healing and growth.

CREATING YOUR SECURE ATTACHMENT LEGACY

Creating a secure attachment legacy starts with understanding the essential elements contributing to emotional safety and trust. These include consistent emotional availability, reliable responses to needs, and the ability to repair relationship ruptures. These fundamental components form the building blocks for developing more substantial, resilient family bonds:

1. **Implementation Strategies**: Transforming attachment patterns requires practical strategies that can be implemented in daily life. This includes establishing regular family connection times, developing emotional coaching skills, and creating environments that support open communication. Success often comes through small, consistent actions rather than dramatic changes.

2. **Future-Focused Development**: Supporting secure attachment in future generations involves ongoing education and skill development. Parents and caregivers benefit from understanding attachment theory and its practical applications. This knowledge, combined with emotional regulation techniques and communication skills, helps create an environment where secure attachment can flourish.

Creating a secure attachment legacy involves fostering deep, meaningful relationships that cultivate trust, understanding, and emotional safety. At the core of this process is recognizing how our attachment styles shape interactions and connections with others. Here are some key steps toward establishing a legacy of secure attachments:

1. **Understanding Attachment Styles**: Begin by exploring your attachment style—secure, anxious, avoidant, or disorganized. Understanding your patterns can help you recognize how they influence your relationships and provide insight into how to nurture healthier connections.

2. **Modeling Secure Attachments**: Be intentional about demonstrating trustworthy and reliable behaviors. Show consistency in your words and actions; this builds a foundation of security for those around you. Share your feelings openly and encourage others to do the same, creating a safe emotional space.

3. **Practicing Active Listening**: Make it a habit to listen to others, genuinely validating their feelings and perspectives. This strengthens bonds and reinforces feelings of safety and belonging, essential elements of secure attachments.

4. **Encouraging Vulnerability**: Creating an environment where vulnerability is welcomed is vital. Share your experiences and struggles, showing that expressing emotions and seeking support is okay. This reciprocal openness fosters a deeper connection.

5. **Conflict Resolution**: Embrace healthy conflict resolution techniques. When disagreements arise, approach

discussions with empathy and a willingness to understand the other person's point of view, focusing on solutions rather than blame.

6. **Investing in Relationships**: Dedicate time and energy to nurture your relationships, whether with family, friends, or partners. Regular check-ins and shared experiences can strengthen the ties and foster a sense of community and belonging.

7. **Teaching Future Generations**: Be mindful of the legacy you leave behind. Share the principles of secure attachment with the younger generations in your life. Teach them about empathy, communication, and the importance of emotional health, empowering them to build secure connections.

By consciously implementing these practices, we can create a secure attachment legacy that enriches our lives and influences those around us. We will contribute to a culture of connection, resilience, and emotional well-being that resonates for generations.

CONCLUSION

As we conclude, take a moment to reflect on your journey. This book has been your companion in exploring the nuances of avoidant attachment, guiding you toward the possibility of secure and meaningful connections. We have delved into understanding dismissive patterns, recognizing emotional triggers, and building trust in relationships. Together, we have uncovered strategies for effective communication, emotional intimacy, and the transformative power of vulnerability. Each chapter has been a step toward dismantling the barriers that hinder deep, fulfilling relationships.

The key takeaways from this journey emphasize the importance of self-awareness and emotional literacy. Understanding your attachment style is a cornerstone of transformation. It allows you to identify and address the patterns that might have kept you distant from your desired connections. Trust-building, as we have discussed, is the foundation upon which secure relationships are built. It is about honesty, transparency, and mutual dedication to cultivating your connection with others. Emotional intimacy and effective communication are the threads that weave trust into the fabric of your relationships, fostering a deeper understanding and connection.

Reflect on your personal growth and transformation. Take a moment to recognize the significant changes in how you perceive yourself and interact with others. Every step you have taken, no matter how small, has contributed to a broader shift in how you relate to the world and those around you. Celebrate your progress and the courage it took to confront past patterns and embrace new ways of being. Your journey is a testament to your resilience and the strength within you to change and grow. You should be immensely proud of how far you have come.

Consistency and practice are vital as you continue on this path. The habits and behaviors you have developed need nurturing to become a natural part of your life. Regular reflection will keep you grounded and aware of your progress. Continuous practice will reinforce the new patterns that lead to secure attachment. Think of these practices as the gentle rain that nourishes a garden; they ensure that your growth is sustained and your relationships flourish.

Remember, the journey does not end here. Learning and self-discovery are ongoing processes essential for deepening your understanding and skills. Keep seeking out, reading, or exploring related topics that interest you. This continued exploration will enrich your journey, offering new perspectives and tools to enhance your relationships. Stay curious and open to the lessons life presents, and know that each discovery adds to the richness of your relational tapestry. Your journey is not a destination but a continuous evolution.

As you look to the future, hold on to hope and optimism. Envision a life filled with secure, fulfilling relationships. This vision is not just a dream; it is within your reach and built on the foundation of your work. The insights and strategies from this book are your guide, offering direction and support as you move forward. Allow hope to light your path, and trust in your ability to create the connections you desire.

I invite you to actively apply what you have learned daily. Share your journey and experiences with others, fostering a growth and support community. Your story can inspire others, creating a ripple effect of positive change. Together, we can build a network of people committed to understanding and overcoming avoidant attachment, creating a world where secure relationships are the norm.

Thank you for taking this transformative journey with me. Your willingness to explore and change is a testament to your courage and determination. Remember, you are not alone. Change is not only possible—it is happening within you. I offer ongoing encouragement and support as you grow and build the secure, meaningful relationships you deserve. Your journey is filled with potential for positive change, and I am confident in your ability to realize it.

The overarching goal of this book was to help you overcome avoidant attachment and build loving, secure relationships. Understanding and addressing dismissive patterns has transformative potential. You have taken significant steps toward a more connected and fulfilling life by embracing these insights. As you continue, know you have the tools and the strength to create the relationships you envision. You are capable of building the secure attachments you deserve. Embrace this journey with confidence and compassion, and let it guide you to the secure attachments you deserve.

APPENDIX: DIGITAL COMMUNICATION AND AVOIDANT ATTACHMENT

In today's interconnected world, digital communication offers opportunities and challenges for those with avoidant attachment patterns. While smartphones, social media, and instant messaging can serve as convenient shields against emotional intimacy, they also present unique opportunities for practicing vulnerability in measured, controlled ways. For individuals with avoidant attachment, these digital tools can become either a fortress reinforcing emotional distance or a bridge toward secure connection. This section explores how to recognize and transform avoidant digital patterns into opportunities for genuine connection while respecting your need for emotional safety.

MODERN TECHNOLOGY'S IMPACT ON ATTACHMENT DYNAMICS

For those with avoidant attachment, digital communication can unconsciously become a perfect tool for maintaining emotional distance. The ability to control response timing, craft careful messages, and avoid face-to-face vulnerability often reinforces avoidant patterns. While texting, instant messaging, and social media appear to facilitate connection, they can enable sophisticated forms of emotional withdrawal. Understanding how you might use these tools to maintain comfortable distance is the first step toward transforming digital habits from barriers into bridges for authentic connection.

Digital Activation Signals and Response Patterns

Understanding your digital attachment triggers is not just crucial —it is empowering. By recognizing these triggers, you gain the power to manage your online relationships effectively. Common activation signals in digital communication often manifest as emotional responses to reading receipts without responses or experiencing anxiety when encountering delayed responses to emotionally vulnerable messages. Many find themselves triggered by noticeable changes in communication patterns, whether in frequency, tone, or emojis. The visibility of social media activity without direct communication can also activate attachment concerns, as can seeing someone's online status during periods of non-response. These digital triggers often mirror in-person attachment activations but can feel more intense due to the immediate visibility of digital behavior. Developing awareness of your specific digital triggers allows for more conscious response choices rather than reactive behaviors.

TEXT COMMUNICATION AND EMOTIONAL SECURITY

Common digital avoidant behaviors include using work emails to avoid personal messages, maintaining multiple chat conversations to disperse emotional intensity, and relying heavily on GIFs or emojis to deflect from genuine emotional expression. You might also prefer text-based communication over calls, use lengthy response delays to regulate emotions or become overwhelmed when messages require emotional vulnerability. Recognizing these patterns allows you to consciously choose different responses that gradually build comfort with digital intimacy.

Digital messaging presents unique challenges for attachment dynamics. The lack of nonverbal signals, vocal tone, and physical presence can amplify attachment anxieties and avoidant tendencies. Message timing, length, and frequency often become proxy indicators for relationship security, leading to potential misinterpretations and emotional distress. However, when used mindfully, text communication can also be a tool for maintaining connection and practicing secure attachment behaviors through consistent, clear communication patterns.

Practical Strategies for Secure Digital Communication

Implementing structured approaches to digital communication can help manage attachment anxiety and build security:

1. **Time-boxing**: This is an effective strategy where you set aside specific periods for checking and responding to

messages rather than allowing anxiety to drive constant checking.

2. **Develop Thoughtful Response Templates**. These can help you navigate moments when you feel triggered but want to maintain a connection.

3. **Metacommunication**: This practice of openly discussing your digital communication style and needs proves invaluable. For instance, you might explain to a partner that you need processing time before responding to emotional messages, suggesting a specific emoji as a signal that you have read their message and will respond thoughtfully later.

Common avoidant patterns in digital communication often emerge in subtle ways. These might manifest as consistently using work to justify delayed responses or maintaining predominantly surface-level, fact-based conversations. Some individuals rely heavily on humor or deflection when conversations turn emotional, while others might withdraw entirely during periods of emotional intensity. Another typical pattern involves preferring group chats to one-on-one communication, as this creates natural emotional distance through the presence of others.

SOCIAL MEDIA'S ROLE IN MODERN RELATIONSHIPS

For those with avoidant attachment, social media can substitute for genuine intimacy, offering the illusion of connection without the vulnerability of direct interaction. The ability to maintain surface-level engagement through likes and brief comments while avoiding deeper conversations often appeals to avoidant tendencies. However, this same technology can be deliberately used to practice small acts of vulnerability, such as sharing personal thoughts or expressing appreciation for others in manageable doses.

Maintaining Digital Connection Without Dependency

Virtual relationship maintenance requires a delicate balance between staying connected and avoiding digital dependency. Regular video calls, thoughtful text messages, and shared online experiences can help maintain emotional bonds when physical presence is impossible. These digital tools are crucial in enhancing and maintaining relationships, providing reassurance and a sense of connection. However, developing strategies that complement rather than replace in-person interaction is vital. This includes establishing digital communication rituals that enhance security while respecting personal boundaries and authentic connection needs. It is important to remember that while digital tools can improve relationships, they should not replace the value of in-person interactions.

Online Resources and Virtual Support Systems

The digital age has expanded access to attachment-related support through online therapy platforms, relationship apps, and virtual support communities. These resources can provide valuable tools for understanding and improving attachment patterns, offering flexibility and accessibility that traditional support systems may lack. Online therapy sessions, in particular, can create safe spaces for exploring attachment issues while maintaining the comfort of familiar environments. However, integrating these digital resources effectively requires understanding their benefits and limitations within the broader context of attachment work.

Setting Digital Boundaries for Healthy Attachment

Establishing clear digital boundaries is essential for maintaining healthy attachment patterns in the modern age. This includes defining response expectations, managing online availability, and creating guidelines for social media engagement within relationships. Healthy digital boundaries help prevent technology from exacerbating attachment anxieties while supporting secure connections. These boundaries might include designated off-line times, agreements about public relationship sharing, and protocols for handling digital communication during conflicts. By setting and respecting these boundaries, you can create a digital environment that promotes security and respect in your relationships.

Digital Wellness and Attachment Growth

Developing digital wellness practices that foster secure attachment requires recognizing how technology shapes our relationship patterns and emotional security. This involves the mindful use of digital communication tools, regular evaluation of online interaction patterns, and adapting digital habits to support attachment objectives. By understanding the intersection of technology and attachment, individuals can utilize digital tools to enhance rather than disrupt relationship security.

Digital Connection Building Exercises

Fostering secure attachment through digital means requires intentional practice and structured approaches. Scheduled digital check-ins provide a foundation for a consistent connection. These regular interactions involve sharing meaningful aspects of your day, including successes and challenges while expressing appreciation for your relationship. This predictable structure helps build trust and security in digital communication.

Progressive digital vulnerability offers a pathway to deeper connection while respecting attachment-related fears. It is a strategy and a journey toward a more profound connection. Begin with lower-risk sharing methods, such as voice messages instead of texts, which convey more emotional nuance while maintaining some distance. Sharing photos of meaningful moments and utilizing video calls for important conversations can gradually increase intimate connection. As comfort grows, progress to real-time emotional sharing, composing digital love letters, and practicing spontaneous expressions of feelings. This journey of digital vulnerability can lead to a deeper, more meaningful connection.

Digital repair rituals are crucial for maintaining secure connections during inevitable miscommunications. Establishing clear protocols for managing digital misunderstandings helps prevent escalation and promotes repair. These include agreeing upon specific ways to signal when you need space, establishing requirements for shifting serious discussions to video calls and maintaining regular check-ins about satisfaction with digital communication patterns. These practices help build security while working toward more profound face-to-face vulnerability, remembering that digital tools should enhance rather than replace in-person connection.

INTEGRATION WITH OVERALL ATTACHMENT STRATEGY

The digital age has transformed how we experience and express attachment needs. Video calls, text messages, and social media have created new opportunities for connection while introducing novel challenges to attachment security. The instantaneous nature of digital communication can trigger attachment anxiety or avoidance in unprecedented ways.

"Digital boundaries" have become crucial in managing modern attachment challenges. This involves creating intentional practices around device use, online availability, and digital communication styles. For those with avoidant attachment, the challenge often lies in using digital tools to enhance rather than replace in-person vulnerability.

Digital communication patterns must be integrated thoughtfully into broader attachment strategies. This involves aligning online interaction styles with attachment goals, using digital tools to support rather than replace intimate connection, and maintaining awareness of how technology affects relationship dynamics. Success requires regular evaluation and adjustment of digital communication patterns to ensure they contribute positively to attachment security and relationship growth.

Consider Darla, who recognized her avoidant patterns in using digital communication. She read messages immediately but waited hours to respond, claiming work kept her busy. In group chats, she was quick with jokes and memes but would disappear when conversations turned personal. Through conscious effort, she began using digital tools differently: setting reminders to respond to individual messages within an hour, sharing one genuine feeling daily via text, and gradually increasing her comfort with video calls. While challenging, these small steps helped her transform digital communication from a shield into a bridge for authentic connection.

FURTHER READING

John Bowlby's Attachment Theory, https://www.simplypsychology.org/bowlby.html

Mary Ainsworth: Attachment Theory and the Strange Situation, https://www.attachmentproject.com/attachment-theory/mary-ainsworth/

A tangled start: The link between childhood maltreatment, psychopathology, and relationships in adulthood, https://www.sciencedirect.com/science/article/pii/S014521342100301X/

Disentangle the neural correlates of attachment style in healthy individuals, https://pmc.ncbi.nlm.nih.gov/articles/PMC6998975/

8 Attachment Style Questionnaires & Tests to Assess Clients, https://positivepsychology.com/attachment-style-tests/

Understanding Emotional Triggers and How To Handle Relationship Issues in Therapy, https://www.sunshinecitycounseling.com/blog/emotional-triggers-and-relationship-issues-in-therapy/

Mindfulness and Emotion Regulation, https://pmc.ncbi.nlm.nih.gov/articles/PMC5337506/

Dismissive Avoidant Attachment: Signs, Triggers, & More, https://www.talkspace.com/blog/dismissive-avoidant-attachment/

Cultivating Trust: 8 Essential Components for Relationship Success, https://extension.usu.edu/hru/blog/building-trust-in-relationships-guide-to-lasting-connection/

16 Exercises To Enhance Emotional Intimacy In Relationships, https://www.thewonders.com/post/16-exercises-to-enhance-emotional-intimacy-in-relationships/

Effective Communication Strategies for Couples, https://epiccounselingsolutions.com/effective-communication-strategies-for-couples-a-therapists-guide/

How Do You Fix Emotional Detachment in a Relationship? https://www.marriage.com/advice/relationship/emotional-detachment/

Conflict Resolution in Relationships & Couples: 5 Strategies, https://positivepsychology.com/conflict-resolution-relationships/

Active listening: Hear what people are really saying, https://www.mindtools.com/az4wxv7/active-listening/

Expectations in a Relationship: Reasonable vs Unrealistic, https://anchorlighttherapy.com/expectations-in-a-relationship-a-reality-check/

How to Deal With Perfectionism in Relationships, https://www.verywellmind.com/dealing-with-perfectionism-in-a-relationship-5226092/

Secure Attachment: Signs, Benefits, Plus How to Develop It, https://www.verywellmind.com/secure-attachment-signs-benefits-and-how-to-cultivate-it-8628802/

Contributions of Attachment Theory and Research: A Framework for Future Research, Translation, and Policy, https://pmc.ncbi.nlm.nih.gov/articles/PMC4085672/

14 Proven Ways To Build Emotional Intimacy: The Ultimate Guide In 2024, https://practicalintimacy.com/how-to-build-emotional-intimacy-relationship/

The Importance of Self Awareness in Relationships, https://perthcounsellingandpsychotherapy.com.au/the-importance-of-self-awareness-in-relationships/

The Invisible Thread: Attachment Styles and the Therapeutic Journey in Daily Life, https://www.awakenedpathcounseling.com/attachment-styles/

Therapy for Avoidant Attachment Style, https://michaelhilgerslpc.com/avoidant-attachment-style-therapy/

Integrating Self-Help and Psychotherapy, https://academic.oup.com/book/1256/chapter/140191997/

How Attachment Styles Impact Relationships: Healing Relational Trauma, https://bayareacbtcenter.com/attachment-styles-relationships-relational-trauma/

Culture and Child Attachment Patterns: a Behavioral Systems Synthesis, https://pmc.ncbi.nlm.nih.gov/articles/PMC6901642/

Culture and Child Attachment Patterns: a Behavioral Systems Synthesis, https://pubmed.ncbi.nlm.nih.gov/31976462/

Navigating Cultural Differences in Personal Relationships: Embracing Diversity, https://medium.com/@phyllismoreau_51174/navigating-cultural-differences-in-personal-relationships-embracing-diversity-f562807c64b7/

Effective Attachment Therapy Techniques for Healing and Building Secure Relationships, https://upvio.com/nervous-system/effective-attachment-therapy-techniques-for-healing-and-building-secure-relationships/

Self-Compassion Practices, https://self-compassion.org/self-compassion-practices/

SMART goals, https://www.mindtools.com/a4wo118/smart-goals/

Understanding 4 Attachments Styles and How They Affect Adult Relationships, https://www.abundancetherapycenter.com/blog/understanding-4-attachment-styles-and-how-they-affect-adult-relationships/

Mindfulness exercises, https://www.mayoclinic.org/healthy-lifestyle/consumer-health/in-depth/mindfulness-exercises/art-20046356/

Mental Health Benefits of Journaling, https://www.webmd.com/mental-health/mental-health-benefits-of-journaling/

Mindfulness exercises, https://www.mayoclinic.org/healthy-lifestyle/consumer-health/in-depth/mindfulness-exercises/art-20046356/

Building Networks for Mental Health: A Guide, https://individualcareoftx.com/2024/04/13/building-networks-for-mental-health/

The Role of Consistency in Behavior Support Strategies, https://positivesolutions behaviorgroup.com/the-role-of-consistency-in-behavior-support-strategies/

The Power of Self Reflection: How to Foster Personal Growth, https://everydayspeech.com/blog-posts/general/the-power-of-self-reflection-how-to-foster-personal-growth/

The Role Of Adaptability in Relationships and Social Interactions, https://fastercapital.com/topics/the-role-of-adaptability-in-relationships-and-social-interactions.html

How to Create a Relationship Vision, https://www.lambertcouplestherapy.com/how-to-create-a-relationship-vision/

ELIZA BENNETT

FREEDOM FROM DISORGANIZED
Attachment

The Step-by-Step Guide to Building Secure
Relationships and Lasting Love

INTRODUCTION

In the quiet moments before dawn, Sarah lay awake, tangled in thoughts and sheets. Her mind raced with the fear that the man she loved might leave, though he lay sleeping beside her. She longed for closeness but felt a constant pull to push him away. This internal tug-of-war was exhausting. Sarah often wondered why love felt so complicated, why the fear of abandonment seemed to shadow every tender moment. Like Sarah, many find themselves caught in the web of disorganized attachment, a pattern rooted in early relationships that often leads to chaos in love and connection. This struggle, familiar to so many, inspired me to write this book.

My name is Eliza Bennett, and I have spent years navigating the complexities of attachment theory, both in my personal life and as a professional. I understand the struggles you might be facing because I have been there myself. My journey began with my own battles to appreciate my relationships, a struggle that I am sure many of you can relate to. This personal path, filled with ups and downs, has become a passion for helping others find clarity and healing. Through my research and writing, I have witnessed the profound impact of understanding and transforming attachment styles on people's lives. I am not just an author—I have walked a similar path and am here to guide you.

Disorganized attachment, a more common experience than one might realize, is a pattern marked by fear and a deep longing for connection. It often originates from inconsistent caregiving in childhood and can lead to challenges in adult relationships. The confusion and pain it causes make it a crucial issue to address, and it is essential to remember that you are not alone in this struggle. Many others, like you, are navigating this complex terrain.

This book offers a practical path forward. It is a step-by-step guide designed to help you shift from disorganized to secure attachment —a transformation that can significantly enhance your relationships and improve your emotional well-being. This book is for adults who recognize themselves in these patterns and seek change. It is for those tired of the cycle of fear and confusion who want practical, actionable solutions for real-life challenges. It is a guide that explains the problems those with disorganized attachment face and provides the tools to overcome it, empowering you to take control of your emotional well-being. With this book, you have the power to make a change.

Within these pages, practical guidance fosters a deeper understanding of your disorganized attachment style and equips you to build healthier connections. The chapters will cover, among other topics, emotional regulation, trust-building, and breaking toxic patterns, and each section is crafted to support your journey toward secure attachment. You will learn to navigate emotions, develop trust, and create lasting, fulfilling relationships. This book's unique blend of real-life examples, research-backed strategies, and practical exercises is designed to facilitate personal transformation. By integrating these tools into your life, you can experience genuine change.

I invite you to commit to this journey. Embrace the potential for positive change and the benefits of developing a secure attachment style. This book is about understanding disorganized attachment and creating a life filled with love and connection. Remember, you are not alone on this journey. I am here to guide you every step of the way, offering support and encouragement. As you turn these pages, remember that transformation is within reach. Let this book be your companion as you embark on a new chapter filled with hope and determination. We will journey to healing and secure, lasting love together.

CHAPTER 1
UNDERSTANDING DISORGANIZED ATTACHMENT

A YOUNG CHILD SITS QUIETLY IN A ROOM, TOYS SCATTERED AROUND them. Their eyes dart between the door and the clock, waiting for the moment their caregiver returns. But when the door finally opens, the child hesitates, unsure whether to run forward or stay still. This scene illustrates the complex world of attachment—the invisible bonds that shape our relationships from childhood through adulthood.

ATTACHMENT THEORY SIMPLIFIED

Attachment theory, a cornerstone of understanding human relationships, offers a lens through which we can view the dynamics of our connections. At its heart is the work of John Bowlby, who proposed that children are biologically predisposed to form attachments with caregivers. These bonds are crucial for survival. Bowlby's theory suggests that the quality of these early attachments influences how we relate to others throughout our lives. Mary Ainsworth, a key figure in this field, expanded on

Bowlby's work with her landmark "Strange Situation" experiment. A key part of this research observed how children responded to the presence and absence of their caregiver in a controlled environment, revealing distinct patterns of attachment behaviors. In this experiment, a child and their caregiver are placed in a room with toys. Then, the caregiver leaves the room, and a stranger enters. The child's behavior during these separations and reunions reveals distinct patterns of attachment behaviors. For instance, children with secure attachment styles could explore their environment when their caregiver was present, and they reacted positively when the caregiver returned after a brief absence.

This research revealed four distinct attachment styles: secure, anxious-resistant, avoidant, and disorganized. Each style reflects a unique approach to connecting with others, with disorganized attachment being the most complex and challenging pattern. These patterns shape how we approach relationships, handle conflicts, and experience intimacy. Understanding these patterns within ourselves can provide valuable insights. By understanding our attachment style, we can identify areas for growth and work toward healthier relationship dynamics.

Attachment theory is not just informative—it is transformative. It equips us with the knowledge to improve our relationships consciously. By applying attachment theory to our lives, we can strengthen our relationships. For instance, if you identify with an anxious attachment style, you might focus on building self-reliance and seeking reassurance from within rather than relying solely on external validation. This might mean trusting your partner's love and support in a romantic relationship without constantly seeking reassurance. In a work setting, it could mean taking on a challenging project without needing constant validation from your supervisor. If avoidant, you might practice vulnerability by sharing your feelings and thoughts with loved ones you trust. This could be as simple as expressing your feelings about a particular situation to a friend or family member. And for those with disorganized attachment, acknowledging the internal conflict and seeking consistency in relationships can be a step toward healing. This might mean seeking a supportive and consistent mentor in a work setting or maintaining a stable and supportive friendship. These practical applications of attachment theory empower us to make informed choices that foster security and connection, offering a hopeful path to healthier relationships.

Attachment theory also helps us understand our interactions with others and deepens our understanding of ourselves. It encourages us to reflect on our upbringing and how it continues to influence our adult relationships. More importantly, it provides a framework for change. By recognizing our patterns and tendencies, we can shift our attachment style toward one that promotes stability and fulfillment. This understanding is not about assigning blame or dwelling on the past but about using these insights to create a more secure and loving relational future. However, it is essential to note that attachment theory, like any psychological theory, has limitations. It primarily focuses on the relationship between a child and their primary caregiver, which may not fully capture the complexity of adult relationships. It also tends to be culturally biased, as it was developed based on research in Western cultures. But with this essential foundation, we can approach our relationships with empathy, understand the complex interplay of attachment styles, and be confident we have the tools to build the connections we genuinely desire.

THE NEUROSCIENCE BEHIND SECURE AND DISORGANIZED ATTACHMENT

The impact of attachment patterns is not just psychological—it is woven into the very structure of our brains. Modern neuroscience reveals how early relationships shape neural pathways, particularly in regions responsible for emotional regulation and social bonding. The amygdala, hippocampus, and prefrontal cortex—our brain's emotional command center—develop differently based on our attachment experiences.

In secure attachment, these brain regions work in harmony. The prefrontal cortex regulates the amygdala's threat response, producing balanced emotional reactions. However, in disorganized attachment, this neural dance becomes disrupted. Brain scans show heightened amygdala activity, suggesting an overactive threat-detection system. This explains why those with disorganized attachment might perceive danger in neutral situations or struggle to trust safe relationships.

The stress response system, regulated by cortisol and other hormones, also adapts to early experiences. Children in unpredictable environments develop hypersensitive stress responses that persist into adulthood. Their bodies maintain higher baseline cortisol levels, preparing for potential threats. This biological adaptation explains the hypervigilance and difficulty relaxing in relationships that many people with disorganized attachment experience.

The brain's plasticity offers hope, however. While early experiences create neural patterns, our brains remain capable of change throughout life. Consistent positive relationships and therapeutic interventions can reshape neural pathways. This process, known as neuroplasticity, means that new, healthier attachment patterns can be learned and integrated at the biological level. Understanding this biological basis helps validate the real challenges of disorganized attachment while affirming the possibility of change. This knowledge can inspire optimism and motivate us to work towards healthier relationships.

Recent research in interpersonal neurobiology shows how secure relationships can help regulate our nervous systems. Through "co-regulation," supportive relationships can help calm overactive stress responses and create new neural patterns for security. Co-regulation is how two individuals in a relationship, often a caregiver and a child, regulate each other's emotions. For example, a caregiver might soothe a child who is upset, which in turn helps the child learn to regulate their emotions. This biological perspective explains why healing often requires understanding our patterns and experiencing consistent, safe relationships that contradict our early programming.

THE ORIGINS OF DISORGANIZED ATTACHMENT

Imagine a world where a caregiver's embrace one day transforms into a cold shoulder the next. Such inconsistency leaves a child uncertain, unsure whether to seek comfort or brace for rejection. This unpredictability, often stemming from the caregiver's emotional struggles, teaches the child that relationships are inherently unstable. For instance, a child who witnesses domestic violence or experiences neglect may learn to associate closeness with danger. This creates a paradox where the child craves connection but fears the potential harm it might bring. The emotional unpredictability within the family environment reinforces this perception, making it difficult for the child to trust and feel secure.

The emotional state of the primary caregiver plays a pivotal role in shaping a child's attachment style. If a caregiver is preoccupied with their unresolved trauma, they may be unable to provide the consistent support a child needs. This can foster an environment where the child feels responsible for managing the caregiver's emotions, further complicating their understanding of healthy relational dynamics. The child may become hyper-aware of the caregiver's mood shifts, leading to heightened anxiety and a constant need to adapt to the caregiver's emotional state. Without consistent emotional support, these children develop survival strategies that, while protective in childhood, often complicate their adult relationships.

Without a secure base during childhood, we often struggle to develop a sense of safety in our adult relationships. A secure base is a reliable support figure who provides comfort and reassurance, allowing the child to explore the world confidently. Without this foundation, trusting others and establishing meaningful connections may be difficult. They may approach relationships cautiously, always on guard for signs of instability or abandonment. This can result in a pattern of pursuing relationships that mirror the unpredictability of their early experiences, perpetuating the disorganized attachment style into adulthood. Understanding these origins is crucial for breaking the cycle and moving toward the security and stability of healthier attachment patterns.

RECOGNIZING THE SIGNS OF DISORGANIZED ATTACHMENT IN ADULT RELATIONSHIPS

As children with disorganized attachment grow into adults, they often carry these early lessons into their relationships. The difficulty in trusting others can result in a constant push-pull dynamic, where the desire for closeness is frequently at odds with the fear of potential betrayal or rejection. Recognizing these signs in our adult relationships is the first step towards understanding and addressing disorganized attachment, empowering us to take proactive steps towards healthier relationships.

In adult relationships, disorganized attachment reveals itself through a tapestry of behaviors that confuse their partner. Emotional volatility is a hallmark of this attachment style. We might shower our partner affectionately one week only to retreat into cold detachment the next. This unpredictability can make relationships feel like a rollercoaster ride, leaving both people uncertain of the ground they stand on. Emotional regulation becomes a significant challenge, as we may struggle to manage the intense emotions that emerge due to perceived threats to our relationships. This difficulty often manifests as emotional volatility, where seemingly minor events can trigger profound reactions. This push-pull dynamic can be exhausting, leading to relationships fraught with tension and uncertainty.

We yearn for closeness yet dread the intimacy that closeness brings. This paradox manifests as a fear of abandonment, where the thought of losing a partner triggers intense anxiety. Simultaneously, there is a fear of engulfment, a worry that becoming too close might result in losing our identity or being overwhelmed by the relationship.

Trust issues also accompany disorganized attachment, further complicating relationship dynamics. We may overanalyze our partner's actions, interpreting innocent remarks or gestures as signs of betrayal or impending rejection. This constant scrutiny can erode the foundation of trust. As a result, there is often a reluctance to commit fully to the relationship, fueled by the fear that doing so might lead to inevitable heartbreak. The impact extends beyond romantic relationships into friendships, work relationships, and family dynamics. Each connection becomes an opportunity for either healing or reinforcing old wounds.

The impact of disorganized attachment extends beyond just relationships; it seeps into self-perception, leading to low self-esteem and chronic self-doubt. We may view ourselves as unworthy of love, attributing relationship struggles to personal shortcomings rather than recognizing the influence of their attachment style. This negative self-view can become a self-fulfilling prophecy, where believing our inadequacy leads to behaviors that sabotage potential happiness. As the years pass, this erodes confidence, making it even harder for us to trust our ability to maintain healthy, loving relationships.

Reflection Section: Recognizing Patterns

Take a moment to reflect on your relationship behaviors. Consider how emotional volatility, trust issues, or fears of intimacy and abandonment manifest in your interactions with others. Write down any recurring themes or patterns you notice. Acknowledge how these might relate to disorganized attachment. This awareness is the first step toward understanding and transforming your relational experiences.

REAL-LIFE EXAMPLES OF DISORGANIZED ATTACHMENT

Let us look at three different people with disorganized attachments. Let us begin with Alex, whose relationships often start with an intense connection, a whirlwind of passion and shared dreams. But as weeks turn into months, a creeping doubt takes root. He starts questioning their partner's intentions, scrutinizing every word and action for hidden meanings. Misunderstandings escalate into arguments, and Alex begins to pull away, convinced that retreat is safer than vulnerability. With Taylor, she oscillates between dependency and detachment. She relies heavily on others in friendships and romances for support and validation. Yet, when things become too intimate, she feels suffocated and fears the loss of independence. Taylor's relationships are characterized by intense closeness followed by sudden distancing. Finally, in the workplace, Tom's disorganized attachment hinders him. He excels in his role but struggles with teamwork. He perceives feedback as criticism and reacts defensively or withdraws from collaboration.

These real-world scenarios reveal how we find ourselves in relationships or situations that mirror our early inconsistent experiences. We may be drawn to partners who are emotionally unavailable or unpredictable or perhaps even misread situations. The result may be a relationship that feels like a battlefield, where both partners struggle to find common ground. Or we might interpret a partner's busy work schedule as a sign of waning interest, leading to accusations and defensiveness. Yet, as we will see in subsequent chapters, resolution is possible. Through self-awareness and open communication, we can begin to address these patterns.

THE ROLE OF TRAUMA IN ATTACHMENT AND THE ROAD TO HEALING

Trauma imprints a lasting impact on our psyche, influencing how we relate to ourselves and others. Imagine a child who learns that love can hurt when it should heal. Whether through witnessing domestic violence or enduring emotional neglect, these early experiences teach the child to associate closeness with danger or unpredictability.

The resulting hypervigilance manifests as constantly scanning the environment for signs of danger or betrayal, even when nonexistent. This heightened alertness stems from a survival mechanism honed in chaotic or threatening environments. Hypervigilance leads to misinterpretations of a partner's actions, seeing threats where none exist. Again, we oscillate between intense intimacy and sudden withdrawal. A partner may wonder why we pull away when things seem to be going well. Closeness can trigger memories of past trauma, leading to overwhelming anxiety. Understanding how trauma shapes attachment provides insight and opens the door to potential change.

The path to healing requires understanding trauma responses and developing new coping strategies. Recognizing the impact of trauma on attachment is crucial for recovery. Trauma-informed therapy offers valuable tools for this journey. (We explore therapy options more fully in Chapter 11.) Therapists understand the deep connection between past trauma and present attachment behaviors. They create a safe environment for us to explore their experiences without judgment, assisting them in unraveling these patterns. Practices like somatic experiencing or EMDR (eye movement desensitization and reprocessing) can help process traumatic memories.

Emotional regulation plays a pivotal role in trauma recovery. Developing emotional management skills is an essential step toward healing. Mindfulness, grounding techniques, and deep breathing can help us stay present and calm when we experience strong emotions. Developing emotional regulation skills also enhances relationship dynamics. In the next chapter, we will examine this in more depth.

CHAPTER 2
EMOTIONAL INSTABILITY AND EMOTIONAL REGULATION

IMAGINE STANDING IN A CROWDED ROOM, SURROUNDED BY THE HUM of conversation, when suddenly someone mentions your name in a critical tone. Your heart races, your palms sweat, and a flood of emotions threaten to overwhelm you. This is the power of emotional triggers—those seemingly small cues that can provoke significant emotional responses. They are often rooted in past experiences and deeply tied to our attachment styles. For those with disorganized attachment, these triggers can feel like invisible landmines scattered throughout their daily lives. But here is the key—understanding and managing these triggers is possible and a liberating step in fostering emotional stability, putting you in the driver's seat of your emotional journey.

UNDERSTANDING AND MANAGING EMOTIONAL TRIGGERS

Understanding and managing emotional triggers is crucial for those with disorganized attachment patterns. These triggers often stem from conflicting early experiences with caregivers, such as a caregiver who is physically present but emotionally distant or inconsistently responsive to the child's needs. This creates a simultaneous need for closeness and fear of intimacy, making emotional regulation particularly challenging in relationships. However, by understanding these contradictory impulses, we can empower ourselves to develop healthier attachment patterns and take control of our emotional journey.

Emotional triggers are stimuli that evoke strong emotional reactions, often disproportionately intense compared to the trigger itself. They can stem from sudden changes in plans, which may unsettle your sense of stability and control. Perhaps a friend cancels plans at the last minute, leaving you feeling abandoned or unimportant, reminiscent of past experiences of unpredictability. Criticism or perceived rejection is another potent trigger, striking at the heart of self-worth and stirring fears of inadequacy. Even a casually delivered remark can feel like a personal attack, sparking a cascade of defensive emotions. These reactions are not just psychological but physiological—activating the body's fight-or-flight response. This ancient survival mechanism floods the system with adrenaline, preparing you to confront or escape the perceived threat. While this response was invaluable to our ancestors, in modern settings, it often leads to overreactions and conflict.

Identifying your emotional triggers is the initial step toward managing them. A valuable tool in this process is keeping an emotional diary, where you can document situations that provoke strong emotions. Note the context, your immediate feelings, and any physical sensations you experience. Over time, patterns will emerge, revealing the specific triggers that disrupt your equilibrium. Reflecting on past conflicts can also shed light on recurring themes, helping you identify the roots of your emotional responses. This self-assessment requires honesty and introspection, as it involves confronting the vulnerabilities that underpin your reactions. But with this awareness, you gain the power to anticipate and prepare for your triggers, reducing their power over your emotions and putting you in control of your emotional well-being. This empowerment instills confidence in your ability to manage your emotional health.

While the physiological response to triggers is automatic, mindfulness can help us recognize the signs before they escalate. We can create a space between the trigger and our reaction by paying attention to our body's physical cues, such as a racing heart, clenched fists, or a tightening in the chest. This pause is an opportunity to choose a response rather than react impulsively. With practice, mindfulness can help retrain the brain to respond with greater calm and control, even in the face of triggers, allowing us to manage emotional responses more effectively. This sense of calm and control brings a profound peace to our emotional landscape.

Employing strategies that enhance emotional awareness to monitor and recognize real-time triggers is beneficial. Another practical approach is to engage in regular self-check-ins throughout the day. By setting aside a few moments to assess your emotional state and identify lingering tensions, you can cultivate a habit of self-awareness. This makes it easier to detect and address triggers as they arise. Visualizing a mental map of your emotional landscape can also help when you chart the connections between events, thoughts, and emotions. By mapping these relationships, you can better understand how different triggers are interlinked, allowing you to anticipate their effects more accurately and prepare for them.

Reflection Section: Identifying Your Triggers

Take a few moments to reflect on recent situations that provoked a strong emotional response. Write down the event, your emotions, and any physical sensations. Consider what might have triggered these reactions. As you review your notes, look for patterns or recurring themes. This exercise can help you pinpoint your triggers and develop strategies to manage them effectively.

MINDFULNESS TECHNIQUES FOR EMOTIONAL BALANCE

As we have seen, mindfulness practices are especially valuable for those overcoming disorganized attachment. They help build the internal stability often lacking due to inconsistent early caregiving experiences. By staying present, you can begin to trust your own emotional experiences rather than feel overwhelmed by conflicting impulses in relationships.

Think of moments when stress takes over, your mind racing with worries about work, relationships, or the future. In such times, mindfulness can offer a sanctuary—a way to ground yourself in the present and reduce the whirlwind of anxiety. At its core, mindfulness is about cultivating awareness of the present moment without judgment. It is a practice that invites you to observe your thoughts and feelings with curiosity rather than getting swept away by them. This simple yet profound shift can transform your emotional stability, offering a beacon of hope and optimism in your journey toward emotional balance.

Foundational Practices and Their Benefits

One of the most accessible mindfulness techniques is focused breathing. Focusing on your breath's rhythm can create a calming anchor amid chaos. This practice reduces stress and enhances your ability to regulate emotions by bringing you back to the present.

To embrace mindfulness further, you can also do a body scan meditation, which helps you connect with your physical self. Find a peaceful spot to lie down or sit comfortably. Close your eyes and then take a few deep breaths. Beginning at the top of your head, slowly move your attention down through your body, noticing any sensations, tension, or areas of relaxation. As you progress, breathe into each area, releasing tension with each exhale. For example, you might start by focusing on your forehead, noticing any tension or relaxation there, then move down to your eyes, cheeks, and so on until you reach your toes. This exercise fosters deep relaxation and awareness, helping you attune to your body's signals.

Another effective practice is mindful breathing. Sitting or lying down comfortably, close your eyes and focus on your breath. Notice the sensation of air entering through your nose, filling your lungs, and leaving your body. Gently take your focus back to breathing if your mind wanders. This technique cultivates patience and concentration, allowing you to respond to stress with better composure.

Mindfulness plays a crucial role in reducing emotional reactivity. When faced with a challenging situation, it is easy to react impulsively, allowing emotions to dictate your actions. Mindfulness introduces a pause, a moment to reflect before responding. This pause empowers you to choose a thoughtful response rather than being driven by immediate emotions. Over weeks and months, this practice can lead to a more balanced emotional state, where reactions are measured and intentional. Integrating mindfulness into daily life can weaken the automatic connections between triggers and responses, fostering a sense of control over your emotional landscape.

Consider the story of Emma, who struggled with overwhelming anxiety at work. Deadlines loomed, and the pressure felt insurmountable. Emma began incorporating mindfulness into her routine, dedicating ten minutes each morning to mindful breathing. Over weeks, she noticed a subtle shift. The anxiety that once paralyzed her began to dissipate. She became aware of the tension in her body, using her breath to release it. During meetings, when stress threatened to take over, Emma discreetly focused on her breath, finding calm amid the chaos. This newfound ability to pause and center herself transformed her work experience. Mindfulness became her ally, guiding her through stressful moments with a sense of peace and clarity.

Another story is that of Mark, who frequently argued with his partner. The most minor disagreements would escalate into full-blown conflicts. After learning about mindfulness, Mark decided to apply it during these heated exchanges. By focusing on his breath and observing his emotions, he learned to listen more and react less. Gradually, the arguments decreased, replaced by constructive conversations. Mark realized that mindfulness helped him communicate better and deepened his connection with his partner. These stories illustrate mindfulness's profound impact on emotional regulation, offering tools to navigate life's challenges gracefully and with understanding.

INTEGRATING MINDFULNESS INTO DAILY LIFE

Adding mindfulness to your daily routine does not require setting aside large blocks of time. It can seamlessly integrate into your activities, such as commuting or taking breaks. For instance, while commuting, whether you are driving, taking public transport, or walking, you can practice mindfulness by focusing on the sensations around you—the feel of the steering wheel, the rhythm of your footsteps, or the sounds in your environment. This practice helps reduce stress and makes your journey (in the literal sense) more enjoyable and less rushed. Similarly, during breaks at work, take a minute to center yourself. Close your eyes, take deep breaths, and release any tension. These small moments of mindfulness can break the cycle of stress and help you return to your tasks with a clearer mind and a calmer demeanor.

Introducing simple mindfulness practices into your routine can be straightforward yet profoundly impactful. Consider box breathing during work breaks. This technique involves inhaling for four counts, holding the breath for four, exhaling for four, and pausing again for four. Focusing on this rhythmic pattern can calm your mind, lower stress, and help you return to work with renewed focus. Similarly, mindful stretching before bed can help ease the day's tension, preparing your body and mind for restful sleep. This practice includes gentle stretches combined with deep breathing, encouraging relaxation and promoting peace as you transition into sleep.

Mindful walking offers another practice that can enhance daily life. Often, we move through spaces on autopilot, lost in thoughts about the past or future. Mindful walking invites you to focus on each step, noticing the sensation of your feet meeting the ground, the rhythm of your movement, and the environment around you. By engaging fully with walking, you create a meditation that grounds you in the present moment. This practice encourages you to slow down and connect with your body, transforming routine movements into mindfulness and stress relief opportunities.

Mindful transitions between activities offer another opportunity to integrate mindfulness. These brief moments, often overlooked, can be a chance to pause and reset. For example, when switching tasks at work, take a few deep breaths to clear your mind and refocus your attention. This simple act can increase concentration and smooth the transition, allowing you to approach the following task clearly and purposefully. These mindful pauses serve as mini-reset buttons throughout the day, helping you maintain a state of calm and attentiveness.

The benefits of regular mindfulness practice extend beyond the moments of calm they create. Consistent practice leads to sustained emotional balance, helping you respond rather than react to life's challenges. When mindfulness becomes a habit, you feel peaceful, even in the most chaotic circumstances. This emotional stability is not about eliminating stress or negativity but changing your relationship with these experiences. Mindfulness helps you learn to notice your thoughts and emotions without being swept away, which can contribute to a more balanced and less reactive emotional state.

Consider the story of Lucy, a teacher who found herself overwhelmed by the demands of her job. Between lesson planning and managing classroom dynamics, stress seemed unavoidable. Encouraged by a friend, Lucy started practicing mindfulness during her lunch breaks. She would sit quietly, focus on breathing, and let go of the morning's tensions. As time passed by, Lucy noticed a significant shift. She became more patient with her students and less frazzled by unexpected challenges. Mindfulness provided her with a sense of calm that permeated her entire day. Similarly, Jake, a software engineer, struggled with the fast pace of his work environment. He began using mindfulness while commuting, focusing on the present moment instead of worrying about the day ahead. This simple change transformed his mornings, making him more focused and effective at work.

Overcoming Challenges and Building Consistency

Despite its benefits, maintaining a mindfulness practice can be challenging. It is easy to forget or feel too busy to fit it into a hectic schedule. To overcome these obstacles, start small. Set realistic goals, like dedicating just five minutes a day to mindfulness. Gradually, as it becomes a natural part of your routine, you can extend the time.

Another common challenge is dealing with a wandering mind. It is typical for your thoughts to drift during mindfulness practice. If this occurs, gently bring your focus back to the present moment without judgment. Remember, the goal is not to clear your mind entirely but to cultivate awareness. For those with disorganized attachment, consistency in mindfulness practice can help establish the internal security that may have been missing in early relationships. This stable foundation becomes crucial when building new, healthier relationships.

Consider the story of Lana, a busy professional constantly overwhelmed by her hectic workdays. By incorporating mindfulness into her routine, she transformed her experience. Each morning, she practiced mindful breathing during her commute, setting a calm tone for the day. She used box breathing at work to manage stress, finding that these practices improved her focus and overall well-being. Then there is Jackson, a parent who struggled to be present with his children amid life's demands. By practicing mindful transitions, he learned to leave work stress behind and engage fully with his family. These practices made him more present, deepening his connection with his children and enriching their time together.

COGNITIVE RESTRUCTURING FOR EMOTIONAL HEALTH

In the tapestry of our minds, thoughts weave intricate patterns that shape our emotional landscapes. Cognitive restructuring is a technique that embarks on the journey of unraveling these patterns, offering a new perspective on how we perceive and respond to the world. This approach involves identifying negative thought patterns that often cloud our judgment and skew our emotional responses. Imagine, for instance, the belief that you are inadequate or unworthy. Such thoughts can trigger a cascade of emotions, leading to feelings of anxiety or depression. By challenging these thoughts and replacing them with balanced alternatives, you can alter the fabric of your emotional experience.

As discussed, those with disorganized attachment often struggle with contradictory thought patterns about relationships—simultaneously wanting closeness while fearing it. Cognitive restructuring can help identify and address these conflicting beliefs, making room for more secure attachment patterns. The process begins with recognizing these unhelpful thoughts, often termed cognitive distortions. These distortions include black-and-white thinking, catastrophizing, and overgeneralizing, among others. They can lead us to view situations exaggeratedly or inaccurately, impacting our emotions and reactions. Consider a scenario where a friend cancels plans, leading you to the immediate thought, "They must not value our friendship." This thought may not be grounded in reality, yet it can evoke feelings of rejection and hurt. Cognitive restructuring encourages you to pause and examine these thoughts critically. Are they based on evidence or assumptions fueled by past experiences?

Maintaining thought records can be incredibly useful in navigating this process. These records act as a tool to track and analyze your thoughts, helping you identify patterns and triggers. Start by jotting down situations that elicit strong emotional reactions and the thoughts and feelings they provoke. Next, evaluate these thoughts: Are they realistic? What evidence supports or contradicts them? This reflective practice lets you see your thoughts from afar, offering clarity and insight. As you become more adept at recognizing and challenging cognitive distortions, you can begin to replace them with more balanced, rational alternatives. For example, instead of thinking, *They don't care about me,* you might consider, *Perhaps something came up, and we can reschedule.*

Cognitive restructuring can profoundly impact emotional responses. Shifting thought patterns can transform how you react to situations, leading to healthier emotional outcomes. When you replace negative thoughts with balanced ones, you reduce their emotional charge, allowing you to respond more calmly and confidently. This shift enhances your emotional resilience and improves your interactions with others, fostering more positive and constructive relationships. Over time, cognitive restructuring enables you to cultivate a more reflective and less reactive mindset.

Engaging with exercises or scenarios can be beneficial to practice cognitive restructuring effectively. Consider creating worksheets that prompt you to dissect and reframe your thoughts. These might include sections for identifying the situation, noting the initial idea and emotion, and then challenging and revising the thought with evidence-based alternatives. Role-playing scenarios where you apply these techniques can reinforce your skills, helping you internalize the process. By consistently practicing cognitive restructuring, you can rewire your thought patterns, promoting emotional health and well-being.

Imagine the transformation of viewing life through a more transparent lens, where thoughts no longer dictate your emotional state but rather guide you with wisdom and balance. This transformation is not about ignoring negative emotions but understanding and reshaping the thoughts that underpin them. With practice, cognitive restructuring can become a natural part of your mental toolkit, equipping you to approach life's challenges more easily and clearly.

BUILDING EMOTIONAL RESILIENCE

Emotional resilience becomes particularly important for those healing from disorganized attachment as they learn to trust themselves and others. It provides the foundation to maintain healthy boundaries while allowing for genuine connection. Emotional resilience is the inner strength that enables you to recover from setbacks and adapt to change. Think of it as your inner compass that stays steady even when life gets stormy. It is like having an emotional immune system that helps you recover from setbacks and grows stronger with each challenge. When you develop this inner strength, you will find yourself surviving difficult moments and gaining wisdom from them. This capacity becomes your foundation for maintaining hope and direction, especially when your relationships or circumstances test your limits. For those working to build secure attachments, this resilience becomes particularly valuable—it helps you stay grounded in your worth even when old insecurities surface.

To enhance your emotional resilience, consider adopting a growth mindset. This involves viewing challenges as opportunities rather than threats, believing that abilities and intelligence can be developed through dedication and hard work. When cultivating a growth mindset, you become more flexible and willing to take risks. This mindset encourages you to embrace failures as learning experiences, which can significantly boost resilience. Engaging in regular self-care practices is another strategy to bolster resilience. This means prioritizing activities that nourish your body, mind, and spirit, such as exercise, relaxation, and hobbies. Self-care replenishes your energy. It enhances your ability to cope with stressors, creating a solid foundation for resilience.

Social support plays a pivotal role in building emotional resilience. Having a network of family, friends, or even colleagues who provide encouragement and understanding can significantly strengthen your ability to cope with stress. Feeling supported makes you more likely to persevere through tough times because you know you are not alone. Community and relationships provide a sense of belonging and security, essential to resilience. Nurturing these connections by reaching out, spending time together, and offering support in return is critical. Building and maintaining strong relationships can create a safety net that bolsters your resilience.

Consider the story of Mia, who faced the loss of a job she loved. Initially devastated, Mia leaned on her family and friends for support. She decided to view the situation as a chance to explore new opportunities. By adopting a growth mindset, she enrolled in courses to learn new skills. As months passed, Mia found a new job and discovered a passion for a different field. Her emotional resilience allowed her to navigate the challenge, learn from it, and emerge stronger. Then there is Jason, who faced a breakup that left him feeling lost. Instead of retreating into isolation, he joined a local hiking group, where he met others who shared similar experiences. The community offered understanding and companionship, helping Jason build resilience. He found comfort in nature and the friendships he formed, which provided him with the strength to move forward. These examples illustrate how emotional resilience can transform adversity into a stepping stone for growth.

Building emotional resilience is a dynamic and ongoing process. It involves actively engaging in practices that strengthen your ability to cope with stress and change. By nourishing a growth mindset, prioritizing self-care, and nurturing social connections, you can enhance your resilience and navigate life's challenges more easily. Resilience empowers you to face difficulties confidently and emerge from them with newfound strength and insight. As you develop this inner fortitude, you will find that you are better equipped to handle whatever life throws your way with a sense of calm and determination.

As we conclude this chapter on emotional regulation, we have explored various strategies to cultivate stability, from recognizing triggers to applying mindfulness in everyday life. These tools help you manage emotions and build a foundation for healthier relationships. Next, we will delve into trust-building and overcoming fears, paving the way for more secure attachments.

CHAPTER 3
BUILDING TRUST AND OVERCOMING FEAR

Perhaps you find yourself at a crossroads where the path of trust seems obscured by shadows of doubt and past experiences. Trust issues often arise from deep-seated betrayals or broken promises that have left scars. But remember, these scars are not permanent. They are not the end of your journey but a part of it. Maybe you remember when a friend broke a promise or a partner failed to show up when it mattered most. These moments etch memories of disappointment, fostering skepticism about the reliability of others. As years pass, such experiences can harden into a protective shield that keeps potential pain at bay and blocks out genuine connections. The influence of parental relationships on our trust development cannot be understated. As children, our first lessons in trust often come from our caregivers. If those caregivers were inconsistent or unreliable, the seeds of distrust might have been sown early on, leading us to question the dependability of those around us. These experiences create a framework through which we view the world, making trust seem fragile and elusive. But remember, this framework can be reshaped, and trust can be rebuilt. The potential for growth and change is always within reach.

TRUST ISSUES AND REBUILDING TRUST PERSONALLY AND PROFESSIONALLY

Trust issues can have a deep-rooted impact on both personal and professional relationships. They can act as a barrier to forming close bonds, leaving you isolated even in the company of others. When trust is absent, misunderstandings become frequent companions, as suspicion clouds judgment and twists intentions. In friendships, you might question the motives behind a friend's actions, leading to tension and conflict. In romantic relationships, this suspicion can breed jealousy and insecurity, creating a cycle of doubt that erodes the foundation of love. Professionally, trust issues might make it difficult to collaborate or delegate tasks, as the fear of being let down overshadows the potential for teamwork and innovation. This pervasive sense of distrust not only damages relationships but also hinders personal growth, as it keeps you from fully engaging with the world around you. For those with disorganized attachment patterns, trust issues are often compounded by contradictory experiences with caregivers who were both sources of comfort and fear. This complicated history can make building trust incredibly challenging, as the desire for connection conflicts with the instinct for self-protection.

Recognizing signs of trust issues within yourself or others can be the first step toward addressing them. One telltale sign is a reluctance to share personal information, stemming from the fear that vulnerability might be exploited. You might find yourself holding back details about your life, keeping others at arm's length to protect your heart. Overanalyzing others' intentions is another indicator, where you scrutinize every word and gesture for hidden meanings or potential threats. This constant vigilance can be exhausting as the mind races to uncover betrayals that may not even exist. Such behaviors create an emotional distance that can be difficult to bridge, leaving relationships strained and unsatisfying.

To start restoring trust, it is crucial to engage in self-reflection. This introspective exercise is a powerful tool that puts you in the driver's seat, allowing you to delve into the origins of your distrust and examine the past experiences that have shaped your current perceptions. Reflect on moments when trust was broken and consider how these events have influenced your behavior and beliefs. This process of self-reflection is not about dwelling on past hurts but about understanding how they have shaped you. Ask yourself what assumptions you make about others' trustworthiness and whether these assumptions are based on present reality or past hurts. Journaling can be a powerful tool, letting you articulate your thoughts and feelings, creating clarity and insight. By understanding the roots of your distrust, you can dismantle the barriers it has built, paving the way for healthier, more fulfilling relationships. Self-reflection is a journey of empowerment and control, allowing you to shape your trust narrative.

Reflective Exercise: Uncovering Trust Challenges

Spend some time reflecting on a recent interaction in which you felt distrustful. Write down the situation, your thoughts, and the emotions it stirred. Consider what past experiences might have influenced your reaction. Identify any patterns in your responses to similar situations. This exercise is not about self-criticism but about gaining insight into how trust issues manifest in your life. By recognizing these patterns, you can start challenging and changing them. For instance, if you notice that you often question others' intentions, try to give them the benefit of the doubt. If you tend to hold back personal information, try sharing more with someone you trust. These small changes can help you overcome your trust issues, opening the door to a more trusting and connected future.

STRATEGIES TO BUILD TRUST WITH OTHERS

Building trust is a process that unfolds through consistent and intentional actions. One of the foundational techniques is active listening. This means being fully attentive and present to what the other person is expressing. It means setting aside distractions and allowing them to express themselves without interruption. Picture a conversation where you nod, maintain eye contact, and respond thoughtfully. This simple act of being present can profoundly affect how others perceive your trustworthiness. It shows them you value their thoughts and feelings and respect their right to be heard. Open communication complements active listening by encouraging honesty and transparency. Sharing your thoughts and feelings openly invites others to do the same, creating a reciprocal flow of dialogue that fosters mutual understanding and trust. Consistency is crucial here; when your words align with your actions, it builds a reliable foundation. Imagine the impact of consistently following through on promises or being punctual. Such actions reinforce the message that you are dependable, gradually strengthening the bonds of trust. When healing from disorganized attachment, consistency becomes exceptionally crucial. Small, reliable interactions help rewire the expectation of unpredictability that often characterizes disorganized attachment patterns. Each fulfilled promise, no matter how minor, helps build a new foundation of trust.

Vulnerability plays a pivotal role in deepening connections and fostering trust. You invite others into your world by sharing personal stories or experiences, offering them a glimpse of your authentic self. This openness can be daunting, but it signals trust and can encourage others to reciprocate. Consider when you revealed a challenging moment from your past to a friend or partner. The act of sharing not only deepens your bond but also demonstrates your willingness to be open and honest. This mutual exchange of vulnerability lays the groundwork for a trusting relationship. It is important to remember that vulnerability does not mean oversharing; it is about revealing parts of yourself safely and appropriately.

To practice building trust incrementally, start with small, manageable steps. Group settings, such as team-building exercises or workshops, can provide a safe environment to practice trust-building activities. These might include exercises where you share something about yourself, engage in a problem-solving task, or participate in a trust fall. Such activities foster a sense of camaraderie and collective trust. Setting small, achievable trust-building goals in your relationships is also effective. For instance, you might begin by sharing a minor concern with a friend and observing their response. Over a while, as trust grows, you can gradually open up about more significant issues. These incremental steps help build a strong foundation of trust without overwhelming either party.

Success stories of restored trust can inspire and offer hope. Take the example of a couple who decided to rebuild their relationship after experiencing a breach of trust. They began by committing to open and honest communication by dedicating weekly time to discuss their feelings and concerns. They slowly rebuilt their bond by practicing active listening and being vulnerable about their fears and hopes. After a few months, their relationship grew much more substantial, grounded in a deeper understanding and appreciation of each other. Another story involves a friendship that was tested by a misunderstanding. Through consistent efforts to communicate openly and share vulnerabilities, the friends were able to mend their relationship, ultimately emerging with a stronger connection. These narratives highlight the transformative power of trust-building strategies, illustrating that trust can be restored and relationships revitalized with patience and effort.

OVERCOMING THE FEAR OF ABANDONMENT

Imagine the lingering echo of a door closing, a sound that resonates deeply for someone with a fear of abandonment. This fear often has roots in past experiences, particularly those from childhood. Separation or loss during formative years can leave an indelible mark, teaching a child that love and security might be temporary. Perhaps a parent left unexpectedly, or a significant move disrupted a child's sense of stability. These moments can instill a fear that those you rely on could vanish without warning. As adults, we may relive these early separations through repeated relationship breakups, each one reinforcing the belief that closeness inevitably leads to loss. This pattern can lead to a pervasive sense of insecurity, where the fear of being left alone becomes a constant companion. For those with disorganized attachment, the fear of abandonment often coexists with a fear of closeness, creating a push-pull dynamic in relationships. This contradiction stems from early experiences where caregivers were simultaneously needed yet frightening.

The behavioral manifestations of abandonment fears are varied and can subtly infiltrate everyday interactions. You might find yourself clinging tightly to relationships, driven by an overwhelming need for reassurance. This clinginess can surface as frequent calls or texts, seeking constant confirmation of love and commitment. While seeking closeness is natural, it can suffocate both parties involved due to fear. Overdependence on partners for reassurance is another typical behavior—a reliance on others to validate your worth and dispel the fear of being left behind. This can manifest as needing constant verbal affirmations or requiring a partner to prove their dedication repeatedly. Such dependencies can strain relationships, as the burden of providing continual reassurance becomes exhausting over time.

Practical coping strategies can be invaluable in managing and reducing these fears. Developing self-soothing and grounding exercises is a powerful approach. These techniques help you regain control over your emotions in moments of panic or anxiety. As mentioned, taking deep breaths, focusing on the physical sensations of your body, or even engaging in calming activities like drawing or listening to music can anchor you in the present moment. These practices shift your focus away from the fear of what might happen to what is, providing relief from the grip of anxiety. As we have seen, cognitive reframing is another effective technique. It can alter how you perceive abandonment scenarios. It involves challenging and changing the negative thoughts that fuel your fears. Instead of assuming a partner's silence means they are leaving, consider other possibilities—they might be busy or need time to recharge. This shift in perspective can alleviate unnecessary worry and promote a more balanced view of relationships.

Stories of overcoming abandonment fears can offer hope and guidance. Consider Lisa, who struggled with the fear of losing her partner. She felt panicked whenever he went on business trips, convinced that distance would lead to disconnection. Lisa learned self-soothing techniques through therapy, like practicing mindfulness during absences. She also worked on cognitive reframing, reminding herself of the firm foundation of their relationship. As weeks passed, Lisa found that she could handle his trips with much less anxiety, focusing instead on their joyful reunions. Then there is Ben, who faced a similar fear after a series of failed relationships. He realized that his overdependence on reassurance stemmed from his lack of confidence. By engaging in activities that boosted his self-esteem, like joining a local sports team, Ben found he needed less validation from his partner. These narratives demonstrate that while the fear of abandonment can be deeply ingrained, navigating and overcoming it with understanding, patience, and the right strategies is possible.

SETTING AND RESPECTING BOUNDARIES

Boundaries serve as invisible lines that define where you end and others begin. You set the limits to protect your well-being, ensuring your physical, emotional, and mental needs are respected. Imagine boundaries as a personal space bubble, unique to each person that dictates how close others can get, literally and figuratively. They are crucial for healthy relationships because they establish clear expectations and prevent misunderstandings. Without boundaries, relationships can become enmeshed, leading to resentment and conflict. You communicate your values and needs by setting limits and fostering mutual respect and understanding. These boundaries empower you to take control of your personal space, allowing you to engage with others safely and comfortably.

Identifying and setting your boundaries requires introspection and clarity. A helpful exercise to begin with is journaling, which allows you to reflect on your limits and how they have been respected or violated. Start by writing down situations where you felt uncomfortable or overextended. Consider what triggered these feelings and what actions you wish had been taken differently. This reflection helps you pinpoint your boundaries, giving you a clearer sense of what you need to feel secure. Once identified, practice role-playing scenarios where you assert these boundaries with a trusted friend or therapist. This practice builds confidence, preparing you to communicate your limits effectively in real-life situations. By rehearsing these conversations, you become more comfortable expressing your needs, reducing the anxiety that often accompanies boundary-setting. For those working to overcome disorganized attachment, boundary-setting can feel particularly challenging due to inconsistent early experiences with limits. Learning to establish and maintain healthy boundaries becomes a crucial step in developing secure attachment patterns.

Maintaining boundaries can be challenging, mainly when others are resistant or push back against your limits. You might encounter people who dismiss your boundaries, viewing them as inconveniences rather than necessities. This resistance can come from a lack of understanding or a fear of change. In these instances, it is important to remain steadfast, reiterating your boundaries with clarity and calmness. Remember, boundaries are not about controlling others but about caring for yourself. You have the right to assert your limits, even if others disagree. It is also essential to be flexible, recognizing that boundaries might need to be adjusted over time as relationships and circumstances evolve. This adaptability ensures that your boundaries remain relevant and practical, reflecting your current needs and priorities.

Respecting others' boundaries is equally important and can enhance trust and satisfaction in relationships. When you honor someone else's limits, you respect their autonomy and individuality. This shared respect fosters a supportive environment where everyone feels acknowledged and appreciated. It encourages open communication, allowing for honest exchanges about needs and expectations. Recognizing and respecting boundaries builds a foundation of trust that strengthens your connection. This respect also empowers others to express themselves authentically, knowing that their boundaries will be honored. In turn, you create a relationship dynamic that is supportive and nurturing, where both people thrive in an environment of mutual understanding.

Reflect on boundaries and consider how they manifest in your relationships. Are there areas where your boundaries feel compromised, or do you struggle to respect others' limits? Explore these questions through introspection and dialogue, using the insights gained to foster healthier, more balanced interactions. By prioritizing boundaries, you cultivate relationships grounded in respect and trust, where each person's needs are valued and protected.

SELF-COMPASSION AS A TRUST-BUILDER

Imagine standing before a mirror, not to critique your reflection but to offer kindness to the person looking back. This is the essence of self-compassion, a crucial element in building trust with ourselves. It involves treating yourself with the same understanding and warmth you would offer a dear friend. When you embrace self-compassion, you cultivate an internal sense of security, laying the groundwork for trust. This practice of self-compassion is especially vital for those with disorganized attachment, as it helps create the internal security that may have been missing in formative relationships. This nurturing approach to ourselves can soften the harshness of self-criticism, allowing us to forgive past mistakes and see them as opportunities for growth rather than failures. By practicing self-forgiveness, we break the cycle of guilt and blame, replacing it with acceptance and learning.

Self-compassion plays a significant role in reducing self-criticism, which often acts as a barrier to personal growth. Many of us have an inner critic scrutinizing every action and decision, overshadowing achievements with doubt. By countering this voice with self-kindness, you can mitigate harsh self-judgment. Instead of fixating on perceived failures, self-compassion encourages you to focus on your efforts and intentions. This shift in perspective can be liberating, freeing you from the shackles of perfectionism. It allows you to recognize your inherent worth, independent of external validation or success. Through this lens, personal growth becomes a journey of exploration and acceptance, not a relentless pursuit of flawlessness.

To nurture self-compassion, consider engaging in meditations specifically designed to foster kindness toward yourself. Find a quiet space, close your eyes, and focus on your breath. As you breathe in, imagine filling yourself with warmth and acceptance. As you exhale, release any tension or judgment. Visualize yourself as you would a close friend, offering words of encouragement and support. This practice helps internalize a compassionate mindset, gradually replacing self-criticism with understanding. Another effective exercise is writing compassionate letters to yourself. In these letters, address your struggles and challenges with empathy and care. Acknowledge your efforts and reassure yourself that it is okay to make mistakes. Writing can reinforce inner dialogue, transforming how you relate to yourself.

Consider the story of Anna, who once struggled with debilitating self-doubt. She often felt paralyzed by the fear of making mistakes, leading her to avoid growth opportunities. Through self-compassion practices, Anna began to view her imperfections with kindness. She started each day with a self-compassion meditation that grounded her in acceptance. As the days went by, Anna noticed a shift in her mindset. She became more willing to take risks and embrace new experiences, trusting her ability to learn from setbacks. Similarly, David found himself trapped in a cycle of self-criticism that hindered his creativity. By writing compassionate letters to himself, David discovered a newfound freedom to express himself without fear of judgment. These narratives highlight the transformative power of self-compassion, illustrating how it can rebuild trust in yourself and unlock potential.

As you cultivate self-compassion, you create a foundation of trust within. This internal security empowers you to face challenges with resilience and courage. It also enhances your relationships, as the kindness you extend to yourself naturally extends to others. By nurturing self-compassion, you foster peace and confidence permeating all aspects of your life. This chapter has delved into the intricacies of trust, offering tools to build and sustain it within and with others. As we journey forward, we will explore strategies for breaking unhealthy relationship patterns, paving the way for deeper connections.

CHAPTER 4
BREAKING UNHEALTHY RELATIONSHIP PATTERNS

PICTURE YOURSELF IN A DIMLY LIT ROOM, SEARCHING FOR A WAY OUT. You feel along the walls, hoping for a door or a window, but all you find are more barriers. This is what it can feel like to be trapped in a cycle of toxic relationships. These patterns can be as elusive as they are damaging, often hidden beneath layers of emotions and interactions that, on the surface, seem ordinary. Yet, they can lead to a profound sense of entrapment, where the prospect of change feels like an unreachable dream. The first step toward breaking free is understanding what constitutes a toxic relationship and learning to recognize the signs.

IDENTIFYING AND PROCESSING RELATIONSHIP TRIGGERS

For those with disorganized attachment patterns, understanding relationship triggers is like turning on a light in a dark room. It often manifests as intense, seemingly contradictory reactions to intimate situations. These triggers can stem from early experiences where caregivers were simultaneously sources of comfort and fear. This understanding is crucial for breaking unhealthy patterns and developing secure relationships, and it can bring a sense of enlightenment to your journey.

Relationship triggers commonly surface in various situations that challenge our sense of safety and connection. When a partner becomes temporarily unavailable, it might trigger deep-seated fears of abandonment. Paradoxically, unexpected displays of affection can also become triggers, as they might feel threatening to those who learned early that intimacy could lead to harm. Conflict situations, particularly involving disagreement or criticism, often activate these triggers, as do moments of emotional vulnerability when sharing feelings. Even physical proximity can become challenging, as we feel uncomfortable when others are too close or distant.

When these triggers activate, we often experience a complex web of reactions. The most distinctive is the simultaneous urge to seek closeness while pushing away—a hallmark of disorganized attachment. This internal conflict can lead to emotional flooding, where feelings become overwhelming, or conversely, to emotional numbness, where feelings shut down entirely. Emotional flooding is when we become overwhelmed by one or more emotions. It can feel like a wave of intense feelings that is difficult to manage or control. Physical symptoms frequently accompany these emotional states, including a racing heart, shallow breathing, or feeling frozen. Many struggle to maintain present awareness, instead becoming lost in memories or future fears. The mind might race with conflicting thoughts about the relationship, creating a state of confusion and anxiety.

Processing these triggers requires a gentle, step-by-step approach. The journey begins with developing the ability to recognize triggers as they arise rather than getting lost in reactive patterns. This awareness creates space for implementing grounding techniques, such as focused breathing, progressive muscle relaxation, or physical anchoring to the present moment. Learning to name emotions without judgment helps create distance from overwhelming feelings, making them more manageable. As awareness grows, we can identify the core fears or needs underlying their triggers, such as the need for safety or fear of vulnerability.

Clear communication becomes essential in this process, though it often feels challenging. When possible, sharing these experiences with partners helps create understanding and support. This might involve explaining triggers beforehand or developing signals when feeling overwhelmed. However, it is equally important to recognize when professional support is needed, particularly when triggers feel too overwhelming to process alone. Whether through therapy, support groups, or trusted friends, building a support network provides crucial resources for this healing journey.

IDENTIFYING TOXIC RELATIONSHIPS AND PATTERNS

Toxic relationship patterns are often characterized by manipulative behaviors that undermine trust and respect. One such behavior is gaslighting, a form of psychological manipulation where a person seeks to make you doubt your perceptions or reality. This tactic can erode your sense of self as months or years pass, leaving you questioning your judgment. Emotional abuse is another hallmark of toxic relationships, manifesting through yelling, ridicule, or belittling. These behaviors can be subtle, cloaked in sarcasm, or disguised as jokes, but their impact is deeply corrosive. Emotional neglect, where one partner consistently ignores the emotional needs of the other, can be equally damaging. Emotional neglect can manifest in various ways, ranging from a partner consistently dismissing your feelings to a lack of emotional support during difficult times. It fosters feelings of invisibility and worthlessness. Recognizing these behaviors is crucial, as they often form the foundation of an unhealthy relationship dynamic. For those healing from disorganized attachment, toxic patterns may feel familiar or even comfortable, making them particularly challenging to identify and change.

The impact of toxic patterns on mental and emotional health is significant. Chronic stress becomes a constant companion, as the unpredictability of the relationship keeps you on edge. This stress can manifest physically, with symptoms like muscle tension or insomnia, and emotionally, leading to anxiety or depression. As time passes, these patterns can erode self-esteem, creating a cycle where the more you endure, the less worthy you feel. This erosion of self-worth can make it difficult to imagine a healthier relationship, trapping you in negativity and despair. The effects can be far-reaching, impacting your relationships and capacity to connect with the world.

Reflecting on your relationship history can illuminate patterns that might otherwise go unnoticed. This introspection is not about assigning blame but about gaining clarity. Consider keeping a relationship journal to document interactions, conflicts, and resolutions. This practice can reveal recurring themes or behaviors that contribute to the toxicity. Your relationship history includes all your past relationships, not just your current one. Reflect on past conflicts, asking yourself what triggered them and how they were resolved. Were there patterns of communication that perpetuated misunderstandings? Did certain behaviors consistently lead to feelings of hurt or inadequacy? This reflection can provide valuable insights, helping you identify the dynamics that need to change. To aid in this introspection, here is a checklist for identifying toxic patterns in your relationships:

1. First, consider whether you frequently feel drained or unsupported by your partner. Healthy relationships should be a source of mutual support and energy, not exhaustion.
2. Next, assess your communication. Do you find yourself reluctant to share your thoughts or feelings openly? This hesitation can indicate a lack of trust or fear of judgment. Evaluate the balance of power in the relationship. Are decisions made collaboratively, or does one person consistently dominate?
3. Finally, consider whether your boundaries are respected. Can you assert your needs and have them honored, or are they dismissed or ignored?

Use this checklist to diagnose unhealthy dynamics, bringing awareness to areas that need attention and change.

Interactive Element: Toxic Patterns Checklist

- Do you frequently feel drained or unsupported in your relationships?
- Are you reluctant to communicate openly with your partner?
- Is there a fair balance of power and decision-making in your relationship?
- Are your boundaries respected, or are they often dismissed?
- Do you experience manipulative behaviors like gaslighting or emotional neglect?

Recognizing toxic patterns is a decisive step toward breaking free from them. You can identify unhealthy dynamics by reflecting on your relationships and using this checklist. This awareness is a foundation for change and a powerful tool for making choices that foster healthier, more fulfilling connections.

TOOLS FOR BREAKING THE CYCLE OF TOXICITY

In the labyrinth of relationships, finding your way out of toxic patterns often begins with the cornerstone of establishing clear personal boundaries. As discussed in the previous chapter, these boundaries act as invisible guardrails, guiding your interactions and protecting your emotional well-being. They are not walls meant to isolate but guidelines that define what is and is not acceptable. To establish these boundaries, identify what makes you uncomfortable or unhappy in your interactions. Are there specific behaviors that consistently leave you feeling overwhelmed or undervalued? Once identified, communicate these boundaries clearly and assertively to those around you. Expressing your needs without ambiguity is essential, ensuring others understand your limits. When establishing boundaries seems challenging due to disorganized attachment, start with small, manageable limits that feel safe to enforce. This process is not a one-time event but an ongoing practice of self-respect and self-care, reinforcing your right to a healthy relational space.

Honest and open communication is another powerful tool in disrupting toxic cycles. It requires you to express your feelings and thoughts transparently, without fear of judgment or retaliation. This means engaging in conversations that might feel uncomfortable but are necessary for growth and understanding. Honest communication involves speaking your truth and being willing to listen—truly listen—to the perspectives and emotions of others. It is about creating a dialogue where both people feel heard and valued. This openness can dissolve misunderstandings and foster a more profound connection when practiced regularly, replacing toxicity with trust and respect. Remember, communication is a two-way street, and being receptive to feedback is as crucial as sharing your experiences.

The role of support systems in fostering change cannot be overstated. Breaking free from toxic patterns often requires the strength and perspective that a supportive network can offer. Understanding friends and family can provide encouragement and a sense of belonging, reinforcing that you are not alone in your journey toward healthier relationships. Turning to professional support, such as therapy or support groups, can be highly valuable. These resources create a safe environment to explore emotions, reflect on behaviors, and develop strategies for personal growth. A therapist can help steer you through complex emotions and equip you with tailored tools. In contrast, support groups foster connection with others who have faced similar challenges, offering mutual understanding and encouragement.

Engaging in exercises to practice healthier behaviors can reinforce your commitment to change. Daily affirmations are a straightforward but powerful way to bolster your self-worth and shift your mindset. Begin each day by affirming your value and potential, using statements that resonate with you, such as "I am worthy of love and respect" or "I choose to create healthy relationships." These affirmations can counteract the negative self-talk that often accompanies toxic patterns, gradually changing the narrative you hold about yourself. Role-playing difficult conversations is another practical exercise. By rehearsing these interactions, you can build confidence and prepare for real-life scenarios, ensuring that you approach them with clarity and calm. Such practice can help you navigate challenging discussions with poise, reducing the likelihood of falling back into old, unhealthy patterns.

Success stories of breaking toxic cycles can inspire and motivate, illustrating that change is possible. Take Elizabeth, who spent years in a relationship marked by manipulation and control. She found the courage to establish firm boundaries, clearly articulating what she would no longer tolerate. With the support of a therapist, Elizabeth learned to communicate her needs assertively and left the toxic relationship behind. Over time, she rebuilt her life, fostering new relationships grounded in mutual respect. Another story is that of James, who grew up in a family where emotional neglect was the norm. As an adult, he realized this pattern had seeped into his relationships, leading to unfulfilling connections. By joining a support group, James found a community that encouraged him to break free from these patterns. He practiced open communication and learned to express his emotions honestly, transforming his relationships into sources of joy and support.

These narratives, though unique, share a common thread: the power of intentional change. They demonstrate that by employing tools like boundaries, communication, and support systems, you can disrupt the cycle of toxicity. Whether through personal determination or with the aid of others, breaking free from unhealthy patterns is achievable and deeply rewarding.

EMPOWERMENT THROUGH SELF-AWARENESS

Picture yourself standing at a crossroads, feeling confident in your choice of direction because you understand your destination and the path that resonates with you. This clarity comes from self-awareness, a powerful tool that enables you to make informed and empowered relationship choices. When you are attuned to your personal needs and desires, you can navigate the complexities of relationships with a sense of purpose and confidence. Recognizing what you truly want from your connections allows you to set boundaries that protect your well-being and align with your values. This self-knowledge empowers you to enter relationships not from a place of need or uncertainty but from strength and clarity. It helps you identify what adds value to your life and what does not, making it easier to walk away from situations that no longer serve you.

Developing greater self-awareness often begins with introspection, which involves turning your focus inward to explore your thoughts, feelings, and motivations. Once again, mindfulness practices can be a valuable tool in this exploration, helping you observe your internal landscape without judgment. By regularly setting aside time to sit quietly and pay attention to your breathing, you can become more aware of the thoughts and emotions that arise. Notice patterns or recurring themes, and consider what they might reveal about your current state of mind. This mindfulness technique encourages you to remain in the moment, reducing the noise of external distractions and allowing you to connect with your genuine self. Keeping a self-reflection journal can further enhance this process. As you write, explore your daily experiences, challenges, and successes. Reflect on how they align with your core values and aspirations. This ongoing dialogue with yourself can illuminate your true priorities, helping you make choices that reflect who you are and what you want. For those with disorganized attachment, self-awareness allows us to recognize the push-pull dynamic in relationships and understand that reactions stem from past experiences rather than present reality.

Self-awareness also plays a crucial role in recognizing external influences and pressures that may impact your decisions. In today's fast-paced world, it is easy to be swayed by the expectations of others or the pressures of societal norms. By cultivating self-awareness, you can distinguish between your desires and those imposed by external forces. This discernment allows you to resist pressures that do not align with your authentic self, enabling you to make choices that are true to your inner convictions. For example, you might notice that a friend's opinion affects your decision about a relationship. With heightened awareness, you can step back and assess whether their influence aligns with your values or if it is causing you to act against your better judgment. This clarity helps you remain true to your path, fostering relationships built on authenticity rather than conformity.

The transformative power of self-awareness is profound, as it has the potential to bring about meaningful positive changes in your life. We can learn from the story of Emily, who realized that her constant need for approval was rooted in a lack of self-awareness. She began to understand her underlying fears and motivations through mindfulness and journaling. This insight allowed her to break free from the cycle of seeking external validation, giving her the confidence to pursue relationships that honored her true self. Similarly, Alex discovered that his tendency to avoid conflict was linked to a more profound fear of rejection. By cultivating self-awareness, he learned to face his fears and engage in open, honest communication, transforming his relationships and strengthening his emotional resilience. These examples illustrate how self-awareness can catalyze growth and empowerment, leading to healthier, more fulfilling connections.

As you embark on this journey of self-discovery, remember that self-awareness is a continuous process. It requires curiosity, patience, and a desire to explore the depths of your inner world. Embrace this exploration with an open heart and mind, knowing each insight brings you closer to the empowered, authentic life you envision. Self-awareness is key to unlocking your potential and creating relationships that reflect your best self.

BEHAVIOR MODIFICATION TECHNIQUES

Behavior modification is vital in personal relationships to foster healthier dynamics. At its core, behavior modification involves intentionally changing specific behaviors that may be contributing to relational discord. By focusing on altering these behaviors, you create a ripple effect that can transform how you interact with others, ultimately leading to more fulfilling relationships. Positive reinforcement is a cornerstone of this approach. It encourages desired behaviors by rewarding them, thereby increasing the likelihood of their recurrence. Imagine the satisfaction of receiving a genuine compliment or a small token of appreciation from a partner after a meaningful gesture. These positive reinforcements serve as powerful motivators, strengthening the behavior and increasing the likelihood that it is repeated.

To modify behavior effectively, setting achievable goals is crucial. These goals should be specific and realistic, providing a clear roadmap for change. Start by identifying a behavior you want to alter, such as improving your conversation-listening skills. Break this goal down into small, manageable steps, like committing to maintain eye contact or practicing active listening techniques. Focusing on one aspect at a time can build confidence and momentum as you progress. Another practical tool is the use of habit trackers. These can help monitor your progress by visually representing your efforts. Every day you successfully implement the desired behavior, mark it on your tracker. Over weeks and months, this visual record serves as a testament to your dedication, highlighting patterns and areas for improvement.

To further support behavior modification, engaging in exercises that reinforce new, healthier behaviors can be beneficial. Developing a reward system is one such exercise. This involves identifying rewards that are meaningful to you and using them to celebrate milestones. For instance, if your goal is to express gratitude more often, treat yourself to something special each time you reach a set target, like writing a thank-you note or verbally acknowledging someone's efforts. This practice not only incentivizes the behavior but also creates positive associations, making it more enjoyable. (We explore the role of gratitude further in Chapter 9.) Visualization is another effective exercise. Spend a few minutes each day visualizing successful interactions where you embody the behaviors you wish to cultivate. Picture yourself communicating with empathy and patience, and imagine the positive responses from others. This mental practice can enhance your confidence and prepare you for real-life situations.

The power of behavior modification is evident in stories of personal transformation. We can look at the case of Laura, who struggled with interrupting others during conversations. She recognized this habit as a barrier to deeper connections. By setting a goal to improve her listening skills, Laura began practicing active listening techniques and used a habit tracker to monitor her progress. She also developed a system of rewards, treating herself to a favorite activity each week she met her targets. Within a year, Laura noticed a significant change in her interactions. Conversations became more meaningful, and her relationships strengthened as others felt heard and valued. Another example is

Mark, who aimed to reduce his tendency to procrastinate essential discussions with his partner. Mark gradually overcame his avoidance by visualizing successful conversations and setting small goals to address issues promptly. These stories illustrate that altering relationship behaviors is within reach with determination and the right strategies.

Behavior modification is not just about changing actions but reshaping the way we engage with others. It empowers you to break free from patterns that no longer serve you, paving the way for healthier connections. As you embrace these techniques, remember that change is a process, and progress may be gradual. Celebrate each step forward and remain patient with yourself. Applying these strategies consistently can help you transform interactions and cultivate rewarding and resilient relationships.

With the tools and insights gained from behavior modification, you are well-equipped to navigate the complexities of relationships. Each step toward change contributes to a broader personal growth and connection journey. As we conclude this chapter, consider how these new behaviors can impact your life, setting the stage for deeper exploration in the chapters to come.

CHAPTER 5
CULTIVATING SELF-WORTH AND SELF-COMPASSION

THINK OF A MOMENT WHEN YOU FELT THE WEIGHT OF SELF-DOUBT pressing heavily on your shoulders. Perhaps it was after receiving criticism at work, or the whisper of inadequacy crept in during a social gathering. These feelings are all too familiar for many of us, and they can become a constant companion if left unchecked. Yet, there is a powerful antidote to this internal struggle: self-compassion. We touched on self-trust briefly in Chapter 3. This chapter will guide you through a deeper understanding and cultivating self-compassion, a transformative practice that can significantly enhance your mental well-being. For those with disorganized attachment stemming from inconsistent or unpredictable caregiving during childhood, developing self-worth can feel particularly challenging due to conflicting early experiences with caregivers. This chapter offers specific tools such as self-compassionate letter writing and daily self-kindness reflections to help rebuild a stable sense of self.

UNDERSTANDING AND CULTIVATING SELF-ACCEPTANCE AND SELF-COMPASSION

Self-compassion and self-acceptance are intertwined practices that form the foundation of healthy self-worth. Self-compassion is treating yourself with the kindness you would offer a friend, while self-acceptance means embracing your strengths and limitations without judgment. These two practices work hand in hand, with self-compassion providing the emotional support and understanding needed to accept oneself fully. For those healing from disorganized attachment, these practices become essential tools for establishing internal stability and breaking cycles of self-criticism.

Research, including Kristin Neff's work, shows that these practices positively influence mental health by reducing anxiety and depression. They involve three key components: self-kindness, recognition of common humanity, and mindful awareness. Accepting yourself fully while offering compassion for your struggles creates an internal environment that supports healing and growth.

The journey toward self-acceptance and compassion often faces barriers, particularly for those with disorganized attachment patterns. These might include fear of vulnerability, difficulty trusting yourself, and conflicting internal messages about self-worth. Overcoming these barriers involves building trust in your own experiences and emotions while learning to quiet the harsh inner critic that may have developed from inconsistent early relationships.

Interactive Element: Exercises to Cultivate Self-Compassion

Here are some practical exercises to help you develop self-compassion:

1. **Self-Compassionate Letter Writing**: This exercise involves setting aside time to write a letter to yourself, addressing a challenge or mistake with empathy and understanding. The key is to acknowledge your feelings and offer comfort and encouragement as you would to a dear friend. This exercise can shift your perspective and foster a more compassionate view of yourself, allowing you to practice self-compassion tangibly. It reinforces the idea that you are worthy of kindness and understanding, even in difficult situations.

2. **Daily Self-Kindness Reflections**: Each evening, reflect on your day and identify moments when you were self-critical. Consider how you could have approached these situations with more kindness and understanding. Write down your reflections and set an intention to practice self-kindness the following day. This practice is crucial to your journey toward self-acceptance. It fosters a more compassionate view of yourself and encourages you to be kinder to yourself.

These exercises can cultivate self-compassion and nurture a more supportive inner dialogue. This practice enhances your mental health and enriches your relationships and overall quality of life.

EMBRACING SELF-ACCEPTANCE

Picture yourself standing in front of a mirror, seeing your reflection and the essence of who you are, with all your strengths and flaws. This is self-acceptance. It means embracing yourself fully and acknowledging both your talents and your imperfections. Self-acceptance is crucial to personal growth because it allows you to live authentically without the constant pressure to conform to unrealistic ideals. When you accept yourself, you let go of perfectionism, understanding that having limitations and making mistakes is okay. This acceptance fosters a sense of peace, freeing you from the relentless pursuit of an unattainable standard of perfection and empowering you to live on your terms, feeling confident and in control of your personal growth.

However, achieving self-acceptance is often easier said than done. Many barriers stand in the way. One of the most significant obstacles is the fear of judgment or rejection. The worry about how others perceive you can be paralyzing, leading you to hide your true self. This fear often stems from past experiences where you felt judged or excluded, leaving a lasting impact that makes you cautious about revealing your authentic self. Internalized criticism from past experiences is another formidable barrier. Negative comments or failures can linger in your mind, creating a harsh inner critic that constantly undermines your confidence and self-worth. These internalized voices can be relentless, and viewing yourself with kindness and understanding is challenging.

To cultivate self-acceptance, it is essential to practice forgiveness for past mistakes. This means acknowledging errors without letting them define you or your worth. Instead of dwelling on what went wrong, focus on what you learned and how you have grown. Forgiveness allows you to release guilt and move forward with a lighter heart. Celebrating small victories and progress is another effective strategy. These "small victories" could be as simple as maintaining a healthy habit, completing a task at work, or showing kindness to others. Recognize and appreciate your achievements, no matter how minor they may seem. This practice helps shift your focus from shortcomings to accomplishments, reinforcing a positive self-image. By celebrating your progress, you build a foundation of self-worth that supports your journey toward acceptance.

We can learn from Michael, who spent years battling negative self-talk. He constantly compared himself to others, feeling inadequate and unworthy. Michael learned to challenge these thoughts through therapy and embrace his unique qualities. He began practicing daily affirmations and celebrating small victories, such as completing a challenging project at work or learning a new skill. Over the months, Michael found peace in his identity, realizing that his worth was not determined by external validation but by his acceptance. Similarly, Stacy struggled with accepting her body image after years of criticism. She started a journey of self-acceptance by forgiving herself for past mistakes and focusing on her strengths, like her creativity and compassion. Through mindfulness and self-reflection, Stacy learned to love herself wholly, imperfections and all.

These stories illustrate the transformative power of self-acceptance. Embracing who you are opens the door to personal growth and fulfillment. You become free to pursue your passions and live life on your terms without the constraints of societal expectations or self-imposed limitations. Self-acceptance allows you to build a strong foundation of confidence and resilience, empowering you to navigate life's challenges with grace and authenticity. As you embrace your true self, you cultivate an inner peace that enhances your well-being and enriches your relationships.

GRATITUDE JOURNALING FOR SELF-WORTH

Have you ever woken up in the morning with a sense of dread about the day ahead, your mind instinctively listing all that might go wrong? Now, picture starting your day differently—by focusing on what you are thankful for. A gratitude journal is a simple, powerful tool that can shift your perspective from focusing on flaws to recognizing strengths. By documenting daily moments of gratitude, you train your mind to seek the positive, fostering a sense of appreciation that boosts self-esteem. This practice is about shifting your focus from what you lack to what you cherish, reshaping how you perceive yourself and the world around you. Even in small doses, focusing on the good nurtures a more positive self-image and enhances your overall sense of self-worth. For those healing from disorganized attachment, gratitude journaling can help anchor positive experiences that might otherwise feel threatening or confusing.

Starting a gratitude journal is straightforward and requires only a few minutes daily. Begin by choosing a notebook that feels inviting—something you look forward to opening. Each day, write down three things you are grateful for. These do not have to be monumental; they can be as simple as the sun's warmth on your face or a kind word from a colleague. The key is to be specific, capturing what made those moments memorable. Regularly reflecting on these positive experiences can help cement them in your mind, making gratitude a natural part of your thought process. Over months and years, this practice can cultivate a habit of looking for the good in everyday situations, fostering a more optimistic and resilient mindset.

The psychological benefits of gratitude practices are well-documented and profound. Focusing on gratitude has improved my mood and fostered a more positive outlook. When you regularly write in a gratitude journal, you notice increased optimism and happiness. This change in perspective lets you approach challenges with a more hopeful attitude, believing in the possibility of positive outcomes. Additionally, gratitude enhances your sense of connectedness to others as you become more aware of the kindness and support present in your life. This increased awareness can lead to deeper, more meaningful relationships as you express appreciation for those around you, strengthening bonds and fostering mutual respect and affection.

Consider the story of Jane, who struggled with persistent feelings of inadequacy. She began gratitude journaling at the suggestion of a friend, skeptical at first about its potential impact. Slowly, Jane noticed a transformation. She started to see herself in a new light, focusing on her strengths and the positive aspects of her life rather than her perceived shortcomings. This shift helped her overcome negative self-perceptions, allowing her to build confidence in her abilities. Another example is Tim, who had always doubted his skills at work. He learned to appreciate his achievements and contributions through gratitude journaling, boosting his self-esteem and confidence. These stories illustrate the transformative power of gratitude, showing how it can elevate self-worth and foster personal growth.

Gratitude journaling can be a gratifying practice that enhances your self-worth and enriches your daily experiences. As you cultivate gratitude, you create a positive foundation supporting your mental and emotional well-being. This practice encourages you to celebrate the small victories in life, recognizing the beauty and abundance surrounding you. It is about acknowledging the good, even amid challenges, and allowing that recognition to fuel your sense of worthiness and joy. As you continue to explore gratitude journaling, remember that it is a personal journey that invites you to discover the richness of your life and the inherent value you hold within.

AFFIRMATION PRACTICES FOR PERSONAL GROWTH

Do you wake up each morning with a chorus of negative thoughts echoing in your mind, telling you what you cannot do or who you are not? This negativity can be relentless, impacting how you view yourself and your potential. That is where positive affirmations come into play. They serve as powerful tools in personal development, helping to challenge and reshape those deep-seated negative self-beliefs. You create a positive self-image that reflects your true potential by consistently affirming your worth and abilities. Affirmations can help resolve conflicting internal messages about self-worth when dealing with disorganized attachment patterns. They reinforce the belief that you are capable and deserving of growth and success, shifting your mindset from doubt to possibility.

Crafting effective affirmations requires thoughtful consideration. Begin using the present tense and positive language, as if what you affirm is already true. For instance, say, "I am confident and capable," rather than "I will be confident someday." This approach helps your mind accept these statements as reality, creating a sense of immediacy and certainty. Focus on specific goals or qualities that resonate deeply with you, ensuring that your affirmations align with your values and aspirations. This personalization makes the affirmations more meaningful and impactful, as they speak directly to your unique journey and desires.

The science behind affirmations supports their effectiveness. Research indicates that affirmations can influence neural pathways, promoting positive thinking and altering the brain's response to stress. When you repeat affirmations, you engage the brain's reward system, reinforcing positive beliefs and reducing the impact of negative ones. This neural reprogramming helps cultivate a more resilient and adaptable mindset, enhancing overall psychological well-being. By inserting affirmations into your daily routine, you can harness the brain's plasticity to foster growth and transformation, paving the way for a more empowered self.

Daily affirmations in your life can be simple yet transformative. Start with morning affirmation practices, setting aside a few minutes each day to recite your affirmations aloud or in your mind. It sets a positive tone for the day, grounding you in the beliefs that you wish to cultivate. Consider using affirmation cards, which you can place around your home or workspace as constant reminders of your intentions. These visual cues can reinforce your affirmations throughout the day, helping to keep your mindset aligned with your goals. As you fold these practices into your routine, you may notice a shift in how you perceive yourself and interact with the world, embracing opportunities for growth with confidence and clarity.

BUILDING AN INNER SUPPORT SYSTEM

Envision a world where you possess an unwavering sense of stability and support, no matter the external circumstances. This is the essence of an inner support system—a network of personal resources that bolsters your confidence and resilience. Developing self-reliance is the cornerstone of this system. It involves trusting your abilities and judgments and knowing that you have the strength to face challenges independently. This self-confidence acts as a buffer against the uncertainties of life, providing a sense of security that is not reliant on external validation. Reinforcing this system is the cultivation of inner resilience. It is the ability to adapt and recover from adversity, and it is fortified by a strong inner support system that can gracefully weather life's storms.

The benefits of a robust inner support system are manifold. Chief among them is increased self-trust. When you trust yourself, you navigate life's challenges with assurance, knowing you have the necessary tools to succeed. This trust fosters a sense of autonomy, allowing you to confidently make decisions, free from the paralyzing fear of making mistakes. Additionally, an inner support system equips you to self-soothe during times of stress. Instead of seeking external comfort, you can draw upon your internal resources to calm and center yourself. This self-soothing ability is invaluable in maintaining emotional equilibrium, helping you manage stress and anxiety effectively. For those with disorganized attachment histories, building an inner support system is crucial for developing the consistent internal presence that may have been missing in early relationships.

Creating and maintaining your inner support system begins with identifying your strengths and resources. Take some time to reflect on your abilities, talents, and past successes. What qualities have helped you overcome challenges? Perhaps it is your perseverance, creativity, or empathy. Recognize these strengths and use them as the foundation of your inner support system. Once you have identified your strengths, consider creating a personal mantra or support statement. This mantra should encapsulate your core values and beliefs, providing motivation and encouragement during difficult times. Repeat this mantra regularly to reinforce your inner support system, making it a central part of your self-care routine.

Consider Rachel, who found herself at a crossroads in her career. Faced with uncertainty, she relied on her inner support system to navigate the transition. Rachel confidently approached the situation by focusing on her strengths, such as her adaptability and problem-solving skills. Her mantra, "I am capable and resourceful," became a guiding light, helping her maintain composure and clarity. Similarly, David faced a challenging family situation that tested his emotional resilience. He strengthened his inner support system through meditation and self-reflection, allowing him to remain calm and composed. These stories illustrate the power of internal support, demonstrating how it can provide stability and strength in the face of adversity.

As you cultivate your inner support system, remember it is a dynamic and evolving structure. Like any other relationship, it requires regular attention and nurturing. Investing in your internal resources creates a bedrock of strength and resilience that empowers you to face life's challenges confidently and gracefully. This inner support system enhances your well-being and enriches your interactions with others, fostering more profound and meaningful connections.

In this chapter, we have explored various strategies to cultivate self-worth and self-compassion. As you build on these concepts, you will be better equipped to handle life's challenges. Next, we will examine how managing emotional closeness and vulnerability can further enhance relationships and personal growth.

CHAPTER 6
MANAGING EMOTIONAL CLOSENESS AND VULNERABILITY

PICTURE YOURSELF STANDING BEFORE A WINDOW, THE LIGHT streaming softly, illuminating the room with warmth. This moment is akin to emotional closeness in relationships—a gentle, illuminating presence that fosters connection and understanding. Emotional closeness is the heart of any meaningful relationship. It involves sharing personal thoughts and feelings, creating a bridge of understanding between individuals. When you share your inner world with someone, you invite them into your life in a way that builds a profound bond. This sharing is about speaking and engaging in meaningful conversations where both people feel heard and valued. These interactions become the threads that weave the fabric of your connection, each exchange strengthening the relational tapestry. As we have discussed, emotional closeness can feel simultaneously desired and threatening for those with disorganized attachment patterns. Understanding this paradox is crucial for developing healthier relationship dynamics.

UNDERSTANDING AND FOSTERING EMOTIONAL CLOSENESS

The benefits of emotional closeness are manifold. When two people connect on this level, trust naturally flourishes. In a world of uncertainty, having someone you can rely on is invaluable. This trust provides support and a safety net for life's challenges. But it is not just about leaning on each other in tough times. It is also about the joyous moments, the celebrations, and the shared laughter that make life beautiful. Greater empathy, a key ingredient in fostering emotional closeness, emerges from this connection, allowing you to understand your partner's perspective with clarity and compassion. As empathy deepens, so does relational satisfaction, as both feel seen and understood. This satisfaction is not fleeting; the deep contentment comes from knowing you are accepted and loved for who you are.

Yet, achieving emotional closeness is not without its challenges. Fear of rejection or judgment can act as a formidable barrier. You might hesitate to open up, worried that revealing your true self could lead to criticism or distancing. Past experiences of betrayal can also cast long shadows, making it difficult to trust again. These fears create walls that hinder intimacy, leaving you isolated even when surrounded by loved ones. It is a paradox of wanting closeness but fearing the vulnerability it requires. Understanding these barriers is crucial, allowing you to approach them with awareness and intention. Those working through disorganized attachment patterns, which can show as a fear of intimacy or a tendency to push people away, may find that emotional closeness triggers conflicting impulses to both seek and avoid intimacy.

Recognizing these patterns is the first step toward building more secure connections.

Intentional strategies can be employed to foster emotional closeness. One practical approach is to put aside dedicated time for deep conversations. It is easy to let meaningful dialogue fall by the wayside in our busy lives. By prioritizing these moments, you signal to your partner that they are essential and that their thoughts and feelings matter. This dedicated time creates a space free from distractions where you can explore each other's inner worlds. Again, another strategy is practicing active listening and empathy. It is a powerful way to enhance emotional closeness. This means not just hearing the words spoken but understanding the emotions behind them. It is being fully present, offering undivided attention, and responding empathetically. Doing so creates an environment where emotional closeness can thrive, nurtured by mutual understanding and respect.

Reflection Section: Cultivating Closeness

Take a moment to reflect on a recent conversation in which you felt emotionally close to someone. What exchange fostered that closeness? Consider how you can replicate these conditions in future interactions. Write down a list of actions or attitudes contributing to this connection. This reflection can guide you in nurturing emotional closeness in your relationships, helping you build more profound and meaningful connections.

TECHNIQUES TO EMBRACE VULNERABILITY

Vulnerability is the hidden strength in relationships, the quiet courage that builds deep, lasting connections. When you are vulnerable, you let go of the need for perfection. You open the door to authenticity by showing your true self and flaws. By sharing your weaknesses and fears, you invite others to do the same, fostering a space of mutual openness. It is in these shared imperfections that genuine connections form. Vulnerability allows you to be seen for who you are, not just the polished version you present to the world. This transparency can strengthen bonds, encouraging others to reciprocate with their truths and creating a foundation of trust and understanding.

Becoming comfortable with vulnerability is a journey that requires self-compassion. It is a practice of gradual self-disclosure in environments where you feel safe. Start small. Share a personal story or an emotion with someone you trust. Notice how it feels to open up and how the other person responds. Safe environments, like close friendships or supportive family gatherings, are ideal places to practice this. You can expand this practice to other areas as you become more comfortable. Alongside this, cultivate self-compassion. When you feel exposed or unsure, remind yourself that vulnerability is a strength, not a weakness. This self-compassion is a cushion, softening the edges of exposure and encouraging further openness. It is important to remember that self-compassion is not just a tool but a comforting companion in embracing vulnerability.

Vulnerability plays a pivotal role in resolving conflicts. Disagreements escalate because people hide their true feelings behind defensiveness or anger. By expressing emotions honestly, you can break down these barriers. Saying, "I felt hurt when you did that," rather than lashing out, invites understanding and resolution. This openness can transform conflict from a battleground into a space for growth and healing. Vulnerability fosters dialogue, allowing both people to express their feelings without fear of retribution. It requires courage but can lead to healthier, more constructive resolutions. When both people approach conflict with vulnerability, they pave the way for empathy, compassion, and a deeper connection. This power of empathy in resolving disputes can lead to a profound sense of growth and healing in your relationships.

Let us consider Esther, who found herself constantly clashing with her partner. Their arguments seemed to go in circles, leaving them both frustrated and disconnected. One day, Esther decided to try something different. Instead of pointing fingers, she shared her fears and insecurities, expressing how certain behaviors made her feel unloved. Her partner, taken aback by her candor, responded with his vulnerabilities. This exchange marked a turning point in their relationship. By embracing vulnerability, they discovered a new level of understanding and intimacy. Then there is Matthew, who struggled with being open about his mental health challenges. After years of silence, he confided in a close friend, revealing his struggles with anxiety. To his surprise, his friend responded with empathy and shared his experiences with similar issues. This moment of vulnerability deepened their friendship, creating a support system Matthew had not realized he needed. These stories illustrate the transformative power of vulnerability, showing that when you dare to be open, you invite others to connect with you profoundly and empower yourself.

PRACTICES FOR HEALTHY EMOTIONAL INTIMACY

As we have seen, emotional intimacy is the delicate art of deeply understanding another person while being understood yourself. It forms the core of profound relationships, fostering a solid framework of mutual respect and acceptance. When you comprehend your partner's inner world *and* your own, you create a bond that withstands time and change. Emotional intimacy transcends physical presence; it is about truly knowing each other and sharing life's vulnerabilities and joys. This deeper understanding allows you to anticipate each other's needs and respond with compassion and care, strengthening the relational fabric woven between you.

Consider incorporating practices that invite connection into your daily life to enhance emotional intimacy. One simple yet powerful exercise is sharing daily highs and lows with your partner. This practice encourages open dialogue about the day's events, fostering a deeper understanding of each other's experiences and emotions. Another effective method is creating rituals of connection. A weekly check-in, where you discuss your feelings, aspirations, and concerns, can be a dedicated space for intimacy to flourish. These rituals remind you to pause and focus on your relationship, reinforcing the importance of maintaining a strong emotional connection amid distractions.

However, maintaining emotional intimacy can be challenging, especially as routine and complacency set in over the years. Long-term relationships often fall into predictable patterns, where the initial excitement fades, and the daily grind takes over. This can lead to neglecting the emotional needs that once came so naturally. When life becomes a series of routines, intimacy can erode, leaving both partners feeling distant and disconnected. Recognizing this drift is crucial, allowing you to take proactive steps to reignite the emotional spark that initially drew you together.

To sustain emotional intimacy, regular expressions of appreciation and gratitude are vital. Taking the time to acknowledge and thank your partner for their efforts and qualities can breathe new life into your relationship. Simple acts like leaving a thoughtful note or verbally expressing gratitude can make your partner feel valued and loved. Additionally, engaging in new and shared experiences together can rekindle the connection. Whether trying out a new hobby, exploring a new place, or even taking a class together, these activities create shared memories and deepen your bond. They break the monotony and remind you of the joy of discovery that brought you together in the first place.

Incorporating these practices into your relationship nurtures the emotional intimacy that sustains lasting bonds. As you strive to understand and connect with your partner on a deeper level, you build a resilient and fulfilling relationship capable of weathering life's changes and challenges. This commitment to intimacy requires intention and effort, but the rewards—a profound connection and enduring love—are well worth it.

BALANCING CONNECTION AND INDEPENDENCE

Maintaining a balance between connection and independence is crucial in the tapestry of relationships. You want to preserve your individuality while building a close bond with your partner, but it can feel like walking a tightrope. Independence allows you to pursue personal interests and hobbies, giving you space to grow and explore. This freedom fuels your sense of self, ensuring you do not lose sight of who you are outside the relationship. Encouraging your partner's autonomy is equally essential. It is about supporting their need for personal space and respecting their pursuits. For those with disorganized attachment histories, finding this balance can be particularly challenging, as early experiences may have created confusion about appropriate boundaries and connections. But when both partners find space to flourish independently, they bring more to the relationship, enriching the connection with new experiences and growth.

Yet, achieving this balance is not without its challenges. The fear of losing yourself in a relationship is common. You might worry that merging too closely with your partner could lead to losing your identity. This fear can create an internal conflict, where the desire for connection clashes with the need for independence. Conversely, dependency on a partner for emotional fulfillment can stifle both people. When one person relies too heavily on the other for happiness or validation, it can lead to feelings of suffocation and imbalance. This dependency can erode the relationship's foundation, making it difficult to maintain a healthy dynamic. Recognizing these challenges is the first step toward finding a harmonious balance.

As discussed in an earlier chapter, consider setting boundaries for personal space and time to nurture independence and connection. Boundaries create a protective bubble where you can recharge and pursue individual interests without guilt. Express your intimate needs and expectations directly to your partner to ensure you understand and respect each other's boundaries. This transparency fosters trust and prevents misunderstandings, allowing the relationship to thrive without compromising personal freedom. Practicing open communication involves regular check-ins where you discuss what is working and what is not. These conversations provide an opportunity to adjust and realign, ensuring both partners feel valued and understood. You create a framework supporting individuality and togetherness by setting clear boundaries and maintaining an open dialogue.

Consider the story of Lily and Sam, a couple who balanced their independence with their deep connection. A passionate artist, Lily needed time alone to create, while Sam thrived on social interactions and adventures. They established a routine where Lily had dedicated studio time, and Sam enjoyed outings with friends. They also set aside time for shared activities, strengthening their connection. This arrangement allowed them to support each other's passions while nurturing their relationship. Another example is Eveline and Joshua, who found balance by pursuing separate hobbies. Eveline loved yoga, while Josh was an avid cyclist. They encouraged each other to follow these interests and often shared stories and insights from their experiences, enriching their bond with new perspectives. These couples demonstrate that with intentional effort, it is possible to maintain individuality while cultivating a deep, fulfilling connection.

NAVIGATING VULNERABILITY IN NEW RELATIONSHIPS

Starting a new relationship is often an exhilarating yet daunting experience. The thrill of discovery mingles with the trepidation of revealing yourself to another person. In these early stages, vulnerability can feel particularly challenging. The fear of being hurt or rejected looms large, casting shadows over moments of budding intimacy. You may wonder if your new partner will accept you as you are or if showing too much too soon might drive them away. This fear is natural, as new relationships often bring uncertainties that test our willingness to open up. Vulnerability, however, is not about baring your soul all at once; it is about gradually taking measured steps to build trust and openness. Those healing from disorganized attachment may find new relationships particularly challenging as they navigate between intense desires for connection and equally intense fears of vulnerability.

Share small, personal details with your new partner to navigate these waters. This might be a childhood memory, a hobby you enjoy, or an emotion you felt during your day. Observe how they respond to these disclosures. Are they interested? Do they reciprocate with their own stories? Their responses can offer meaningful insights into the potential for a deeper connection. This gradual self-revelation allows you to gauge their capacity for empathy and understanding without overwhelming either party. As trust builds, you can slowly increase the depth of your disclosures, fostering a safe environment where both of you feel comfortable being yourselves.

In the context of new relationships, trust is the bedrock upon which vulnerability rests. As we saw in Chapter 3, building trust is a gradual process that demands patience and consistency. Trust is earned through actions that demonstrate reliability and integrity. Consistent behavior, such as keeping promises and punctuality, reinforces the belief that your partner is dependable. As your relationship grows, these actions create a secure foundation, allowing you to feel safe in your vulnerability. As trust grows, so does the willingness to share more intimate thoughts and feelings. This mutual trust paves the way for a more profound emotional connection, transforming initial uncertainty into a lasting bond.

Consider the story of Arthur and Mia, who met through mutual friends. Initially, Arthur hesitated to share his passion for poetry, fearing it might be seen as frivolous. Encouraged by Mia's genuine interest in his hobbies, he started sharing his favorite poems. Mia responded with enthusiasm, sharing her love for literature. This exchange marked the beginning of a deeper connection. As their trust in each other solidified, Arthur and Mia opened up about more personal topics, such as family dynamics and aspirations. Their relationship blossomed as each disclosure brought them closer, proving that vulnerability can be a powerful catalyst for intimacy when embraced thoughtfully.

Similarly, consider Claire, who entered a new relationship cautiously after a previous heartbreak. She explored the idea of vulnerability by sharing her love for painting, something she had kept private for years. Her partner, Ben, reacted with curiosity, asking questions and suggesting they visit an art gallery together. Encouraged by his supportive response, Claire gradually shared more about her artistic journey, including her dreams and fears. With each shared story, their bond deepened, and Claire realized that being vulnerable did not weaken her; it enriched her connection with Ben. These narratives illustrate that embracing vulnerability, even in small doses, can lead to meaningful and lasting relationships.

CHAPTER 7
EFFECTIVE COMMUNICATION IN RELATIONSHIPS

IN THE ORCHESTRA OF HUMAN INTERACTION, COMMUNICATION ACTS AS the conductor, guiding the symphony of words, gestures, and emotions that connect us. Yet, amid the cacophony of modern life, our ability to genuinely listen often falls silent, drowned out by the relentless tempo of distractions and responsibilities. Imagine a conversation where the speaker's words drift into an abyss of inattentiveness—their meaning lost in the noise of unending notifications and mental clutter. This scenario is all too familiar in a world where our attention is a prized commodity, constantly sought after by the demands of daily life. As we have mentioned in other chapters up to this point, active listening offers a beacon of clarity in this fog of distraction, inviting us to engage with others on a deeper, more meaningful level. For those with disorganized attachment patterns, communication can feel particularly challenging as it may trigger conflicting impulses to both connect and withdraw. Understanding these patterns is crucial for developing more consistent and secure communication styles.

THE ART AND IMPORTANCE OF ACTIVE LISTENING

Active listening is much more than hearing words; it is the art of fully engaging with the speaker and focusing intently on their message and emotions. Unlike passive listening, where words merely pass through our consciousness, active listening requires deliberate attention and presence. It involves reflecting on what is being said, not just the words but the emotions and intent behind them. By paraphrasing or summarizing the speaker's message, you can demonstrate understanding and empathy, creating a space where the other person feels honestly heard. This practice enhances communication and fosters intimacy and trust, laying the foundation for stronger relationships. The emotional benefits of active listening are significant, making it a skill worth mastering.

Despite its importance, active listening is often hindered by various barriers. Distractions are among the most common obstacles, drawing our focus away from the speaker and onto other stimuli. Whether it is the ping of a smartphone or the mental checklist of tasks yet to be completed, these interruptions can sever the connection thread, leaving the speaker feeling undervalued and ignored. Multitasking further compounds this issue, as dividing attention between multiple activities diminishes our capacity to engage with any task fully. Prejudgments and assumptions also pose significant barriers, as preconceived notions about a person's intentions or abilities can color our perception of their words, leading to misunderstandings and conflicts. These assumptions act as filters, distorting the speaker's message and preventing genuine communication. However, active listening can help overcome these barriers, as it encourages us to focus on the speaker's message and emotions rather than our distractions or assumptions. Those healing from disorganized attachment may find active listening incredibly challenging, as past experiences may have created heightened sensitivity to verbal and non-verbal cues. Learning to distinguish between past triggers and present communication becomes essential.

Practical techniques can overcome these barriers and enhance active listening skills. One of the most effective methods is maintaining eye contact. It shows the speaker you are fully present and engaged. This simple act can convey a sense of respect and attentiveness, encouraging open and honest dialogue. Using verbal affirmations, such as "I understand" or "That makes sense," can reinforce your engagement, demonstrating that you are actively processing the speaker's message. These affirmations serve as verbal nods, acknowledging the speaker's thoughts and emotions and fostering a deep connection. Additionally, reflecting on the speaker's words through paraphrasing can clarify understanding and ensure that both parties are on the same page.

Consider the story of a team leader, Spencer, who transformed a work environment plagued by misunderstandings through the power of active listening. He created a culture of respect and understanding by encouraging open dialogue and practicing attentive listening during meetings. Team members felt valued and heard, leading to increased collaboration and productivity. Similarly, active listening can bridge the gap between friends or partners in personal relationships, strengthening bonds and resolving conflicts. The transformative power of active listening to resolve disputes can bring hope and optimism to any relationship. We can learn from a couple who began practicing active listening after years of miscommunication. By genuinely hearing each other's concerns and perspectives, they were able to address underlying issues and foster a more harmonious relationship.

Interactive Exercise: Active Listening Practice

Try this simple exercise to hone your active listening skills. Pair up with a friend or partner and set a five-minute timer. One person speaks about a topic of their choice while the other listens attentively. The listener should maintain eye contact, refrain from interrupting, and use verbal affirmations. After the person speaking finishes, the listener paraphrases what was said to confirm understanding. Switch roles and repeat. Reflect on how this exercise changes the dynamic of your conversation and the connection you feel with your partner.

CLEARLY EXPRESSING EMOTIONS

Imagine sitting down with someone you care about, eager to share a moment of vulnerability, only to find the words tangled in your throat. This is a familiar scene for many, where the unspoken emotions create a barrier, leaving both people feeling distant and misunderstood. The ability to express emotions is a cornerstone of trust and intimacy. When you articulate your feelings openly, you invite transparency into the interaction, paving the way for deeper connections. For those with disorganized attachment histories, expressing emotions clearly can feel particularly risky, as early experiences may have taught that emotional expression leads to unpredictable responses. Building a new framework for emotional expression becomes crucial. By reducing misunderstandings, you create an environment where both people feel safe to share their authentic selves, fostering a bond built on mutual respect and understanding—transparent emotional expression bridges two hearts in a dance of empathy and compassion, reassuring both people of their security in the relationship.

Consider employing strategies that clarify and own your feelings to articulate emotions effectively. One powerful method is using "I" statements, which allow you to express your emotions without casting blame. For instance, saying, "I feel hurt when plans change unexpectedly," focuses on your feelings rather than accusing the other person of wrongdoing. This approach encourages open dialogue and reduces defensiveness, making it easier for the other person to engage with your perspective. Additionally, distinguishing between thoughts and feelings is crucial. Often, what we perceive as emotions are judgments or assumptions in disguise. By separating these elements, you gain clarity and can communicate more authentically. For example, instead of saying, "I feel like you're ignoring me," consider stating, "I feel lonely when you don't respond."

Despite its importance, many struggle to express emotions clearly due to various challenges. A common hurdle is the fear of vulnerability, where sharing emotions feels like exposing a tender underbelly. This fear can come from past experiences where vulnerability led to hurt or rejection. As a result, we may suppress our emotions, choosing silence over the risk of being misunderstood. Another significant challenge is the lack of an emotional vocabulary. We often resort to vague expressions without words to describe complex feelings, leaving our emotions open to misinterpretation. This lack of precision can lead to frustration and conflict, as neither party fully understands the other's emotional landscape.

Engaging in specific exercises can be beneficial to navigate these challenges and enhance clarity in emotional communication. Emotion journaling offers a private space to explore and articulate your feelings. By regularly writing about your emotions, you become more attuned to their nuances and can identify patterns or triggers. This practice improves your emotional vocabulary and provides insights into your inner world, enabling you to communicate more precisely. Additionally, role-playing emotional conversations can be an effective way to practice expressing emotions in a safe environment. By simulating real-life scenarios with a trusted friend or therapist, you can experiment with different ways of articulating your feelings, receiving feedback, and refining your approach. This rehearsal can build confidence, making expressing emotions clearly in actual situations easier.

The journey of expressing emotions is not about achieving perfection but embracing authenticity. It is about finding the courage to share your inner world with another, knowing that doing so can deepen your connection. As you practice articulating your emotions, you create a space where you and your partner can engage in meaningful dialogue, navigating the complexities of your relationship with openness and grace. In this dance of communication, each step toward clarity and honesty strengthens your bond, enriching your relationship and fostering a love grounded in understanding and trust.

CONFLICT RESOLUTION STRATEGIES

In every relationship, conflict is as inevitable as the changing seasons. Yet, how we approach and resolve these disagreements can significantly influence the health of our connections. Conflict resolution is not merely about finding a middle ground but is a vital component that strengthens relationships. Addressing issues constructively enhances mutual understanding, ensuring everyone feels heard and respected. This approach prevents resentment from festering, which, if left unchecked, can erode the foundation of even the strongest bonds. Consider conflict an opportunity to deepen your relationship, explore different perspectives, and grow together. Those working through disorganized attachment patterns may find conflict particularly triggering, as it can simultaneously activate both fight and flight responses. Understanding these reactions helps in developing more balanced conflict resolution strategies.

Effective conflict resolution relies on strategies to navigate disagreements with empathy and clarity. Finding common ground and reaching compromises are pivotal techniques. They involve identifying shared values or goals that can serve as a foundation for agreement. When both people focus on these commonalities, it becomes easier to negotiate solutions that respect each person's needs. Also, establishing fair fighting rules can prevent conflicts from escalating into heated arguments. These rules might include agreeing to take breaks when emotions run high or committing to speak calmly and respectfully. These guidelines create a structured environment where issues can be addressed without fear of personal attacks.

Setting and timing play crucial roles in the success of conflict resolution. Discussing sensitive issues at the wrong time can lead to misunderstandings and heightened emotions. Choosing the right moment—when both people are calm and receptive—ensures the conversation is productive. Similarly, the setting can influence the outcome of a discussion. A neutral, comfortable environment can help both people feel safe to talk about their thoughts and emotions. Creating a space free from distractions is vital, where the focus remains on resolving the conflict. This careful consideration of timing and setting sets the stage for meaningful dialogue, allowing for the possibility of resolution and reconciliation.

Consider the story of Dustin and Louise, whose relationship faced turbulence due to differing priorities. Their arguments often spiraled into blame games, leaving both people frustrated and disconnected. However, they transformed their disagreements into collaborative discussions by implementing conflict resolution strategies. During one such dispute, Dustin suggested they list their shared goals, which revealed more commonalities than differences. They agreed to compromise, aligning their priorities to accommodate each other's needs. This shared exercise resolved their immediate conflict and strengthened their bond, reinforcing the importance of teamwork and empathy.

In another instance, Sam and Alex navigated a conflict regarding household responsibilities, which had become a source of tension. By agreeing to rules for fair fighting, they approached the issue calmly, each taking turns articulating their feelings without interruption. They chose a quiet evening at home to discuss their concerns, ensuring a relaxed setting that encouraged openness.

This thoughtful approach allowed them to express their frustrations without escalating into personal attacks. Through mutual understanding and compromise, Sam and Alex created a chore schedule that balanced their contributions, resolving the conflict amicably and enhancing their sense of partnership.

Resolving conflicts constructively requires patience, empathy, and a willingness to see beyond immediate disagreements. It is about recognizing that beneath the surface tension lies an opportunity for growth and understanding. By employing effective strategies, you can transform conflicts into moments of connection, reinforcing the bonds that hold your relationship together.

BUILDING EMOTIONAL INTELLIGENCE

Imagine being in a crowded room filled with chatter and overlapping conversations. Yet, somehow, your attention zeros in on one person's expression—a subtle brow furrow and a slight downturn of the lips. This skill to pick up on emotional cues, to not only recognize but also understand the emotions of others, is a vital part of emotional intelligence (EQ). Emotional intelligence is knowing and controlling our feelings and handling interpersonal relationships judiciously and empathetically. It enhances interactions by allowing us to navigate the emotional terrain of relationships with insight and sensitivity. Recognizing our emotions and those of others enables us to manage them effectively, paving the way for smoother communication and deeper connections.

At the center of emotional intelligence lies self-awareness and self-regulation (as discussed in Chapter 2). Self-awareness is recognizing your emotions and understanding how they affect your behavior and thoughts. It is about acknowledging your strengths and weaknesses without judgment. When you are aware of your emotional states, you can manage them more effectively. Self-regulation follows naturally, enabling you to control impulsive reactions and healthily manage emotions. This skill allows you to pause before reacting, choosing responses central to your values and goals. Together, these elements form the foundation of EQ, providing stability and control in the face of emotional challenges. Another critical component is empathy— the ability to understand and share the feelings of another. Empathy bridges the emotional gap between people, fostering connection and trust. Coupled with social skills, which involve managing relationships and building networks, empathy allows you to communicate more effectively and resolve conflicts gracefully.

Developing emotional intelligence is an ongoing process involving deliberate practice and reflection. Again, mindfulness is a powerful tool in this endeavor, as it enhances self-awareness by encouraging you to observe your feelings and thoughts non-judgmentally. Practicing mindfulness can help you be more attuned to your emotional states, allowing you to respond rather than react. Engaging in perspective-taking exercises further sharpens your EQ, challenging you to see situations from another's viewpoint. This practice deepens empathy and enriches your understanding of diverse perspectives, enabling more nuanced and compassionate interactions. Adding these strategies into your daily life can cultivate more emotional intelligence, leading to more harmonious and fulfilling relationships.

For those healing from disorganized attachment, developing emotional intelligence includes learning to trust their emotional experiences while building the capacity to regulate intense reactions that stem from early attachment wounds. Consider the story of Michelle, who navigated complex social dynamics at work with newfound ease after enhancing her emotional intelligence. Previously, office politics left her feeling overwhelmed and isolated. By focusing on self-awareness and practicing mindfulness, Michelle learned to identify her triggers and manage stress more effectively. Her improved self-regulation allowed her to approach challenging colleagues calmly and poised, transforming tense interactions into productive dialogues. Another tale is that of Joaquin, who struggled to connect with his partner on an emotional level. Through empathy-building exercises, he learned to listen and validate his partner's feelings, leading to stronger, more empathetic connections. These transformations demonstrate the profound impact of enhanced emotional intelligence on professional and personal relationships, creating a ripple effect of understanding and connection. Emotional intelligence is not a destination but a path that enriches every interaction, guiding you toward more profound, meaningful connections.

DEVELOPING EMPATHIC COMMUNICATION SKILLS

While those with disorganized attachment patterns may have developed a heightened sensitivity to other's emotions as a survival mechanism, learning to channel this sensitivity into healthy empathic communication requires practice and patience.

Empathic communication is the bridge that connects one heart to another, fostering a deep mutual respect and understanding that transcends mere words. Hearing someone, truly understanding them, and sharing their emotional experience. This communication transforms interactions by reducing conflict and enhancing cooperation, encouraging openness and vulnerability. Empathy allows partners to feel seen and valued in relationships, creating a haven where both can express themselves without fear of judgment. Empathic communication is about tuning into the person's emotional frequency, resonating with their feelings, and responding with genuine care. It builds trust, allowing the relationship to flourish through shared understanding and compassion.

Specific techniques can be employed to cultivate empathic communication to nurture empathy in interactions. Practicing active listening with empathy involves being fully present and attentive to the other person's words and emotions. It is about setting aside your thoughts and focusing entirely on the speaker, acknowledging their feelings and experiences. Validating others' emotions is another critical aspect. By affirming their feelings, you show that you understand and respect their emotional state, even if you do not necessarily agree with their perspective. This validation creates a sense of security and acceptance, encouraging open dialogue and reducing defensiveness. Empathy becomes a natural part of your communication style through these practices, enriching your relationships with depth and understanding.

However, developing empathic communication is not without its challenges. Personal biases and assumptions can be significant barriers, clouding your judgment and keeping you from fully engaging with the other person's experience. These biases often stem from past experiences or ingrained beliefs, influencing how you perceive and interpret others' emotions. Overcoming these barriers requires consciously setting aside preconceived notions and approaching each interaction with an open mind and heart. Emotional reactivity is another obstacle that can block empathy by triggering defensive responses. When emotions run high, it can be difficult to remain empathetic and objective. Managing your emotional reactions is crucial for maintaining empathy, allowing you to respond calmly and thoughtfully rather than impulsively.

Specific exercises can be highly beneficial for practicing and strengthening empathic communication. Reflective listening exercises are an excellent way to hone your empathic skills. In these exercises, you listen to someone express their thoughts and emotions, then reflect on what you have heard to ensure understanding. This practice strengthens your ability to tune into the speaker's emotional state and respond effectively. Storytelling and role-playing are also effective methods for building empathy. By stepping into someone else's shoes and experiencing their story firsthand, you gain a deeper understanding of their emotions and perspectives. These exercises encourage you to empathize with a wide range of experiences, broadening your capacity for compassion and connection.

I often reflect on a couple I know who regularly use storytelling to strengthen their empathic communication. They create a rich tapestry of shared understanding and empathy by sharing personal anecdotes and exploring each other's emotional landscapes. This practice allows them to navigate challenges gracefully and patiently as they have cultivated a deep reservoir of compassion and insight. Another example involves friends who, through reflective listening exercises, have learned to support each other with empathy and care. This skill has transformed their friendship, allowing them to communicate openly and honestly, free from the constraints of judgment and misunderstanding. Empathic communication is not just a skill but a way of being that enriches every interaction and deepens every connection.

In this chapter, we have explored various communication techniques that can transform relationships, from active listening and expressing emotions clearly to resolving conflicts constructively and building emotional intelligence. These skills improve communication and foster deeper connections and understanding. Developing these skills will make your relationships more fulfilling and resilient. In the next chapter, we will explore how to cultivate secure attachments, building on the foundation of effective communication to create lasting and meaningful connections.

CHAPTER 8
SECURE ATTACHMENT AND HEALTHY RELATIONSHIPS

IMAGINE A WORLD WHERE RELATIONSHIPS FLOW LIKE A HARMONIOUS dance, each partner moving gracefully and understanding. This equilibrium is the essence of secure attachment, where love is a partnership built on trust and mutual respect. A securely attached person approaches relationships with a sense of balance, seamlessly integrating independence with the joys of connection. They walk through life with a harmonious rhythm, assured that they are worthy of love and capable of giving it. In such relationships, there is no need for pretense or games; authenticity and empathy take center stage, creating a stable foundation that weathers life's storms. For those healing from disorganized attachment, the journey toward secure attachment requires understanding that seemingly contradictory needs for closeness and distance are normal responses to early experiences.

UNDERSTANDING SECURE ATTACHMENTS

Secure attachment stands apart from other styles due to its core attributes. At its heart is the confidence in relationships that stems from a deep-seated belief in our value and the trustworthiness of others. This confidence allows us to engage fully with those around us, knowing that our worth does not hinge on the approval of others. This assuredness fosters resilience, enabling us to approach conflicts with calm and clarity. Securely attached individuals also master the art of balancing independence and interdependence. They understand the importance of maintaining their own identities while cherishing the connections they form. This equilibrium ensures they can pursue personal goals without fear of losing themselves in relationships, making room for personal growth and meaningful connection.

The emotional benefits of secure attachment weave a tapestry of stability and well-being. Reduced anxiety and fear of abandonment are prominent, as secure individuals trust in the strength of their relationships and have faith in their ability to navigate challenges. This emotional stability creates a sense of peace, allowing them to engage with others from a place of authenticity rather than fear. Their confidence in the resilience of their relationships reduces the need for excessive reassurance, freeing them to focus on the joy and fulfillment that connections bring. This foundation of trust and security enhances their well-being, providing a steady anchor in an unpredictable world. While those with disorganized attachment histories may initially find secure attachment traits foreign or frightening, these patterns can be learned through consistent, supportive relationships.

Behavioral indicators of secure attachment are transparent and observable. Effective communication is a cornerstone, as securely attached individuals prioritize open dialogue and active listening. They engage in conversations with empathy and respect, ensuring everyone feels heard and valued. Conflict resolution is approached with patience and understanding, as they seek to address differences constructively rather than defensively. This communication skill fosters an environment where issues can be resolved without resentment. Secure individuals are also willing to seek and offer support, understanding that relationships thrive on reciprocity. They know when to lean on others and when to be a source of strength, creating a dynamic of mutual empowerment.

Consider the scenario of a couple discussing their plans. Both partners approach the conversation with mutual respect, eager to understand each other's dreams and aspirations. They listen actively, offering encouragement and support as they explore possibilities together. Their dialogue is characterized by honesty and openness, free from the fear of judgment or rejection. In another example, friends supporting each other through life changes demonstrate secure attachment. Whether a career transition or a personal milestone, they stand by each other, offering reassurance and understanding. Their relationship is a safe space where they can express vulnerability and receive unwavering support.

Reflection Section: Identifying Secure Attachment in Your Life

Reflect on your relationships and consider moments where you felt secure and grounded. Write about the qualities that contributed to this sense of security and how you can nurture these traits further. Consider how you communicate, resolve conflicts, and offer support. This reflection can help you identify areas where secure attachment thrives and where it may need nurturing.

STEPS TO DEVELOP SECURE ATTACHMENT

Developing a secure attachment begins with understanding your personal attachment style. Recognizing whether you lean toward anxious, avoidant, or disorganized patterns can offer valuable insights into how you approach relationships. This self-awareness is the key to identifying behaviors that may hinder connection and working toward cultivating secure attachment traits. It is like holding a map of your emotional landscape, helping you navigate toward healthier interactions. Identifying patterns may reveal seemingly contradictory behaviors for those with disorganized attachment—both pursuing and avoiding closeness. For instance, you might find yourself craving intimacy but feeling overwhelmed when it becomes too intense. Understanding these patterns is crucial for transformation. Begin by reflecting on past relationships and noting recurring patterns. Ask yourself, "Do I often feel anxious about your partner's commitment? Do I tend to withdraw when intimacy deepens?" Understanding these tendencies is the first step toward a more secure attachment style.

As pointed out, setting and respecting personal boundaries is crucial once you have identified your attachment style. Boundaries are the invisible lines that protect your emotional and mental space, ensuring that your needs and values are honored.

They create a sense of safety and autonomy, allowing you to engage in relationships without losing yourself. Start by defining what feels comfortable for you in a relationship and communicate these boundaries to others. For instance, you might set a boundary around the amount of time you need for yourself each day or the level of emotional support you can provide without feeling overwhelmed. Respecting your boundaries reinforces self-worth, and respecting others' boundaries fosters trust and mutual respect. This practice lays the groundwork for secure, balanced relationships where both people feel valued and understood.

Again, self-awareness plays a pivotal role in this transformative process. Through self-reflection, you can recognize and transform attachment patterns that no longer serve you. Journaling is a powerful tool in this endeavor. You gain insights into triggers and habitual reactions by tracking your emotional responses. Writing down your feelings and thoughts lets you process emotions constructively, creating a space for growth and change. This practice enhances self-awareness and fosters emotional regulation, as well as managing and healthily responding to your feelings. It helps you react to situations more calmly and clearly. As you become more attuned to your internal landscape, you can make conscious choices that align with secure attachment behaviors.

To reinforce secure attachment traits, engage in practical exercises encouraging growth. Role-playing can be effective in practicing assertiveness. You can rehearse responses that honor your boundaries and needs by simulating challenging interactions. This practice builds confidence and prepares you for real-life situations. It enables you to communicate effectively and assertively. Also, mindfulness exercises can enhance emotional regulation, allowing you to navigate emotions easily. Deep breathing or meditation cultivates a sense of presence and calm, reducing reactivity and fostering emotional balance. These exercises equip you with the skills to approach relationships from a place of security and self-assurance.

Consider the story of Alisha, who once struggled with fears of vulnerability. She often felt exposed when opening up to others, fearing judgment or rejection. Through therapy and self-reflection, Alisha began to understand her anxious attachment style. She started journaling daily, which helped her identify fear and avoidance patterns. Over weeks and months, Alisha practiced role-playing with a friend, learning to assert her needs and express her feelings without anxiety. By consistently applying these strategies, she noticed a shift in her interactions. Her relationships became more fulfilling, characterized by trust and open communication. Alisha's journey illustrates how understanding and transforming attachment patterns can lead to a secure attachment style.

In another example, consider John, who faced difficulties with trust. His avoidant attachment style led him to withdraw emotionally, fearing dependency on others. Through mindfulness practices, John learned to stay present with his emotions rather than shutting down. He embraced exercises that encouraged openness, gradually building trust through consistent actions. John became more comfortable with intimacy by practicing assertiveness and respecting personal boundaries. His relationships became more supportive and stable as he learned to trust himself and others. John's story highlights the transformative power of cultivating secure attachment traits through intentional effort and practice.

BUILDING A SECURE BASE IN RELATIONSHIPS

In any relationship, the concept of a secure base holds immense significance. The emotional foundation provides safety and support, allowing us to explore the world confidently and grow personally. Imagine a tree with deep roots, anchoring it firmly while its branches stretch out freely. This secure base acts similarly, offering stability that encourages us to go beyond our comfort zones, ensuring they have a reliable place to return to. Emotional safety within a secure base means we feel accepted and valued, free to express ourselves without fear of judgment or rejection. This creates an environment where vulnerability is welcomed and authentic connections can thrive. Building a secure base is particularly important for those with disorganized attachment, as it provides the consistency and safety needed to develop new relationship patterns.

Creating a secure base requires intention and effort but is achievable through practical strategies. Maintaining open and honest communication is fundamental. This involves sharing thoughts and feelings transparently, fostering trust and understanding. When we communicate openly, we invite our partners into our inner world, allowing for deeper connections. Additionally, offering consistent reassurance and validation is crucial. This means acknowledging and affirming each other's emotions and experiences, reinforcing the idea that each person is valued and understood. Consistent reassurance helps to dispel doubts and insecurities, creating a nurturing environment where both people feel supported.

As discussed, mutual trust and respect are the cornerstones of a secure base. Trust-building activities, such as setting shared goals, engaging in cooperative tasks, or spending quality time together, can play a pivotal part in strengthening these elements. Through these experiences, we learn to rely on each other, deepening our bond and reinforcing trust. Respect is equally vital, ensuring that each person's boundaries and autonomy are honored. A secure base is constructed by upholding these values, providing a strong foundation for healthy and fulfilling relationships.

Consider a mentor-mentee relationship where growth is fostered through a secure base. The mentor provides guidance and support, encouraging the mentees to explore new opportunities and challenge themselves. This dynamic allows the mentee to take risks, knowing they have a real source of wisdom and encouragement to fall back on. Similarly, in family dynamics, a secure base can support individual autonomy. Family members provide a safety net, offering love and acceptance that empowers us to pursue our passions and make independent decisions. This support nurtures self-confidence and fosters a sense of belonging, reinforcing the secure base that underpins familial relationships.

In friendships, a secure base might manifest through unwavering support during life changes. Friends offer a listening ear, providing comfort and encouragement as one navigates transitions. This consistent presence instills a sense of security, knowing someone is there to lean on when needed. In romantic relationships, a secure base is evident in partners who champion each other's dreams. They celebrate successes and provide solace during setbacks, ensuring the A relationship is a sanctuary of support and understanding. Mutual encouragement nurtures growth and resilience, allowing each person to thrive individually and together.

A secure base is more than just a concept; it is a dynamic and evolving aspect of relationships. It requires active participation from everyone. We can cultivate a secure base that enriches relationships by prioritizing communication, reassurance, trust, and respect. This foundation allows for exploration, growth, and the joy of authentic connection, creating a relational environment where we are free to be our true selves.

TRANSFORMING RELATIONSHIP DYNAMICS

Changing the dynamics of a relationship often begins with recognizing and addressing negative behaviors that have become habitual. These behaviors might include patterns of communication that lead to misunderstandings or actions that inadvertently hurt one another. It is about becoming aware of these tendencies and consciously trying to change them. Encouraging positive communication habits is crucial. This means actively listening, speaking with empathy, and being open to feedback. It creates a space where both people feel safe to discuss their feelings and thoughts without fear of criticism or dismissal. This transformation does not happen quickly; it requires dedication and a willingness to shift old patterns into healthier ones.

Implementing regular check-ins can be incredibly practical in fostering change in relationship dynamics. These are dedicated times when you and your partner can openly discuss the state of your relationship. It is a chance to address concerns, celebrate successes, and plan for the future. Check-ins help prevent issues from festering and becoming more significant problems. They also reinforce the bond between partners by showing commitment to the relationship's health. During these conversations, it is vital to approach topics with curiosity rather than judgment. This openness encourages honest dialogue and mutual understanding, laying the groundwork for lasting change.

Patience and persistence are vital in this process. Relationship dynamics that have been in place for years will not change overnight. Unlearning old habits and building new ones takes time. Patience allows for the inevitable mistakes and setbacks, while persistence ensures you keep moving forward. Both partners must commit to the long-term goal of a healthier relationship. This means being willing to try again despite failures and remaining hopeful that change is possible. Over a year, these efforts can lead to profound shifts in how you relate to one another, resulting in a more fulfilling and harmonious partnership.

Consider the story of Liz and Cal, a couple in constant conflict. They realized that their arguments were fueled by miscommunication and unaddressed grievances. By committing to regular check-ins, they better understood each other's perspectives. They practiced active listening and learned to express their needs without blame. Within a year, their conflicts became less frequent and more constructive. They discovered a newfound understanding and respect for each other, strengthening their relationship. Similarly, friends like Cynthia and Carla, who experienced a betrayal, rebuilt their trust by addressing the hurt openly. They committed to transparency and consistency, restoring their friendship to mutual support and care.

REPAIRING ATTACHMENT RUPTURES

Attachment ruptures—moments when the emotional connection is temporarily broken—are inevitable in any relationship. For those healing from disorganized attachment, these ruptures can feel particularly threatening, often triggering intense fears of abandonment or rejection. Understanding that ruptures are opportunities for repair and strengthening bonds, rather than signs of relationship failure, is crucial for building secure attachments.

The repair process has several key steps:

1. Acknowledging the rupture without shame or blame
2. Creating space for both partners to express their emotional experience
3. Taking responsibility for our role in the disconnection
4. Working together to understand triggers and patterns
5. Developing specific strategies to prevent similar ruptures
6. Rebuilding emotional connection through small, consistent actions

Consider Maria and James, who experienced a rupture when James withdrew during a conflict. Instead of interpreting his withdrawal as rejection, Maria recognized it as a trauma response. They worked together to understand their triggers and developed a "time-in" protocol—a structured way to maintain connection even when needing space. This approach transformed their ruptures from threats to opportunities for deeper understanding.

MAINTAINING SECURE ATTACHMENTS AS PARTNERS

Maintaining secure attachments requires continuous effort and intention in the ever-evolving landscape of relationships. It is easy to assume that once a secure attachment is formed, it will remain strong without further nurturing. However, like a garden that flourishes with regular care, relationships thrive when they are consistently tended to. Sustaining secure attachments involves continuously nurturing emotional intimacy, ensuring the bonds of connection remain vibrant and resilient. This means actively engaging with your partner, sharing experiences, and staying attuned to each other's emotional needs. When both partners invest in maintaining this closeness, they create a space where love and understanding can grow unimpeded by neglect or complacency.

Relationships inevitably face challenges that can disrupt even the most secure attachments. Life transitions, such as moving to a new city or changing jobs, can introduce stress and uncertainty. These changes can alter the dynamics of a relationship, testing its strength and adaptability. During these times, secure attachments may be threatened by the anxiety of the unknown or the demands of new responsibilities. It is crucial to acknowledge these potential obstacles, and addressing them with openness and empathy is just as important. By recognizing the impact of these transitions, couples can work together to navigate them, ensuring that their connection remains strong despite external pressures. This forward-thinking approach helps reduce the risk of drifting apart during periods of change.

There are practical strategies that couples can employ to reinforce secure attachments. Regular relationship check-ins provide an opportunity to connect deeply and address any concerns before they escalate. These check-ins are moments to express gratitude, share feelings, and discuss future aspirations. They allow partners to align their goals and reaffirm their commitment to one another. Also, engaging in shared activities and experiences can strengthen the bond between partners. Whether it is a weekend getaway, a cooking class, or a walk in the park, these shared moments create cherished memories and deepen the emotional connection. By prioritizing quality time together, couples can fortify their attachment, making it more resilient to external stressors.

Consider the story of Phyllis and Jack, a couple celebrating decades of mutual support and love. Over the years, they have faced numerous challenges, including career changes and family responsibilities. Yet, they have remained steadfast in their commitment to each other, regularly setting aside time for one another. Their relationship check-ins have become a cherished ritual, allowing them to maintain a deep understanding of each other's needs and desires. Similarly, lifelong friends Stella and Bob have weathered various life stages together. They have supported each other through personal and professional milestones, always trying to stay connected despite geographical distances. Their friendship is a testament to the power of consistency and shared experiences in maintaining secure attachments.

Setting the Pace in New Relationships

Beyond the initial foundations discussed, pacing in relationships requires a delicate balance of self-awareness and communication. Consider Marcus's experience: He previously rushed into relationships only to feel overwhelmed and withdrawn. After working on his attachment patterns, he developed a personal "relationship speedometer"—checking in with himself regularly about his comfort levels with emotional and physical intimacy.

Key aspects of healthy pacing include the following:

- Creating space for individual growth while building connection
- Discussing expectations about time spent together
- Maintaining outside friendships and interests
- Gradually increasing emotional vulnerability
- Respecting each person's need for space and processing time

For example, Sally and Ken agreed to have "pace-setting conversations" every few weeks, openly discussing their comfort levels with the relationship's progression. This helped them navigate differences in their preferred speeds of emotional intimacy and prevented either partner from feeling pressured or held back.

Building Trust Gradually

Trust-building resembles constructing a bridge —it requires careful attention to foundation, regular maintenance, and patience. Steve and Mel demonstrated this by starting with small trust exercises: sharing minor vulnerabilities and observing how others handled them before moving to more profound disclosures.

Practical trust-building steps might include the following:

- Making and keeping small commitments consistently
- Being transparent about availability and boundaries
- Acknowledging and repairing minor ruptures promptly
- Demonstrating reliability in day-to-day interactions
- Respecting stated limits and preferences

Consider developing a "trust portfolio" by documenting instances where trust was honored. This will help you maintain perspective during challenging times and create a concrete reference point for the relationship's reliability and growth.

SECURE ATTACHMENT IN FAMILY RELATIONSHIPS

Family relationships often serve as the blueprint for our attachment styles, yet they also offer opportunities for healing and growth. Picture a family dinner where tension simmers beneath polite conversation. The patterns you develop in childhood may still influence these interactions, but understanding them provides a chance for transformation. Through conscious effort and practice, you can begin to create more secure bonds with family members, even if past relationships were marked by insecurity or trauma.

Creating secure attachments within families requires intentional effort and understanding, particularly when transforming established patterns. The Chen family exemplifies this transformation, having shifted from anxiety-driven interactions to more secure connections through conscious effort and professional guidance.

Secure family attachment manifests through consistent emotional availability and clear communication about needs and boundaries. It requires a delicate balance between respecting individual autonomy and maintaining strong connections. Regularly repairing ruptures and celebrating individual differences become cornerstones of family security. These elements create a foundation where family members feel safe expressing themselves authentically.

The Martinez family demonstrates how to implement these principles through structured connection points. They established daily one-on-one time with each child, creating spaces for undivided attention and emotional attunement. Weekly family meetings provide forums for open discussion, while monthly individual parent-child outings strengthen specific relationships. Quarterly family reviews help track progress and set new goals for a deeper connection.

Families must acknowledge inherited patterns without assigning blame when addressing multigenerational attachment patterns. This process involves creating new family rituals that support security and developing a shared language for emotional needs. Regular opportunities for repair and celebrating small shifts toward security become essential. These steps help break negative cycles while building stronger family bonds.

Extended family relationships add another layer of complexity to attachment dynamics. Success requires setting clear boundaries while maintaining meaningful connections. Families must learn to respect different attachment styles while creating safe spaces for difficult conversations. Establishing protocols for managing conflicts helps navigate challenging situations while building new traditions can support security across the extended family network.

NAVIGATING WORKPLACE ATTACHMENTS

Professional relationships significantly impact our daily well-being and often mirror our attachment patterns. Understanding and managing workplace attachments can enhance both professional success and personal growth. These relationships require careful attention to boundaries and communication while supporting professional development.

Secure leadership demonstrates consistent and clear communication while maintaining appropriate professional boundaries. Effective leaders recognize team members' needs while balancing autonomy and support. Regular feedback and acknowledgment foster a workplace where team members feel safe taking risks and growing professionally.

Holly's transformation of her department illustrates attachment-aware leadership in action. She established consistent communication channels with each team member through regular one-on-one check-ins. Clear expectations and structured feedback processes created predictability, while support for professional growth demonstrated investment in team development. Her attention to work-life boundaries helped maintain appropriate professional relationships.

Managing professional boundaries requires careful attention to role definition and appropriate emotional distance without withdrawal. This balance includes thoughtful sharing of personal information and maintaining consistent professional boundaries. Regularly reviewing professional relationships helps ensure they remain healthy and productive.

Authority figure relationships often trigger attachment patterns in our personal lives. Successfully managing these relationships involves balancing needs for autonomy and guidance while handling feedback and evaluation. Power dynamics require careful navigation, and building professional trust takes time and consistency.

Peer relationships in the workplace present unique challenges in maintaining appropriate closeness while managing competitive elements. Supporting colleague growth while handling workplace conflicts requires emotional intelligence and clear boundaries. Building collaborative relationships strengthens team effectiveness and our professional development.

Remote work has also added new dimensions to workplace attachment. Building connections through digital means requires intentional effort to maintain a presence without physical proximity. Creating virtual team cohesion while managing digital boundaries has become increasingly important. Supporting remote team attachment often requires new approaches to communication and connection.

Success in workplace attachments ultimately depends on self-awareness of attachment patterns and maintaining professional boundaries. Regular relationship assessment and ongoing professional development support healthy workplace connections. Understanding these dynamics helps create workplace environments that support individual and organizational growth while maintaining appropriate professional distance.

As this chapter draws to a close, it is clear that secure attachments are not static; they are dynamic, living entities that require ongoing care and attention. By continuously nurturing these connections, we can ensure that our relationships remain healthy and fulfilling. The effort invested in maintaining secure attachments pays dividends in the form of emotional stability, trust, and enduring love. As you reflect on these insights, consider how to apply them to cultivate lasting connections in your life. In the next chapter, we will explore the broader implications of secure attachments and how they influence personal growth and fulfillment, offering a deeper understanding of relationships' role in our lives.

CHAPTER 9
INTEGRATING PERSONAL GROWTH INTO DAILY LIFE

ENVISION AWAKENING EACH DAY WITH A CLEAR SENSE OF DIRECTION, where every moment presents an opportunity to draw nearer to your aspirations. The seemingly insignificant daily habits can silently revolutionize your life over time. Consider the British Cycling Team, whose remarkable achievements were not the result of drastic changes but the refinement of their daily routines. This chapter delves into how you can implement similar strategies to your personal growth, redefining success as a steady accumulation of progress rather than sporadic leaps.

CREATING DAILY HABITS FOR PERSONAL GROWTH

The power of daily habits is the backbone of long-term success that can transform your aspirations into achievable realities. Starting your day with a purposeful morning routine can create an uplifting atmosphere that carries through and resonates throughout the hours ahead. Consider the difference between waking up to a cluttered mind versus beginning with a clear plan. A morning ritual, such as spending a few minutes setting intentions or engaging in light exercise, can sharpen your focus and boost productivity. These practices anchor you, offering a sense of control and readiness for whatever the day holds. At the other end of the day, evening reflections serve as a moment of pause, allowing you to assess daily progress and recalibrate as needed. By taking stock of what went well and identifying areas for improvement, you cultivate a growth mindset that keeps you motivated and aligned with your goals. These reflections are not about self-criticism but about fostering self-awareness and celebrating small wins.

Incorporating practical daily habits can significantly support your personal development journey. For instance, reading a chapter of a self-development book each day expands your knowledge and inspires new ideas and perspectives. This habit can be a source of daily motivation, prompting you to think differently and consider new approaches to challenges. Similarly, setting daily intentions can focus your energy and efforts toward specific goals. By starting each day with a clear intention, you direct your actions with purpose, transforming vague aspirations into concrete achievements. These habits, though simple, have the potential to create a powerful momentum that catapults you forward. Consistency matters more than perfection when establishing habits to overcome past emotional attachment wounds. Small, regular steps toward security build new neural pathways.

Consider the concept of habit stacking, a powerful tool that can further enhance your growth efforts. This involves linking new habits to established routines, making them easier to adopt and maintain. For instance, you can integrate a gratitude practice with your morning coffee ritual. As you savor the warmth of your drink, take a moment to reflect on three things you are grateful for. This practice enriches your morning routine and cultivates a mindset of appreciation that can positively influence your day. Similarly, pairing daily walks with listening to motivational podcasts is another effective strategy. Combining physical activity with learning maximizes the benefits of simultaneously nurturing your mind and body. Habit stacking leverages the power of current routines to support the adoption of new, beneficial behaviors, increasing the likelihood of long-term success. It is a tool that empowers you to take control of your growth journey.

Maintaining consistency in daily habits can be challenging, but it is essential for sustained growth. Using habit trackers can provide visual motivation by allowing you to monitor your progress. Each tick on the tracker represents a step forward, offering tangible evidence of your commitment and effort. This visual record can inspire persistence, especially when progress feels slow or stagnant. Celebrating small wins is another strategy to reinforce habit formation. Acknowledge and reward yourself for each milestone, no matter how minor it may seem. These celebrations create positive associations with your efforts, encouraging you to continue and build on your successes. They are the fuel that keeps your motivation burning bright.

Interactive Element: Creating Your Daily Habit Tracker

Design a simple habit tracker to monitor your progress. List your daily habits and mark each day you complete them. Reflect on patterns or challenges you notice, and adjust your approach as needed. Use this tool to celebrate your achievements and stay motivated on your growth journey.

CONTINUOUS SELF-REFLECTION PRACTICES

Imagine standing in front of a mirror, reflecting your outward appearance and the intricate tapestry of your thoughts, emotions, and aspirations. This is the essence of self-reflection—a powerful tool that fosters growth by shining a light on your inner world. Regular self-reflection encourages a deeper understanding of yourself, guiding you toward personal development. Weekly journaling allows for capturing insights and reflections, providing a written record of your thoughts and feelings. This practice enables you to observe patterns, notice shifts in perspective, and gain clarity on issues that might have seemed daunting. Self-reflection helps identify secure and insecure attachment patterns, allowing for conscious relationship choices. By dedicating time each week to journaling, you create a habit of introspection, turning the act of writing into a ritual that nurtures self-awareness and encourages emotional release.

Monthly reviews take self-reflection a step further, offering an opportunity to reassess your goals and progress. This practice invites you to step back and view your life from a broader perspective, evaluating where you stand concerning your aspirations. By reviewing the past month, you can acknowledge accomplishments, recognize areas for growth, and refine your goals as needed. This continuous reflection and adjustment cycle helps align your goals with your evolving values and priorities. It becomes a compass that guides your life's direction, keeping you on track and motivated to pursue growth with intention and purpose. Through these structured moments of reflection, you cultivate a mindset of continuous improvement, transforming challenges into opportunities for learning and development.

To enhance your self-reflection practices, consider employing SWOT analysis tools. Often used in business, this technique can be adapted to explore your "strengths, weaknesses, opportunities, and threats." You can use your strengths to navigate challenges and seize growth opportunities by identifying them. Acknowledging weaknesses allows for targeted improvement, while recognizing external opportunities and threats can inform your decision-making. Reflective prompts also serve as a valuable aid in self-reflection, guiding you to explore emotions and thoughts profoundly and honestly. These prompts might include questions like, "What am I grateful for today?" or "What challenges have I overcome this week?" By responding to such questions, you delve into your inner experiences, gaining insights that might otherwise remain hidden.

Self-reflection plays a vital role in setting goals and achievement. It informs and refines your goals, ensuring they are grounded in reality and aligned with your authentic self. Through reflection, you gain clarity on what truly matters to you, allowing you to set goals that resonate with your core values. This clarity enhances your motivation and increases the likelihood of achieving your objectives. Reflecting on your progress, you may find that some goals need adjustment based on personal insights. This flexibility is key to maintaining momentum and ensuring that your path to growth remains dynamic and responsive to change. Regularly reassessing your goals creates a feedback loop that supports sustained personal development, turning aspirations into actionable steps toward fulfillment.

To deepen your self-reflection practices, consider engaging in exercises that encourage introspection and understanding. Meditation focused on self-inquiry is one such practice that invites you to explore your inner world with curiosity and openness. Through meditation, you quiet the mind and create space for insights to emerge, allowing you to connect with your true self. This practice fosters a sense of peace and acceptance, facilitating a deeper understanding of your thoughts, emotions, and desires. Creative expression, such as drawing or painting, offers another avenue for self-reflection. By engaging in artistic activities, you tap into your subconscious mind, giving form to thoughts and feelings that might not be easy to articulate verbally. This expression lets you explore your inner landscape non-linearly, revealing new perspectives and insights.

These practices make self-reflection a powerful ally in your growth journey. It encourages you to look within, delve into your inner self, and discover profound wisdom. As you continuously self-reflect, you develop a deeper understanding of yourself, strengthening your foundation for growth and transformation. This process is not about achieving perfection but embracing the fullness of who you are, with all your strengths and vulnerabilities. Through self-reflection, you cultivate a relationship with yourself that is grounded in authenticity, compassion, and a commitment to lifelong learning.

THE ROLE OF GRATITUDE IN PERSONAL DEVELOPMENT

Imagine a day when you pause amid the chaos to give thanks for a stranger's smile, the warmth of the sun on your face, or the quiet comfort of your home. These small acts of gratitude can profoundly affect your mindset, turning ordinary moments into sources of joy and contentment. Gratitude is more than just a word of "thanks"; it is a mindset that fosters resilience and optimism. When you consciously focus on what you have rather than what you lack, it shifts your perspective from scarcity to abundance, enhancing your well-being and satisfaction. This focus on the positive can build mental resilience, enabling you to face challenges with a stronger, more optimistic outlook.

Embracing gratitude can increase resilience, helping you bounce back from adversity more robustly. When faced with difficulties, gratitude allows you to see beyond the immediate pain and recognize the silver linings. It shifts attention from what is wrong to what is right, fostering a sense of optimism that fuels perseverance. This shift enhances personal satisfaction and helps maintain a balanced emotional state. Acknowledging the good in your life can serve as an anchor in turbulent times, providing a sense of stability and hope. By regularly practicing gratitude, you cultivate a mindset that sees challenges as opportunities for growth instead of insurmountable obstacles.

To cultivate gratitude, consider maintaining a daily gratitude journal. This practice entails dedicating a few moments daily to writing down things you appreciate. It could be as small as enjoying a tasty meal or having a heartfelt conversation with a friend. Over time, this habit helps train your mind to recognize and hone in on the positive aspects of daily life, fostering a mindset that nurtures personal growth. Writing thank-you notes is another powerful way to express appreciation. By taking the time to acknowledge the kindness of others, you not only strengthen your connections but also reinforce your gratitude mindset. These practices can transform your outlook, making gratitude a natural part of your daily life.

The transformative power of gratitude is its ability to shift negative thought patterns. When you approach life with gratitude, you begin to reframe challenges as opportunities for growth. Instead of viewing obstacles as setbacks, you see them as stepping stones toward personal development. This perspective can diminish frustration and helplessness, empowering you to take proactive steps toward your goals. Gratitude encourages you to adopt a growth mindset, where you perceive difficulties as chances to learn and evolve. This change in outlook can enhance resilience and promote a more flexible approach to life's challenges.

Consider the story of Carl, who faced unexpected job loss. Initially overwhelmed by anxiety and uncertainty, Carl decided to focus on gratitude. Each day, he wrote down three things he appreciated, from the support of his family to the opportunity to explore new career paths. This practice helped him remain optimistic and open to possibilities, eventually leading him to a fulfilling new position. In another example, the Johnson family began a weekly tradition of sharing what they were grateful for. This simple ritual brought them closer, fostering stronger bonds and a shared appreciation. These stories illustrate how gratitude can lead to positive transformations, turning adversity into a catalyst for growth and connection.

Gratitude is not just an emotion but a powerful tool for personal development, reshaping how you interact with the world. By incorporating gratitude into your daily life, you enhance your resilience, foster deeper connections, and cultivate a mindset of abundance. This chapter has explored various aspects of personal growth, from building daily habits to practicing mindfulness and self-reflection. As you continue integrating these practices into your life, remember that gratitude can guide your journey and pave the way for lasting fulfillment.

MANAGING SETBACKS AND RELAPSES

Healing is not linear—it is a journey of progress and occasional steps backward. Picture yourself implementing new communication strategies in a relationship when suddenly, under stress, you fall back into old patterns. This moment is not a failure but an opportunity for deeper learning. Understanding that setbacks are standard growth parts can help you maintain momentum even when progress feels elusive. These moments often contain valuable lessons about your triggers and areas needing additional attention.

Setbacks in attachment healing are not only expected but can be valuable learning opportunities when approached with self-compassion and curiosity. The path to earned secure attachment often includes regression periods, particularly during stress or significant life changes. Understanding this natural ebb and flow helps maintain perspective during challenging periods.

Emma's experience illustrates this dynamic. After months of progress in managing her anxious attachment patterns, a job loss triggered old abandonment fears in her relationship. Initially, she felt devastated by what she perceived as "falling back" into previous patterns. However, working with her therapist, she came to understand that setbacks often contain important information about unresolved attachment needs and remaining growth areas.

The key difference between early recovery and later setbacks lies in developing awareness and tools. While the emotional intensity might feel similar, those who have done attachment work typically recover more quickly and can more effectively identify triggers. This awareness allows for faster implementation of coping strategies and a return to security.

During setbacks, the brain's threat response system can temporarily override newer, more secure attachment patterns. Understanding this neurobiological response helps reduce shame and enables a more constructive approach to recovery. The goal shifts from preventing all setbacks to building stronger recovery muscles.

Creating a setback response plan before challenges arise can provide a crucial roadmap during difficult times. This plan might include identifying early warning signs, establishing communication protocols with key supporters, and outlining specific self-care practices that have proven effective. Regular review and updating of this plan strengthens its effectiveness.

The concept of "productive regression" suggests that sometimes, moving backward temporarily allows for more profound healing. These periods often reveal subtle patterns that were not visible before, offering opportunities for a more complete resolution of attachment wounds. Viewing setbacks through this lens transforms them from failures into stepping stones toward greater security.

BUILDING RESILIENCE THROUGH CHALLENGES

Each challenge in your healing journey builds resilience, like a muscle growing stronger through exercise. Consider the story of Lisa, who faced intense anxiety when attempting to form new relationships. Rather than avoiding connections entirely, she learned to view each interaction as practice in building resilience. In six months, she developed a toolkit of coping strategies, transforming challenges into opportunities for growth. This resilience became her foundation for maintaining progress even during difficult times.

Resilience in attachment work develops by facing and processing challenges rather than avoiding them. Successfully navigating difficulties builds confidence in our ability to maintain a connection through adversity. This process strengthens both individual capacity for regulation and relationship durability.

James discovered this while working through trust issues with his partner. Each time they successfully resolved a conflict, his nervous system recorded a new experience of repair and return to connection. Within months, these experiences created a foundation of resilience that helped him maintain perspective during triggering situations.

Developing attachment resilience involves strengthening both internal and external resources. Internal resources include emotional regulation skills, self-awareness, and cognitive flexibility. External resources encompass supportive relationships, professional help, and environmental factors promoting security. The interaction between these resources creates a robust support system for navigating challenges.

The concept of "stress inoculation" applies particularly well to attachment resilience. Gradually facing attachment challenges in a supported way helps build tolerance for relationship stress. This process must be calibrated carefully - too much challenge overwhelms the system, while too little provides insufficient opportunity for growth.

Creating a personal resilience inventory helps track growth and identify areas for development. This inventory might include successful navigation of past challenges, current coping strategies, and available support systems. Regular updates to this inventory provide concrete evidence of progress and help maintain motivation during difficult periods.

Advanced resilience is developing the capacity to connect with yourself while navigating relationship challenges. This dual awareness allows for emotional engagement and wise perspective, reducing the likelihood of becoming completely overwhelmed by attachment triggers.

I cannot overstate the role of community in building resilience. Connecting with others who understand attachment work provides validation, shared wisdom, and living examples of earned security. These connections create a broader context for individual healing and demonstrate the possibility of lasting change.

Time perspective plays a crucial role in building resilience. Understanding that healing follows a spiral rather than a linear path helps maintain hope during setbacks. Each return to familiar challenges brings new insights and opportunities for deeper integration of secure attachment patterns.

The ultimate goal of resilience building is not to eliminate all attachment anxiety or avoidance but to develop confidence in our ability to return to security. This confidence comes from repeated experiences of successfully navigating challenges and maintaining connection through difficulties. With time, this creates a foundational sense of security that can weather significant life challenges while maintaining healthy attachment bonds. In the next chapter, we will explore embracing a new relational identity and how these personal growth practices can transform our interactions with others.

MEASURING AND TRACKING PROGRESS

Understanding your growth in attachment healing requires both quantitative and qualitative measures. Progress often appears in subtle shifts—a calmer response to triggers, quicker recovery from attachment wounds, or increased comfort with emotional intimacy. Creating structured ways to track these changes helps validate your journey and identify areas needing attention.

Consider implementing these tracking methods:

1. **Weekly Attachment Journal**: Document specific interactions, emotional responses, and recovery times from triggering events
2. **Monthly Security Scale**: Rate your sense of security in relationships across different domains (1-10 scale)
3. **Relationship Pattern Tracking**: Note the frequency of secure versus insecure responses to everyday situations
4. **Recovery Time Log**: Monitor how quickly you return to baseline after attachment triggers
5. **Connection Capacity Chart**: Track duration and quality of emotional intimacy in relationships

Sarah's experience illustrates effective progress tracking. She maintained a detailed journal of her attachment responses, noting that her recovery time from abandonment triggers decreased from days to hours over six months. This concrete evidence of progress helped maintain motivation during challenging periods.

CHAPTER 10
EMBRACING A NEW RELATIONAL IDENTITY

IMAGINE WAKING UP ONE MORNING AND DECIDING TO WEAR A NEW pair of glasses through which you view the world. Everything appears more precise and more vibrant, and the contours of your surroundings take on a refreshed significance. This act of clarity parallels the process of redefining your relational identity. Just as glasses can correct vision, embracing a new relational identity can transform how you perceive and engage in relationships. It is about stepping back and examining the roles you have unconsciously assumed, the labels you have worn, and deciding which ones to keep and which to shed. For those healing from disorganized attachment, embracing a new relational identity involves integrating seemingly contradictory aspects of self—the part that yearns for connection and the part that fears it. This integration is essential to developing a coherent sense of self in relationships, empowering you to take control of your relational journey.

UNDERSTANDING AND CRAFTING YOUR RELATIONAL IDENTITY

Relational identity is the self-concept you hold in the context of relationships. It encompasses how you see yourself, believe others see you, and your roles in your interactions. Past relationships often shape this identity, carrying the imprints of joyful and painful experiences. Perhaps you have been the caregiver, always putting others first, or the peacemaker, smoothing conflicts. These roles, while familiar, can limit your growth and fulfillment if not consciously examined. Recognizing these patterns is the first step in understanding how they influence your current self. Acknowledging their origins can redefine your identity to align with your true self and desires.

Crafting a new relational identity is a conscious and deliberate process. Start by identifying your core beliefs and values. These guiding principles define what matters most to you in relationships. Consider what qualities you admire in others and wish to embody yourself. Next, envision your ideal relational self. Picture how you want to interact with others—are you more assertive, compassionate, or open? This vision acts as a compass, directing your relationship behaviors and decisions. Setting clear intentions allows you to step confidently into this new identity, shedding roles that no longer serve you. When crafting a new relational identity after disorganized attachment, it is essential to acknowledge the protective function of old patterns and the possibility of new, more secure ways of relating. This involves gradually expanding your "window of tolerance for emotional intimacy," which refers to the range of emotional experiences you can comfortably manage. Expanding this window allows you to engage in deeper, more fulfilling relationships. A wider window will enable you to handle more intense emotional interactions, leading to deeper, more fulfilling relationships.

Self-perception plays a pivotal role in shaping your relational identity. How you view yourself influences your interactions and expectations in relationships. A positive self-image attracts compatible partners who resonate with your true self. Conversely, a negative self-view might lead you to accept less than you deserve. Understanding your self-concept clarity—the extent to which your self-beliefs are clearly defined and consistent—can enhance relationship satisfaction and commitment. You create healthier, more fulfilling connections by cultivating a clear and positive self-view and realizing the power of your thoughts and beliefs in shaping your relational journey. This empowerment allows you to take control of your relationships and foster personal growth.

To support this identity transformation, engage in exercises that align with your vision. One potent activity is writing a letter to your future self. In this letter, describe your ideal relational identity and your steps to achieve it. Reflect on the changes you wish to see and the emotions you hope to experience. This exercise solidifies your intentions and serves as a source of motivation and guidance. Another effective tool is creating a vision board for your relational goals. Use images, words, and symbols representing the qualities and relationships you aspire to cultivate. Place this board somewhere visible to remind you of your journey and keep you focused on your path. And once again, practicing mindfulness can help you stay present in your relationships and align your actions with your desired identity. Reflecting on your interactions at the end of each day can also provide valuable insights and help you track your progress.

Reflection Section: Craft Your Relational Identity

Take a moment to reflect on your current relational identity. What roles and labels have you unconsciously adopted? For instance, you might see yourself as the "caretaker" who always puts others' needs before your own or the "people-pleaser" who avoids conflict at all costs. How do these roles impact your interactions and relationships? Write down your core values and envision your ideal relational self. Consider making a vision board or writing a letter to your future self-detailing your desired relational identity. This exercise will help clarify your intentions and guide you in redefining your relational identity for personal growth and fulfillment.

CELEBRATING PROGRESS AND MILESTONES

Imagine standing at the top of a hill, gazing back at the winding path you have traversed. Each step forward, each challenge overcome, represents the progress you have made. We often forget to pause and appreciate these milestones in our personal growth. Yet, acknowledging achievements is vital. It motivates you and boosts self-esteem, reinforcing the positive changes you have worked hard to achieve. For those with disorganized attachment histories, celebrating progress might initially feel threatening or unfamiliar. Starting with small, private acknowledgments can help build comfort with recognition and success. When you take the time to celebrate, you affirm these changes, making them a permanent part of your identity. This celebration is not just about the significant victories. It is about recognizing the small, everyday steps that contribute to your growth, each a building block in the foundation of your new self. By acknowledging your progress, you validate your efforts and recognize the steps you have taken toward personal growth, making you feel validated and recognized.

Reinforcing positive behaviors through celebration is like watering a plant; it encourages continued growth and resilience. Acknowledging your progress strengthens the neural pathways associated with positive behaviors, making them more likely to recur. This creates a cycle of positivity, where each success breeds further success. Celebrating these moments also boosts your confidence and morale. By recognizing your accomplishments, you remind yourself of your capabilities and potential. This self-assurance propels you forward, empowering you to tackle future challenges more easily. In essence, celebration is a powerful tool for fostering a growth-oriented mindset that embraces change and transformation.

There are many ways to recognize and celebrate milestones in your journey. Journaling personal achievements is a simple yet effective method. By documenting your progress, you create a tangible record of your growth, one you can revisit whenever you need a boost of motivation. This practice helps you track your development and provides insight into the patterns and habits contributing to your success. Sharing these milestones with supportive friends or family amplifies their impact. When you involve others in your celebration, you create a sense of community and accountability. These shared moments of joy strengthen your relationships, reminding you that you are not alone in your quest for growth.

Acknowledging progress has profound psychological benefits. It enhances your well-being and commitment to change by reinforcing your efforts and encouraging further development. Celebrations strengthen the neural pathways for positive behavior, making these actions more automatic and ingrained. This neurological reinforcement is crucial for sustaining long-term growth, as it helps you internalize the changes you wish to see. By celebrating your achievements, you create a feedback loop of positivity, where each acknowledgment fuels further motivation and dedication.

Consider the story of Leanne, who marked her personal growth by hosting a small gathering of close friends. She shared her journey, highlighting the challenges she had overcome and the lessons she had learned. This celebration affirmed her progress and inspired her friends to embark on their paths of self-discovery. Another example is Justin, who reflected on his development through art. He created a series of paintings representing different aspects of his growth, each piece a visual testament to his transformation. These stories illustrate the diverse ways we can celebrate our achievements, using creativity and community to honor our progress.

Reflection Section: Celebrate Your Milestones

Reflect on your recent achievements, big or small. Consider how you can celebrate these milestones meaningfully. You might journal your progress, share it with a friend, or create something tangible to commemorate your journey. Remember, celebration is not a luxury but a vital part of personal growth. It reinforces the positive changes you have made and motivates you to continue on your path of transformation.

BUILDING A SUPPORTIVE COMMUNITY

Imagine a garden thriving with diverse plants, each contributing to the ecosystem as a garden flourishes with variety and personal growth blossoms within a supportive community. A network of encouraging people offers a fertile ground for development and resilience. Friends, family, and even mentors provide the accountability that keeps us on track. They cheer our victories and nudge us forward when we falter. This collective journey nurtures a sense of connection, a reminder that we are not alone. Through these relationships, insights are exchanged, and experiences are shared, enriching our understanding and broadening our perspectives. Building community can be particularly challenging for those with disorganized attachment, as trust and consistency may feel foreign. Starting with structured, time-limited interactions can help develop comfort with sustained connection.

Identifying and cultivating supportive relationships requires intention. Begin by seeking out groups or clubs that resonate with your interests. Whether it is a book club, a sports team, or an art class, these gatherings are fertile ground for forming connections with like-minded individuals. Such settings encourage exchanging ideas and experiences, sparking inspiration and camaraderie. Additionally, consider seeking out mentors or role models who embody the qualities you aspire to nurture. Their guidance and wisdom can be invaluable as you navigate your path. Building a community is not just about finding support; it is about contributing to the lives of others and creating a reciprocal flow of encouragement and growth.

A community rich in diverse perspectives enhances understanding and empathy. Interacting with people from various backgrounds and experiences challenges our assumptions and broadens our worldview. It encourages open dialogue, where differing opinions can coexist and enrich the conversation. This exchange fosters shared learning; each person brings unique insights and stories. Embracing these differences deepens our empathy and strengthens our ability to connect with others meaningfully. Engaging with diverse perspectives creates a more inclusive and compassionate approach to our relationships and personal growth.

To strengthen community bonds, consider organizing regular meet-ups or discussions. These gatherings, such as a monthly coffee chat or a book club meeting, can be informal. The key is to create a space where open dialogue and connection can flourish. Another way to deepen relationships within your community is by participating in group challenges or projects. Whether it is a volunteer initiative, a creative collaboration, or a fitness goal, working together toward a common objective fosters a sense of unity and shared purpose. These activities strengthen bonds and provide opportunities for people to learn from one another, enhancing the group's collective growth.

Interactive Element: Strengthening Community Bonds

Consider organizing a monthly meet-up with friends or becoming part of a local club that matches your interests. Use these opportunities to engage in open discussions, share experiences, and learn from one another. Alternatively, propose a group challenge or project that encourages collaboration and shared goals. This exercise will help you build deeper connections within your community, fostering a supportive network that nurtures personal growth and development.

SUSTAINING CHANGE AND GROWTH

Imagine growth as a living entity that requires nurturing through consistent commitment and ongoing effort. Setting goals and feeling motivated at the start is easy, but sustaining that momentum calls for dedication. Actual change is not a one-time event but an ongoing process that unfolds over months and years. Setting long-term relational goals can anchor your growth, giving you a clear direction to aim for. These goals include improving communication skills, deepening emotional connections, and cultivating empathy. By having these targets, you create a roadmap for your relational development. This clarity helps keep you motivated and focused, reminding you of the larger picture when daily challenges arise.

Embracing lifelong learning and adaptation is equally vital. The world around us is in constant flux, and so are we. Being open to learning new strategies and adapting to changing circumstances ensures your growth remains dynamic and relevant. Continuous development fosters resilience, equipping you to handle whatever life throws your way. This adaptability is about being flexible and viewing change as an opportunity for further growth. When you approach life with a mindset that welcomes learning, you remain open to new experiences and insights, enhancing your ability to sustain change over time.

Regularly revisiting your goals and values is crucial to maintain momentum in personal growth. Reflect on what truly matters to you and whether your current path aligns with those priorities. Periodic self-assessment helps you stay on track and make necessary adjustments. This reflection is not just about looking back; it is about looking forward and ensuring that your actions are aligned with your aspirations. Engaging in self-assessment allows you to identify areas that need attention and celebrate the progress you have made. It keeps you grounded and focused, providing the clarity needed to navigate the complexities of personal growth.

Adaptability plays a significant role in sustaining change, allowing you to adjust your goals in response to new experiences or insights. Life is unpredictable, and the growth path often has unexpected twists and turns. Being flexible enables you to embrace and use these changes to your advantage. When encountering new opportunities or challenges, reassess your goals and consider how they might evolve. This willingness to adapt ensures that your growth remains relevant and meaningful, allowing you to continue moving forward even when circumstances shift.

Consider the story of Alexander, who initially set out to improve his relationships by becoming a better listener. As he practiced and refined his skills, he discovered a passion for communication and decided to pursue a career in counseling. This unexpected path required him to adjust his goals, but his adaptability allowed him to thrive in this new direction. Additionally, consider Maia, who faced the challenge of relocating to a new city. Instead of viewing it as a setback, she saw it as an opportunity to explore different cultures and perspectives. By maintaining a growth mindset, Maia continued to seek new challenges and opportunities, enriching her personal and relational development.

Those healing from disorganized attachment often need to balance pushing for growth with maintaining emotional safety. This might mean progressing in smaller steps while building internal security. Sustaining change and growth is an ongoing process that requires a willingness to learn, dedication, and adaptability. By setting long-term goals, engaging in self-assessment, and remaining open to change, you can maintain momentum and ensure your growth journey is fulfilling and enduring. As you continue to embrace this dynamic process, remember that growth is not a destination but an evolving journey that unfolds with each step you take.

EMBRACING LASTING LOVE AND SECURITY

Imagine a relationship as a well-built house, standing firm against the tests of time and weather. Lasting love and security form the sturdy framework of this house, offering shelter and warmth. They are not fleeting emotions but enduring states that provide a stable foundation for the lives built within. Mutual respect and understanding are the cornerstones, supporting the structure with a balance of give-and-take. This mutual respect means valuing each other's perspectives and honoring individual differences, while understanding is deeply knowing and accepting each other's inner worlds. Together, they create an environment where both partners feel seen, heard, and valued, nurturing a bond that withstands life's inevitable storms.

Enduring love and security are also about trust and support, the beams that hold the house together. Trust is the unwavering belief in each other's integrity and intentions. It allows for vulnerability without fear of judgment or betrayal. Support is the steadfast presence that reassures both partners they are not alone. When trust and support are woven into the fabric of a relationship, they provide a sense of safety that encourages exploration and growth. This security creates a haven where both partners can express themselves freely and pursue their aspirations, knowing they have a reliable partner. For individuals working through disorganized attachment patterns, embracing lasting love involves learning to trust their capacity for secure attachment and their partner's consistency. This includes developing tolerance for positive experiences and learning to maintain connection during triggering moments.

As we have seen, consistent communication and emotional availability are key traits of relationships that embody lasting love. Think of these as our metaphorical house's open windows and doors, allowing light and fresh air to flow freely. Regular communication keeps everyone aligned, reducing misunderstandings and fostering harmony. It involves not just talking but actively listening and engaging in meaningful conversations. Emotional availability means being present for each other, offering empathy and understanding without judgment. When both partners are emotionally available, they create an environment where feelings can be expressed safely, deepening the emotional connection and trust.

Shared values and long-term commitment are like the solid roof that shelters the house. Shared values provide a common ground and a guiding compass that aligns the couple's goals and aspirations. They ensure that both partners move in the same direction, reinforcing the bond with shared purpose and meaning. Long-term commitment is the promise to weather life's ups and downs together. It is the conscious decision to invest in the relationship, nurturing it through attention, care, and effort. This commitment is not just a vow but a daily choice, a testament to the enduring nature of their love.

To cultivate lasting love and security, it is important to prioritize quality time and shared experiences. These moments add color and warmth to the relationship, creating memories that strengthen the bond. Prioritizing quality time means setting aside distractions and focusing on each other, whether through simple activities like cooking together or exploring new places. Shared experiences deepen the connection by fostering a sense of adventure and discovery. They remind both partners of the joy and excitement that brought them together, reinforcing the bond with shared laughter and wonder.

Continually investing in personal and relational growth is essential for nurturing enduring relationships. This means recognizing that growth is an ongoing process requiring dedication and effort. Personal growth involves self-reflection and self-improvement, ensuring both people bring their best selves to the relationship. Relational growth means actively working on communication, trust, and understanding, addressing challenges with empathy and collaboration. By valuing growth, both partners ensure that their relationship evolves and adapts, remaining resilient and fulfilling over a lifetime.

Consider the story of Anastasia and Nathan, who celebrated their anniversaries with meaningful traditions. Each year, they revisited where they first met, reflecting on their journey together and renewing their commitment to each other. These traditions became cherished rituals, reinforcing their bond with love and nostalgia. Another example is Ellen and Elliot, who supported each other through life's challenges. When Elliot faced a career setback, Ellen provided unwavering encouragement and belief in his abilities. This support strengthened their relationship, proving that love is not just about sharing the good times but standing by each other in adversity. These stories illustrate the power of lasting love, showing that relationships can thrive across a lifetime with mutual respect, understanding, and commitment.

CHAPTER 11
SEEKING PROFESSIONAL SUPPORT

THE JOURNEY OF HEALING ATTACHMENT WOUNDS SOMETIMES REQUIRES more than self-help strategies and personal reflection. Like a skilled navigator helping you chart unknown waters, a mental health professional plays a crucial role in your healing journey. They can provide expertise, guidance, and support that catalyzes profound healing. This chapter explores the vital role of professional support in attachment healing, helping you understand when and how to seek help, what types of therapy might benefit you, and how to make the most of therapeutic relationships. Remember, seeking help is not admitting failure but a courageous step toward growth and healing. For those with disorganized attachment, professional support is particularly crucial as healing often requires help in integrating contradictory survival responses and processing complex trauma. The therapeutic relationship can provide the consistent, regulated presence needed to develop earned, secure attachment.

WHEN TO SEEK PROFESSIONAL HELP

Imagine waking up each morning feeling like you are wearing emotional armor that has grown too heavy to bear. You have read self-help books, practiced mindfulness, and worked on personal growth, yet something still feels unresolved. This experience is common for those with attachment wounds, and recognizing when to seek professional help is crucial in your healing journey. The relief that comes with this recognition is immense, as it validates your experiences and reassures you that you are not alone. Being proactive and recognizing signs indicating professional help is essential, as they often signal the need for professional intervention.

Consider Maria's story: She managed her attachment issues independently for years, using meditation and journaling to cope with relationship anxiety. However, when a new romantic relationship triggered overwhelming fears of abandonment, she found herself unable to sleep, constantly checking her partner's social media, and experiencing panic attacks. These symptoms signaled that professional support could offer tools and perspectives beyond her coping strategies. Similarly, James realized he needed help when his difficulty trusting others began affecting his career advancement, preventing him from forming necessary professional relationships despite his technical expertise.

Those with disorganized attachment may notice additional signs like:

- Simultaneously craving and fearing close relationships

- Experiencing freeze responses during emotional intimacy
- Difficulty maintaining consistent feelings toward others
- Experiencing both anxious and avoidant behaviors
- Struggling with emotional regulation in relationships

Other key indicators that professional help might be beneficial include the following:

- Ongoing emotional distress that disrupts daily life
- Recurring relationship patterns that you cannot seem to break
- Intrusive thoughts or memories about past trauma
- Difficulty maintaining healthy boundaries
- Physical symptoms of anxiety or depression
- Feeling stuck despite implementing self-help strategies
- Isolation or withdrawal from relationships
- Overwhelming emotional responses to ordinary situations

The decision to seek help often involves hesitation and questions. You might wonder if your problems are "serious enough" to warrant professional intervention, or perhaps you feel shame about needing support. These concerns are typical but should not prevent you from seeking help. Remember, seeking help is not admitting failure but a courageous step toward growth and healing. Expert support can provide meaningful insights and helpful resources at any stage of your healing journey, whether you are just beginning to understand your attachment style or working to maintain progress in your relationships.

TYPES OF THERAPY FOR ATTACHMENT ISSUES

The therapeutic landscape offers a variety of approaches to healing attachment wounds, each with its unique benefits and methodologies. Understanding these options is crucial as it can help you make well-informed choices about your healing journey. For disorganized attachment, therapeutic approaches that specifically address trauma and dissociation are often the most effective. It is essential to understand these different types of therapy, as it will empower you to choose the one that best suits your needs and offers unique benefits for your healing journey:

1. **Sensorimotor Psychotherapy**: This form of somatic therapy focuses on healing disorganized attachment by integrating body-based interventions with psychological processing. This approach recognizes that traumatic experiences are stored in our body's nervous system and movement patterns. Therapists help us explore and renegotiate physical sensations and impulses associated with attachment wounds, allowing for gentle, bottom-up healing that supports nervous system regulation and creates new embodied experiences of safety and connection.

2. **Internal Family Systems**: IFS addresses disorganized attachment by understanding our internal psychological system as composed of multiple "parts" with different roles and protective functions. In this approach, the therapist helps us identify and compassionately engage with protective parts that developed in response to attachment trauma. This facilitates healing by accessing

our core "self"—an inherently whole and healing aspect that can integrate fragmented inner experiences and restore emotional balance and relational capacity.

3. **Dialectical Behavior Therapy**: DBT addresses disorganized attachment, providing skills in emotional regulation, distress tolerance, and interpersonal effectiveness. Therapists help us develop mindfulness and self-validation techniques that counteract the invalidating experiences often associated with early attachment trauma. By teaching us to recognize and modulate intense emotional responses, DBT supports healing attachment wounds through improved emotional resilience, more adaptive coping strategies, and the gradual development of healthier relational patterns.

These approaches help integrate fragmented aspects of experience and build coherent narrative understanding. Other therapies include the following:

1. **Cognitive Behavioral Therapy**: CBT focuses on identifying and changing thought patterns and behaviors that maintain attachment insecurities. This approach helps us recognize how early experiences shape our current relationship beliefs and provides practical tools for creating new, healthier patterns. For example, Cindy worked with a CBT therapist to challenge her belief that she was inherently unlovable. She learned to identify negative thought patterns through structured exercises and homework assignments and replace them with more balanced perspectives.

2. **Eye Movement Desensitization and Reprocessing**: This may be particularly effective for processing traumatic experiences that contribute to attachment issues. This therapy uses bilateral stimulation (typically eye movements) while processing difficult memories, helping to reduce their emotional impact. Peter, who experienced childhood neglect, found that EMDR helped him process these experiences in a way that talk therapy alone had not achieved. The treatment allowed him to integrate these memories without becoming overwhelmed by them.

3. **Psychodynamic Therapy**: This approach explores how past relationships and early experiences influence current attachment patterns. It helps us understand the unconscious motivations behind our behaviors and emotions in relationships. This deeper understanding allows us to make different choices in our current relationships. It provides a safe space to explore painful experiences and feelings while developing new ways of relating to others.

4. **Attachment-Based Therapy**: This approach, specifically designed to address attachment issues, focuses on creating a secure therapeutic relationship as a foundation for healing. The therapist serves as a safe base from which we can explore our attachment patterns and experiment with new ways of relating. This therapy helps us understand how our attachment style developed and provides opportunities to experience secure attachment within the therapeutic relationship.

5. **Group Therapy**: This offers unique benefits for attachment healing. It provides opportunities to practice

new relationship skills in a supportive environment. Witnessing others' experiences and receiving feedback from peers can provide valuable insights and normalize our struggles. The group setting allows us to explore attachment patterns in real time while developing healthy relationships with other group members.

WORKING WITH THERAPISTS

The relationship with your therapist is a powerful catalyst for healing attachment wounds. Like learning to dance with a skilled partner, working with a therapist requires trust, communication, and willingness to try new steps. The process begins with finding the right therapist who understands attachment theory and creates a safe space for exploration and growth. When healing from disorganized attachment, seeing a therapist experienced in complex trauma is essential. The therapeutic relationship may initially feel threatening, and a skilled therapist will gradually understand how to build safety while respecting protective responses.

1. **Finding the Right Fit**: The search for a therapist might feel overwhelming, but consider it an investment in your healing journey. Start by researching people who specialize in attachment issues or trauma. Many offer initial consultations, during which you can assess their approach and your comfort level with them. Pay attention to your feelings in their presence: Do you feel heard and understood? Do they explain their approach clearly? Trust your instincts while remaining open to the process.

2. **Building the Therapeutic Alliance**: A strong therapeutic relationship develops gradually, like any secure attachment. Your therapist should demonstrate consistency, empathy, and professional boundaries while creating space for you to explore difficult emotions. This relationship can become a template for secure attachment, showing you what it feels like to have a reliable, attuned presence in your life.

3. **Navigating Challenges**: Therapeutic work often stirs up difficult emotions and resistance. Especially when working on core attachment wounds, you might feel vulnerable, defensive, or tempted to withdraw. These reactions are normal and can provide valuable information about your attachment patterns. A skilled therapist will help you navigate these challenges while maintaining a safe therapeutic environment.

MAKING THE MOST OF THERAPY

Therapy is an investment in your emotional well-being, and like any investment, its success depends partly on how you engage with the process. Think of therapy as a collaborative journey where you and your therapist contribute to the healing process. Your active participation can significantly enhance the benefits you receive from therapy.

1. **Between-Session Work**: Therapy's impact extends beyond the session hour through homework assignments, journaling, or practicing new skills. These activities help integrate therapeutic insights into your daily life. For

instance, Elena's therapist suggested she keep a relationship journal, noting situations that triggered attachment anxiety and her responses. This practice helped her identify patterns and apply therapeutic tools in real time.

2. **Setting Goals and Tracking Progress**: Clear therapeutic goals help you focus your work and measure progress. These goals might include developing better boundaries, reducing anxiety in relationships, or processing specific traumas. Regularly reviewing these goals with your therapist ensures your work aligns with your healing objectives. Remember that progress is often not linear; setbacks are standard parts of the healing journey. For those with disorganized attachment, progress usually involves learning to tolerate positive experiences and connections. Small steps toward consistency and emotional regulation are significant achievements worth noting.

3. **Integration and Application**: The real work of therapy happens as you apply insights and skills in your daily life. This might involve practicing new communication patterns in relationships, setting boundaries with family members, or using self-soothing techniques during moments of attachment activation. Each small step builds confidence and creates new neural pathways for secure attachment.

ALTERNATIVE SUPPORT RESOURCES

Beyond traditional therapy, various resources can complement your healing journey. These alternatives provide different perspectives and support levels, creating a comprehensive healing approach.

1. **Support Groups**:

   - Online and in-person attachment-focused groups
   - Adult Children of Dysfunctional Families (ACoA) meetings
   - Trauma survivor groups
   - Relationship skills workshops

2. **Online Communities**:

   - Moderated forums for attachment healing
   - Social media groups focused on secure attachment
   - Virtual support circles
   - Educational platforms with attachment-focused content

3. **Workshops and Retreats**:

   - Attachment healing intensives
   - Relationship skills workshops
   - Body-based trauma workshops
   - Mindfulness retreats for attachment work

CREATING A SUPPORT TEAM

Building an adequate support network requires coordination and clear communication between different resources. Think of your support team as collaborative, with each member contributing unique perspectives and support.

Core Team Components

1. **Primary Therapist**:

   - Coordinates overall treatment
   - Provides individual support
   - Guides therapeutic process

2. **Support Groups**:

   - Offer peer understanding
   - Provide regular connection
   - Share coping strategies

3. **Personal Relationships**:

   - Trusted friends/family
   - Partner(s)
   - Mentors

Coordination Strategies:

   - Regular check-ins with each support source

- Clear communication about boundaries and roles
- Integration of different perspectives and tools
- Periodic team assessment and adjustment

For example, Maya coordinates with her therapist, attachment support group, and trusted friend. Her therapist helps process deeper issues, her support group provides weekly connections, and her friend offers practical support. This coordinated approach provides comprehensive support for her healing journey.

CONCLUSION

As you reach the end of this book, reflect on your journey from disorganized attachment to secure attachment. Each chapter has been a step on this path, guiding you through understanding your attachment style, recognizing emotional triggers, building trust, and transforming relationships. You have explored how emotional regulation, self-worth, and effective communication can lead to profound personal growth and healthier connections. This transformation is within your grasp, and the tools and insights you have gained are your compass.

Attachment theory offers a foundation for understanding how early experiences shape our relationships. Understanding these concepts opens the door to personal growth. Emotional regulation and trust-building are the bedrock of secure relationships. As you have learned, transforming relationship patterns involves recognizing and breaking free from toxic dynamics. Self-worth and self-compassion are crucial for building a strong foundation, and effective communication is the bridge that connects us to others.

Throughout this book, you have uncovered key takeaways to guide your journey. You have learned to identify emotional triggers and regulate your responses. Mindfulness and cognitive restructuring have offered ways to balance emotions. Trust-building and breaking unhealthy patterns have paved the way for stronger connections. You have embraced self-worth and self-compassion, setting the stage for lasting love. Each chapter has equipped you with practical strategies to foster secure attachments.

Take a moment to celebrate your progress. Your courage and resilience in embarking on this journey are commendable. Embracing a new relational identity is a significant achievement. Each milestone is a testament to your growth, no matter how small. Reflect on how far you have come and the potential that lies ahead. Your journey is not just about what you have achieved so far but about the continuous potential for growth and change.

Remember, this journey is not just about what you've achieved. It is about applying the tools and strategies you have learned every day. Your commitment to personal growth and securing fulfilling relationships is key. Let the insights and practices from this book guide your daily interactions and nurture the connections you value. Your commitment is the driving force behind your success.

Also, remember that ongoing practice and reflection are essential to sustaining change. Make habits like gratitude journaling, and mindfulness exercises a part of your daily routine. Regular self-assessment will keep you aligned with your goals. These practices will help you stay connected and grounded in your journey. Remember, growth is a continuous process that requires dedication, but the rewards are worth it.

You are not alone in this journey. Share your experiences and insights with others. Engaging with a supportive community will encourage you and give you new perspectives. Seek out groups or forums to connect with others on similar paths. These connections can enrich your journey and offer a sense of belonging. Remember, you have a community of support around you as you continue to secure attachment, and your experiences can also inspire others on their journey.

Hold on to hope and inspiration as you continue this journey. Secure attachment can profoundly impact your relationships and overall well-being. With dedication and self-awareness, lasting love and security are attainable. You have the power to create fulfilling connections that enrich your life.

I am deeply grateful that you have trusted this book as a companion on your journey. We share the goal of achieving secure and loving relationships. Your engagement with the material and commitment to personal growth are genuinely inspiring. Thank you for allowing me to be part of your path to transformation.

As you close this book, feel empowered to make lasting changes. Embrace your new relational identity and continue striving for personal and relational fulfillment. The steps you have taken are just the beginning. Your journey toward secure attachment is a path of continuous discovery and growth. May it lead you to the love and security you deserve, and remember, your growth potential is limitless.

FURTHER READING

Attachment Theory, Bowlby's Stages & Attachment Styles, https://positivepsychology.com/attachment-theory/

Transcending childhood trauma in adult relationships, https://www.counselling-directory.org.uk/articles/transcending-childhood-trauma-in-adult-relationships/

Disorganized Attachment: Definition, Causes, & Signs, https://www.choosingtherapy.com/disorganized-attachment/

Mary Ainsworth: Attachment Theory and the Strange Situation, https://www.attachmentproject.com/attachment-theory/mary-ainsworth/

How to Heal Disorganized Attachment: Self-Regulation Tips, https://www.attachmentproject.com/blog/self-regulation-disorganized-attachment-triggers/

Mindfulness and Emotion Regulation, https://pmc.ncbi.nlm.nih.gov/articles/PMC5337506/

Cognitive Restructuring: Techniques and Examples, https://www.healthline.com/health/cognitive-restructuring/

Building Resilience With Mindfulness-Based Stress Reduction, https://www.apa.org/ed/precollege/topss/stress-reduction.pdf/

The Effect of Early Traumatic Experiences and Adult Attachment on Parental Reflective Functioning, https://pmc.ncbi.nlm.nih.gov/articles/PMC5364177/

20 Ways to Rebuild Trust in a Relationship, https://www.choosingtherapy.com/how-to-rebuild-trust/

Understanding Fear of Abandonment, https://www.verywellmind.com/fear-of-abandonment-2671741/

Setting Healthy Boundaries in Relationships, https://www.helpguide.org/relationships/social-connection/setting-healthy-boundaries-in-relationships/

Toxic Relationships Checklist, https://www.mindfulecotherapycenter.com/wp-content/uploads/2017/01/Toxic-Relationships-Checklist.pdf/

What Are the Short- and Long-Term Effects of Emotional Abuse?, https://www.healthline.com/health/mental-health/effects-of-emotional-abuse/

7 Ways to Improve Communication in Relationships, https://positivepsychology.com/communication-in-relationships/

Breaking the Pattern of Painful, Unhealthy Relationships, https://tinybuddha. com/blog/breaking-the-pattern-of-painful-unhealthy-relationships/

Self-Compassion Research, https://self-compassion.org/the-research/

How Gratitude Changes You and Your Brain, https://greatergood.berkeley.edu/ article/item/how_gratitude_changes_you_and_your_brain/

Neural mechanisms of self-affirmation's stress buffering effects, https://academic.oup.com/scan/article/15/10/1086/5815969/

Self Acceptance Therapy: Embrace Your True Self, https://ca4wellbeing.com/self-acceptance-therapy/

An Attachment Theory Perspective on Closeness and Intimacy, https://labs.psych. ucsb.edu/collins/nancy/UCSB_Close_Relationships_Lab/Publications_files/ CollinsFeeney%282004%29-Chapter3.pdf/

14 Proven Ways To Build Emotional Intimacy In 2024, https://practicalintimacy. com/how-to-build-emotional-intimacy-relationship/

How to Balance Independence & Healthy Relationships, https:// mindfulhealthsolutions.com/how-to-balance-your-independence-and-interdependence-for-healthy-relationships/

Active Listening in Relationships: A Path To Deeper Intimacy, https:// holdinghopemft.com/active-listening-a-key-to-deeper-intimacy-and-understanding-in-your-relationship

How to Express Emotions: 12 Ways to Communicate Feelings, https:// positivepsychology.com/express-emotions/

5 Conflict Resolution Strategies, https://www.pon.harvard.edu/daily/conflict-resolution/conflict-resolution-strategies/

Improving Emotional Intelligence (EQ): Expert Guide, https://www.helpguide. org/mental-health/wellbeing/emotional-intelligence-eq/

Secure Attachment: Signs, Benefits, and How to Cultivate It, https://www. verywellmind.com/secure-attachment-signs-benefits-and-how-to-cultivate-it-8628802/

How to Develop a Secure Attachment Style, https://blog.zencare.co/how-to-develop-a-secure-attachment-style/

Relationship Influences on Exploration in Adulthood, https://pmc.ncbi.nlm.nih. gov/articles/PMC2805473/

6 Tips for Ending a Cycle of Unhealthy Relationships, https://www. psychologytoday.com/us/blog/conquering-codependency/202010/6-tips-ending-cycle-unhealthy-relationships/

The Impact of Daily Habits on Long-Term Success - Life Planner, https://

thelifeplanner.co/blog/post/the_impact_of_daily_habits_on_long_term_success.html/

Mindfulness for Your Health, https://newsinhealth.nih.gov/2021/06/mindfulness-your-health/

Self-Reflection: A Pathway to Personal Growth, https://www.linkedin.com/pulse/self-reflection-pathway-personal-growth-adil-mahmoud/

The Transformative Power of Gratitude: A Path To Personal Resilience, https://www.forbes.com/sites/chriswestfall/2024/11/28/the-transformative-power-of-gratitude-a-path-to-personal-resilience/

Disorganized Attachment Style in a Relationship, https://www.thecouplescenter.org/disorganized-attachment-style-in-a-relationship/

Secure Attachment: Signs, Benefits, and How to Cultivate It, https://www.verywellmind.com/secure-attachment-signs-benefits-and-how-to-cultivate-it-8628802/

The Role of Self-concept Clarity in Relationship Quality, https://www.tandfonline.com/doi/full/10.1080/15298860903332191/

How Community Support Fuels Personal Growth, https://advantagecaregroup.org/2023/12/29/building-stronger-together-how-community-support-fuels-personal-growth/

www.ingramcontent.com/pod-product-compliance
Lightning Source LLC
Chambersburg PA
CBHW071658120626
46550CB00001B/28